Gender and Sexuality in Modern Chinese History

Gender and sexuality have been neglected topics in the history of Chinese civilization, despite the fact that philosophers, writers, parents, doctors, and ordinary people of all descriptions have left reams of historical evidence on the subject. Moreover, China's late imperial government was arguably more concerned about gender and sexuality among its subjects than any other premodern state. Sexual desire and sexual activity were viewed as innate human needs, essential to bodily health and well-being, and universal marriage and reproduction served the state by supplying tax-paying subjects who were duly bombarded with propaganda about family values. How did these and other late imperial legacies shape twentieth-century notions of gender and sexuality in modern China? In this wonderfully written and enthralling book, Susan Mann answers that question by focusing in turn on state policy, ideas about the physical body, and notions of sexuality and difference in China's recent history, from medicine to the theater to the gay bar and from law to art and sports. More broadly, the book shows how changes in attitudes toward sex and gender in China during the twentieth century have cast a new light on the process of becoming modern, while simultaneously challenging the universalizing assumptions of Western modernity.

Susan L. Mann is Professor Emerita of History at the University of California, Davis. Her books include *The Talented Women of the Zhang Family* (2007) and *Precious Records: Women in China's Long Eighteenth Century* (1997).

New Approaches to Asian History

This dynamic new series publishes books on the milestones in Asian history, those that have come to define particular periods or mark turning points in the political, cultural, and social evolution of the region. The books in this series are intended as introductions for students to be used in the classroom. They are written by scholars whose credentials are well established in their particular fields and who have, in many cases, taught the subject across a number of years.

Books in the Series

Judith M. Brown, *Global South Asians: Introducing the Modern Diaspora*

Diana Lary, *China's Republic*

Peter A. Lorge, *The Asian Military Revolution: From Gunpowder to the Bomb*

Ian Talbot and Gurharpal Singh, *The Partition of India*

Stephen F. Dale, *The Muslim Empires of the Ottomans, Safavids, and Mughals*

Diana Lary, *The Chinese People at War: Human Suffering and Social Transformation, 1937–1945*

Sunil S. Amrith, *Migration and Diaspora in Modern Asia*

Thomas David DuBois, *Religion and the Making of Modern East Asia*

Gender and Sexuality in Modern Chinese History

Susan L. Mann

University of California, Davis

CAMBRIDGE
UNIVERSITY PRESS

CAMBRIDGE UNIVERSITY PRESS
Cambridge, New York, Melbourne, Madrid, Cape Town,
Singapore, São Paulo, Delhi, Tokyo, Mexico City

Cambridge University Press
32 Avenue of the Americas, New York, NY 10013-2473, USA

www.cambridge.org
Information on this title: www.cambridge.org/9780521683708

© Cambridge University Press 2011

First published 2011

Printed in the United States of America

A catalog record for this publication is available from the British Library.

Library of Congress Cataloging in Publication data

Mann, Susan, 1943–
Gender and sexuality in modern Chinese history / Susan L. Mann.
    p.   cm. – (New approaches to Asian history)
Includes bibliographical references and index.
ISBN 978-0-521-86514-2 (hardback) – ISBN 978-0-521-68370-8 (paperback)
1. Sex role – China. 2. Women – China. 3. Sex – China. I. Title. II. Series.
HQ1075.5.C6M36   2011
305.420951–dc22   2011009040

ISBN 978-0-521-86514-2 Hardback
ISBN 978-0-521-68370-8 Paperback

in memory
William Skinner
1925–2008

Contents

Figures

Acknowledgments

My first debt is to Marigold Acland of Cambridge University Press, who encouraged me to write this book and did not give up while I worked on it. I am also grateful to three anonymous readers for Cambridge University Press, whose suggestions inspired a radical rethinking of the agenda for the manuscript, and to Gail Hershatter for a meticulous critique of the final drafts. In the end, the subject of this book overwhelmed the capacity of a single manuscript, and I am all too aware of its shortcomings.

Many scholars have heard me out as I developed the ideas for each chapter. I thank in particular Guotong Li and her colleagues at California State University Long Beach, whose cross-cultural interests sparked important questions that I have since tried to address. At Indiana University and the Kinsey Institute, I am indebted to comments by Lynn Struve, Klaus Mühlhahn, Heidi Ross, Liana Zhou, and Gardner Bovingdon. At Harvard University's Fairbank Center, Ellen Widmer and Wai-yee Li presided over a seminar at which I benefited from feedback from Henrietta Harrison, Mark Elliott, Vanessa Fong, William Kirby, Peter Bol, and Max Oidtmann. Paul Goldin and Siyen Fei at the University of Pennsylvania and Weijing Lu, her colleagues, and their graduate students at the University of California, San Diego, all helped me to rethink my assumptions. Many others offered advice that proved crucial: Bill Lavely, Mark Halperin, Sheldon Lu, Mrinalini Sinha, Barbara Engel, and – especially – Beverly Bossler. Students in my senior seminar on the history of the body read and criticized two sample chapter drafts with tact and insight. Mona Ellerbrock and the late Mary Lou Wilson supplied support of a different kind that I will never forget. Cheryl Barkey read the complete first draft cover to cover. Credit for the many improvements that resulted belongs to her and to Gail Hershatter; problems that remain can be blamed entirely on me.

The Academic Senate at the University of California, Davis, invited me to deliver the annual Faculty Research Lecture in 2008, during which

I first mapped ideas for this book. It is a pleasure to acknowledge here the intellectual and collegial delights of my years at UC Davis. The manuscript was nearly complete in its first draft when William Skinner died. I wish he had been able to see it finished.

SLM
Winter 2010

Preface: Does Sex Have a History?

> Conversations about sex are always part of a larger current of conversations and arguments. Desire's objects, expressions, control, suppression, transgression, relative importance, and the venues in which all of these are expressed, are not "natural" occurrences, but social ones. Like everything else of interest to the historian, they change over time.
>
> Gail Hershatter (1996:78)

Does sex have a history? Almost any teenager coping with a parent who still lives in the dark ages will assure you that it does. But the history of sex is surprisingly difficult to study. Why? Lack of evidence. Most people keep their sex lives to themselves. What people write down, publish, and circulate may be sexual fantasy or invention, with plotlines designed to sell copy. This evidence can tell us a lot about what people like to read or watch or imagine, but little about what they actually do. Ironically, the most reliable evidence for a history of sex is the mass of material (by government officials, religious leaders, parents, doctors, and so on) telling people what *not* to do. We can be certain that *some* people were doing *some* of that.

Sometimes the historical record on sex becomes very noisy, but at other times it is quiet. Clearly that is not because people stopped having sex. Sporadic outbreaks of chatter about sex in the documentary record pose additional problems for historians interested in the history of sexuality. When, where, and why do certain kinds of sex, or certain kinds of sexual relationships, become problematic? And what is going on the rest of the time?

There are many other reasons, besides these obvious ones, why the history of sex is difficult to study. In the case of this book – a history of sexuality in modern China – the usual problems with evidence apply.

But two additional challenges face Western[1] scholars and students who are interested in the history of sex and gender in China. One has to do with time, and the other with culture – and the two are related. The problem of time arises whenever China's cultural history is told in terms drawn from the history of Euro–North America, using "the West" as an implicit template for measuring China's historical "progress." Precisely *when* China made the transition to "modern" culture, and *what* that transition entailed, has been a consuming question for China historians. Such habits of thinking about historical time, and the questions they raise, have invited scholars and students in Euro–North America to imagine that temporal change is not only linear but convergent. In other words, eventually – as time marches on – the Chinese will somehow become "just like us." This kind of thinking casts sexuality in late imperial China as both exotic and backward. It also impedes our understanding of sexual mores and practices in contemporary China, where – despite the hallmarks of modern sexuality that Western readers find reassuringly familiar – sexual culture differs in important ways from a Euro–North American model.

At the same time, being attentive to cultural difference can also produce misreadings of the history of sexuality in China. An example of this can be found in the learned writings of the Dutch intellectual and sinologist Robert van Gulik (1910–1967).[2] After years of research on Chinese erotica, Gulik concluded that before the Manchu conquest of 1644, Chinese culture encouraged "natural" forms of sexual expression that liberated the Chinese from the moralistic constraints of his own time and place. As the chapters that follow will show, however, Gulik was misled by his own yearnings for a different cultural idea of sexuality. In China, as in every culture, there was and is nothing "natural" about sexuality. It was, and still is, strictly regulated and calibrated by rules and conventions, by custom and taboo, by medical and governmental authorities, and by profiteering and preaching (see Goldin's introduction to Gulik [2003], also Furth [1994]). Gulik further maintained that "prudery" associated with Confucian orthodoxy inhibited sexual expression in China after the fall of the Ming dynasty (1368–1644), making it extremely difficult to find out anything about people's private sex lives in the eighteenth and nineteenth centuries (Gulik 1951). As we shall see, this assertion too can be challenged.

---

[1] This conventional term refers to Euro–North America; it is used in this book for convenience whenever it is less cumbersome than the alternatives.

[2] A sinologist is a scholar who studies Chinese culture using sources written in classical Chinese.

The chapters that follow aim to avoid bad habits of thinking about time and culture. They focus on the transition from the nineteenth to the twentieth century, from the "late empire" to the "modern nation." Chapters are divided topically, each foregrounding the nineteenth-century context in which change occurred. During the decades between 1898 and 1949, new ideas about gender and sexuality reshaped the Chinese social order. These new ideas spread during decades of revolutionary conflict and warfare that ended with the founding of the People's Republic in 1949. Over the course of the twentieth century, then, the meaning of the categories "men" (*nan* 男) and "women" (*nü* 女) shifted in many arenas, from the state to the family, from medicine to literature, from labor to law, and from the theater to the gay bar. Yet the heteronormative conventions in the phrase "man/woman" and "husband/wife" remained stable, and the family system in which descent was traced through the male line stayed largely intact. This paradox lies at the heart of the book.

The book is divided into three parts. Part I focuses on the government and its relationship to gender and sexuality, with a focus on the family. Part II shifts the focus from the institutions in Part I to individual persons and their bodies. Part III shifts yet again to consider questions about fantasy, modernity, and globalization, defined in sexualized and gendered terms. In each part, three broad, overarching patterns become clear. First, the movement of women toward work and study outside the home after 1900 was the most significant and sweeping change in China's sex-gender system in centuries.[3] Its repercussions are still being felt. Second, in a culture in which sex was never coupled with sin – in which Adam and Eve had no role in the cultural or historical explanations for sexual desire and its consequences – the Chinese conviction that sexual activity is an essential part of a healthy human life softened and defused the conflicts about homoerotic desire, and about homosexual and transgendered identities, that feed homophobia and even violence in many modern cultures. Third, the Chinese state or government has historically played an overwhelmingly important role in defining the criteria for performing gendered identities. Government policies promoting heteronormative reproductive marriage have merely grown more pervasive, and even coercive, in the course of the twentieth century.

The reasons why any history of gender and sexuality in China must begin by addressing the role of the government will quickly become clear. The prominent role of government in defining gender relations and sexuality is a unique, enduring feature of Chinese history that sets the Chinese experience apart from that of other modern industrial nations. As

---

[3] For a formal model of the concept of sex-gender systems, see Rubin (1975).

for bodies, in China as in Europe and the Americas, physical bodies generally determine who counts as male and who counts as female. But conceptions of the physical body are constructed by culture in historical time and space. Bodies are coded by age, class, race, or ethnicity. Bodies are mutable and subject to transformation through fantasy or imagination, by clothing or costume or disguise, and by injury or surgery or adornment. Finally, physical bodies *perform* gender and sexuality, and those performances are fluid and constantly shifting. Part II, then, gives evidence for the ways in which bodies submit to, resist, challenge, and reshape government and its policies. In late imperial Chinese history, the unstable meanings of "male" and "female" were pushed to extremes in the creative imagination and were in turn deeply shaken by processes of modernization and globalization, including imperialism or colonialism. Part III moves into the other arenas beyond state and body where the meanings of sexuality and gender have been continually transformed at the hands of writers, artists, entertainers, travelers, and tourists.

To anchor the reader as the discussion moves rapidly through time, three temporal signposts appear. The first refers simply to "late imperial," or "Qing dynasty" culture. This signpost signals the broad cultural matrix of social, legal, economic, religious, and medical beliefs and practices of "premodern" China. The Qing dynasty began in 1644 and ended in 1911, in a tumultuous paroxysm of belated reforms that included changing the educational system and raising the status of women. Late Qing reforms anticipated many of the transformations that came in the twentieth century. The second temporal signpost refers generally to "twentieth-century" changes, especially changes in beliefs and practices associated with the new Republican nation, established in the revolution of 1911, which brought down the Qing dynasty. Republican-era changes in gender and sexuality were all shaped by the intellectuals who led the New Culture and May Fourth movements of 1915–1919. These movements, centered in Beijing and Shanghai, called for an end to the authority of Confucian values, especially the authority of elders over youth and men over women. May Fourth intellectuals also hoped to spread their new values by writing in "plain speech" or vernacular Chinese, to reach a broad popular audience. A third major signpost in this book points to the radical shifts that followed the Chinese Communist revolution in 1949. These shifts were manifested in two stages: the Maoist period, from 1949 to 1976, and the post-Mao era, from 1976 to the present. Roughly speaking, readers will find each chapter divided into discussions of late imperial or Qing dynasty cultural forms, followed by briefer comments on changes in the twentieth century from May Fourth through the present era. The aim of these sweeping overviews is to suggest how our understanding of the history of gender and sexuality in contemporary China must take account of pre-twentieth-century beliefs and practices. Despite the massive changes that revolution brought to every person in China, deep-rooted past ideas about sexuality and gender performance are still being reinvented, recirculated, and given new meanings.

What kinds of cultural expectations and rules framed the idea of "man" and "woman" in nineteenth-century China? How did these figure in the new rules and expectations that developed in the twentieth century? Readers will encounter in this book recurrent ideas that shape notions of gender and sexuality. These include the cosmological forces *yin* and *yang*; fantasies and myths about male-female relationships with profound sexual meanings; convictions – philosophical, religious, and medical – about human nature and the body; and, finally – perhaps most important, in the Chinese context – governmental "statecraft" policies promoting civilizing projects. All of these ideas constructed notions of *nan* (male, or men) and *nü* (female, or women) in the late empire. Sometimes, they worked together; often, they worked against each other; over time, they changed. The twentieth century was arguably a period of continual, even tumultuous, change in gender and sexuality. But the foundational ideas did not vanish. In contemporary China, the cosmological forces of *yin* and *yang* still inform the most basic medical conceptions of the human body. Fantasy and myth about past heroes and heroines still figure in popular culture from television and film to comics, fiction, and the Internet. Convictions about human nature and the body from the past have been infused into the vocabulary of Western science, social science, and philosophy. And the government is engaged as never before in the active manipulation of norms governing gender and sexuality.

A final note about the relationship between gender and sexuality that is implicit in this book: Many scholars would argue that by assuming a relationship between gender and sexuality, we have predetermined our findings and trapped ourselves in arbitrary and unexamined (Western) binaries before we start (see, for example, Boellstorff [2007] and Najmabadi [2005]). As this book shows, the discipline and control that ordered the nineteenth-century Qing empire was based precisely on a carefully calibrated and even coercive relationship between sexed bodies (gendered male and female) and the performance and expression of sexuality. This discipline and control was so powerful, so unconsciously embraced, and so skillfully deployed by human agents that the surviving evidence compels the historian to recognize a sex-gender system based on models of "male" and "female." At the same time, the easy slippage between masculine and feminine bodily styles and performances – a central feature of sexuality in Chinese culture – makes even Western notions of "queer" difficult to apply meaningfully in any historical context, including the present (Sinnott 2010). Readers of this book will come away with at least a keen awareness of the extent of sexual control, and of the modes for internalizing that control, in modern Chinese history. Perhaps, on reflection, readers will also become cognizant of the conditions that shape sexual behavior and sexual identity in their own lives and cultures. At the same time, they may also gain a new appreciation for the capacity of the individual person to defy, subvert, or manipulate the powerful hegemonic structures of state, family, and society, given the right historic moment.

Introduction: The cloistered lady and the bare stick

When a family wanted to know more about a girl who had been suggested for a daughter-in-law and asked what kind of a girl she was, the neighbors would answer, "We do not know. We have never seen her." And that was praise.

Ning Lao T'ai-t'ai (Pruitt 1945:29)

If a man plots to have illicit sex in broad daylight, it is usually when he happens to encounter a woman in some lonely village or remote empty place. . . . If he encounters a young girl of fifteen *sui* or under, then he may be able to "join by means of coercion"; but if she is over sixteen *sui*, then it is unlikely that the rape will be consummated. . . . But women who walk alone without any company are rarely chaste.

Magistrate's handbook, early nineteenth century (Sommer 2000:108)

The strict boundaries around young women that were supposed to keep them chaste and pure were the same boundaries that upheld the honor of the family in nineteenth-century China. These boundaries were as salient in the laws of the eighteenth century as they were in the upbringing of respectable women at the turn of the twentieth century, as Ning Lao T'ai-t'ai could testify. Tensions surrounding this ideal of female purity were thoroughly explored in early Chinese texts, one of the most widely read being the classic "Tale of Yingying." Here is a synopsis of that story, written by a Tang scholar named Yuan Zhen (779–831): Yingying is a fair seventeen-year-old when her mother introduces her to the comely scholar Zhang, to whom the mother owes a favor. He falls in love at first sight and attempts to approach Yingying through her maid, Hongniang. Hongniang persuades Zhang to write love poems to Yingying to seduce her. This works so well that Yingying, after an initial display of outrage, climbs over the wall of her compound to Zhang's bed and sleeps with him.

For the next month, he joins her secretly every night in the western wing of her home, where they make love. In the end, though, Zhang abandons Yingying for the capital, where he sits for the exams and rebuffs her tender letters. Stories of the affair spread throughout the capital, many of them richly sensual and romantic, some cruel and hurtful. Yingying ultimately marries another man, and Zhang another woman.

Yingying's story is replete with regret, resentment, and nostalgia. It features passionate accounts of divine union, fearsome images of women as dangerous and polluting, and outpourings of anger and shame. The tale reappeared in many variations on the stage, including a thirteenth-century play called *The Western Wing*. In the seventeenth century its themes were transformed and given a happy ending in the opera *The Peony Pavilion*, which in turn inspired a best-selling American novel by Lisa See.[1] In the tale of Yingying, all of the tensions explored in Part I of this book are revealed: the tension between cloistered women and sexual desire, the shame attached to women who have sex outside of marriage, the enterprise of the single male determined to get access to a woman he desires, the overwhelming power of physical desire and the sublime bliss of its consummation, and the inability of parents, morals, and high walls to contain passion. The figure of the maid as a boundary-crossing intermediary is also a key part of this story. It is Hongniang, after all, who suggests the seduction strategy that allows the plot to unfold.

Yingying's affair with Scholar Zhang gave readers a chance to consider all of these tensions, and to come away with a new, if not cheery, appreciation of the irresolvable nature of the conflicting imperatives. The thing to notice about Yingying, in the original story, is that she is hardly a shrinking violet. In fact, she (not Scholar Zhang) initiates sexual intercourse by coming to *his* bed, despite her apparent awareness of the costs to her that will inevitably follow. He, by contrast, illustrates the relative ease with which men can escape the consequences of lost romance and find comfort in new relationships. Hers is a cautionary tale, but one with enough emotional complexity to give readers' imagination plenty to feed on. The earliest versions of the drama *The Western Wing*, derived from Yingying's story, take full advantage of the sensual language and imagery in the original text, as analyzed by West and Idema: the garden, the full moon, and the flowers all convey *yin* imagery of sexually accessible beauty. Red flowers, especially the red peony, point to the engorged vulva; the flesh is white jade or "mutton fat"; the penis is "the jade one"; zither

---

[1] For a translation and close readings of the original Tang story, see Yu 2000:173–201. On *The Western Wing*, see West and Idema 1991; on *The Peony Pavilion*, Tang 2002; Lisa See's novel is *Peony in Love* (2007).

strings are the frenum of the clitoris; and playing the zither is a method of arousal (West and Idema 1991:142–146, 147). We should not imagine, then, that young girls brought up to conceal themselves deep inside the boudoir were unaware of the world beyond. In fact, mere mention of deep concealment would have sufficed to remind the girls of Yingying's story. Many Yingying-style tales also sent a powerful message: the ideal "female beauty" (*jiaren*) of fiction is talented, virtuous, *and* ill-fated (Grace Fong 1997:273–275).

This introductory chapter examines the central tension in Yingying's story: the historic imperative requiring that women be cloistered at home, juxtaposed against the constant circulation of men through the social, political, and economic systems of the country. The sex and gender system in nineteenth-century China revolved around cloistered women. Boundaries that concealed women defined the system, and the sexuality and status of every man and woman in the empire was measured in relation to those boundaries. The boundaries divided people who were respectable (the Chinese term was "*liang*," or "good") from everyone else. To be a respectable person, you had to belong to a respectable family, and the mark of a respectable family was the purity of its women. A pure woman's respectability was ensured, as Ning Lao T'ai-t'ai tells us in the preceding quotation, if she stayed out of sight. We can construct a map of the entire nineteenth-century social order using this paradigm of concealment. At the center of that social order sat the *guixiu* (ladies cultivated in the boudoir): the wives and marriageable daughters of upper-class men who lived a life concealed from public view. Women in all respectable families tried to follow their example, and those who failed lost status commensurately.

Why were cloistered women so central to the sex and gender system in a society in which the family was based on male descent lines? And why did the end of cloistering make "the woman problem" the burning issue in China's first national revolution in 1911? These are some of the questions this book examines. In doing so, the book takes the long view. That is, we will not be concerned so much with gains and losses, or progress and setbacks, in the so-called status of women, or with questions about gender equality. Rather, we will ask how the relationships between gender and power have been configured in China's modern history, particularly in the transition from the late empire to the modern nation. Our primary focus will be the Chinese cultural context within which those relationships were framed and negotiated over time. This approach enables us to view modern Chinese history through a lens that makes us think differently about the social and cultural costs of the end of the empire and the beginnings of the nation-state. Was the end of the civil service examination system in 1906 more important than programs to send women out of the home for school and work? Why was the one-child family policy a culturally legitimate option in post-Mao China? How much do classical ideas about sexuality and gender performance figure in contemporary sexual behavior? By using sexuality as a category of historical analysis, this book poses and offers answers to these and other questions. The rest of this introduction shows how sexuality was embedded in every aspect of social life in Chinese culture – from marriage to social status and from notions of space to patterns of mobility – and, especially, in Chinese politics and government.

Sexuality and social life

Sexuality and marriage

In nineteenth-century China, every person was supposed to get married and rear sons to carry on a patriline. Chances for marriage, however, varied with gender and status. Nearly 100 percent of females married; up to 20 percent of males never did. Marriage in respectable families of means was arranged, usually by parents, and a married son ideally lived with his parents in a joint household that included his wife, his married brothers, and all of their children. His sisters would be "married out" into another patriline. Wealthy parents had many advantages in this marriage market. They could marry off their children earlier, attracting desirable young brides with fancy bridal gifts and presents and supplying elaborate dowries for their daughters. The wealthy could afford to add concubines to the family, especially when a wife did not give birth to a son – "the rich got children," as one scholar put it (Harrell 1985). Thus the wealthy could hope to achieve the Chinese family ideal, which was to have many generations under one roof. But even people of modest means aimed at the ideal, and the vast majority of Chinese in the nineteenth century spent at least part of their lives in a joint family household shared by relatives of three generations.

Getting married and having children were social expectations, and the wealthy had a better chance of fulfilling those expectations than did the poor. Similarly, women had a far better chance of living the ideal than did men. Women were almost certain to marry at some point in their lives, even after decades of service as maids or indentured servants, because of the insatiable quest for fertile young women in the marriage market, and because wealthy families enhanced their reproductive success by acquiring concubines. By contrast, large numbers of men died unwed because they could not find or afford a bride. Access to a bride was a defining condition of every young man's life chances. And in every generation, a vast pool of impoverished young men died without marrying at all. Unmarried men without wives or children – rootless "bare sticks," as they were called – were feared by respectable people in settled communities and closely monitored by the government. They were perceived as disruptive, predatory, and undisciplined by the constraints of life in a settled family home.

The demand for brides and concubines was constant, and it rose in times of peace and prosperity. Yet because a male heir was required to continue a patriline, most married couples had a strong preference for sons. This tilted the sex ratio of surviving children, sometimes due to neglect or even infanticide of unwanted baby girls, particularly among the poor and especially in periods of hardship. The result was a marriage crunch that squeezed out poor males. The crunch tightened and loosened with the ups and downs of the dynastic cycle and the regional economy. So in the sex and gender system described here, the cloistered young woman occupies one end of a continuum; at the other end is the rootless young male – the bare stick. She is surrounded by institutions and relationships that hold the social order in place. He is a free-floating marginal figure whose presence is a continuing threat to that social order.

Sexuality and social identity

We can already begin to see how sex and social status were related in the nineteenth century. But sexuality was even more central to social identity than one might suppose. Social status in late imperial China was measured in many ways, but the most fundamental distinction was drawn between people who were considered respectable (called "good" [*liang*]) and people marked as pariahs (called "polluted" [*jian*]). Every household in the registered population was classified under one of these two categories, which also defined the boundaries of marriage markets. Before the eighteenth century, women of pariah status were sexually available for prostitution and entertainment, but not for marriage with respectable commoners; men of pariah status were forbidden to take brides from respectable commoner families. Pariah men were also barred from access to the single most important path of upward mobility: education. They could not enter local academies, nor sit for the civil service examinations.

The vast majority of commoner families were "good" people, members of stable communities whose menfolk worked at respectable jobs in one of the "four occupations" (scholar, farmer, merchant, or artisan). Only a small minority of households appeared in the tax registers under the category "polluted." Men and women in these households were stigmatized by work that was considered degrading or vile (yamen runners, actors, prostitutes and singing girls, butchers, and certain local outcast groups were all counted as *jian*). Although pariah men and women performed necessary services in communities of respectable persons, sometimes in very intimate capacities (such as, for women, preparing a bride for a wedding or, for men, escorting a funeral entourage), they were isolated from the respectable commoner population by residence, dress, and powerful legal barriers.

Among the hundreds of thousands of respectable commoner households, social status was measured by a complex balance of prestige, power, and work, defined differently for men and for women. Among men, a great divide separated "those who labor with their minds" (the scholar elite) from "those who labor with their hands" (farmers and artisans). Male status hierarchies were occupational, ranking scholars/officials first, as the mental laborers, followed by farmers or cultivators,[2] artisans, and merchants, in order of prestige and respectability. Cultivators were considered more respectable than artisans or merchants, even though they often had less prestige and power, not to mention wealth. This was because their work was productive labor, yielding food for the people and tax revenue for the state. Artisans, who simply manipulated raw materials and sold them for a profit, and merchants, who merely profited from the labor of others, ranked below farmers on this scale of social worthiness.

For women, by contrast, status was defined not only by the occupation of father, husband, or son (a woman could inherit a posthumous title based on a son's distinction in office or in the community), but also by sexuality. And both status and sexuality were intimately connected to work. The key status line for women was the line separating brides and wives of respectable commoners from all other women, whether concubines, maids, nuns, courtesans, or prostitutes. Because, by making a good match for their daughter, a woman's natal family could actually improve their status, respectable women intended as brides were groomed with status markers in mind. A respectable young woman might or might not

---

[2] The Chinese term, *nong*, is usually translated "peasant." I prefer the term "cultivator," because many subjects classified as *nong* were in fact farmers with their own plots, whereas others were tenants or even farm laborers. The central meaning of the term refers to manual labor in agriculture as a primary producer.

be educated (to prepare her for the top stratum of the marriage market), but she would invariably be taught how to do respectable "womanly work," that is, to work with her hands inside the home, as a spinner, weaver, or embroiderer. Other kinds of work that had to be performed outside where a woman would come into contact with men, including farm work, threatened a woman's potential to move up in the marriage market. Whether scholars, cultivators, artisans, or merchants, the ability of a family to cloister women, train them for womanly work, and place them in a respectable marriage was a crucial marker of status.

Unmentioned in the occupational hierarchies defining respectable men's work were soldiers and priests or monks. Military service was the lowliest occupation known to nineteenth-century Chinese, summed up in the folk saying "Good iron is not made into nails, good men are not made into soldiers." In the nineteenth century during peacetime, battalions of soldiers – often with their families – were stationed in strategic towns and along critical borders, isolated from communities of ordinary common-ers. When rebellion broke out, or when a dynasty fell, however, bandits and soldiers alike could invade the homes of commoner families and the inner quarters that concealed respectable women. Women trapped inside a walled city under siege committed suicide when the city fell, to protect their own honor and the honor of their families. Women who fled walled cities seeking protection from warfare in rural villages were vulnerable to attack on the road. Either way, times of disorder were times when even the most cloistered women might be exposed and shamed. A crudely illustrated woodblock print deploring the travesties of the Taiping rebels' occupation of Jiangnan in the 1860s is full of examples of such scenes (see Figure 1).

Sexuality and social space

Among upper-class people, rules for sex segregation started within the household. Married sons lived with their parents, and the ideal family housed many generations under one roof. Space had to be arranged, therefore, so that a father would never be alone with one of his son's wives, and so that a senior male's young concubine would be kept away from his sexually active sons. Dining, accordingly, was not a communal family event but was, rather, segregated by sex, with older women and servants attending to men at the table.

Sexual transgression was just one concern. Equally important was the upbringing of daughters as future brides. In upper-class households, in which both sons and daughters were educated, a daughter could study

1a–b. Travesties of the Taiping Rebellion. *Source:* Jiyun shanren [pseud.], *Jiangnan tielei* (Tears from iron in Jiangnan). Taipei: Guangwen shuju, 1974, pp. 7, 17.

1a–b (*continued*)

with her brothers and male cousins up to the age of twelve *sui*,[3] but that was the sole venue for their interaction. As she entered puberty, she was pulled back into the *guige*, or women's quarters, which was set off in the rear of the house, where it was shielded from sight and sound of the entry halls and reception rooms where visitors came and went. There she might continue her education under the supervision of a governess or female relative, while also learning to sew, embroider, play the zither, compose simple poems, write shapely characters with a brush, and possibly try her hand at monochrome ink painting. This transition into the women's quarters coincided not only with puberty but with marriage plans, for young girls of the upper class were betrothed by their parents early in life. Embroidery, then, was not simply a practical skill or an idle pastime, but rather a kind of preparation for marriage in which a young girl began to fashion shoes (see Figure 2) and the elaborate trimmings for her dowry trousseau.

If the spaces of the household were organized to prevent sexual inter-actions and to prepare for sexual interactions, and the sequestering of women was the primary obsession, then an upper-class girl was reared to marry out – to think of herself as the future wife of a particular chosen boy – as soon as she entered puberty. This dedication to a future husband was so complete that some girls committed suicide if a fiancé died before the wedding. They could not conceive of a future without that proper marriage. Why would a young girl have this particular vision of her future life? To understand this, we need to remind ourselves that a daughter's relationship to her natal family was different from a son's. The patrilin-eal rituals of the kinship system presumed that all women married and became ritual members of the marital family, not the natal family. So a daughter was not listed in the family genealogy, and when she died, she had no place on her natal family's ancestral altars. Her permanent ritual place was located in the genealogy and at the ancestral altar of her hus-band. Many young girls, for that reason, were betrothed by their parents at birth, often to the infant son of a family friend. Respectable parents who feared that they could not afford a proper marriage for a daughter, particularly the dowry costs, had recourse to expedient options such as adopting out a daughter as a *tongyangxi*, or "little daughter-in-law." In this arrangement, a baby girl or a very young daughter would be taken in by her future husband's family, reared as one of their own children, and then expected to share a bed with her husband as soon as the marriage

---

[3] Age was calculated in lunar years, and a child was considered one *sui* at the year of her birth. Every person gained one *sui* at the New Year. Thus, a child born just before the New Year might turn two *sui* shortly after birth.

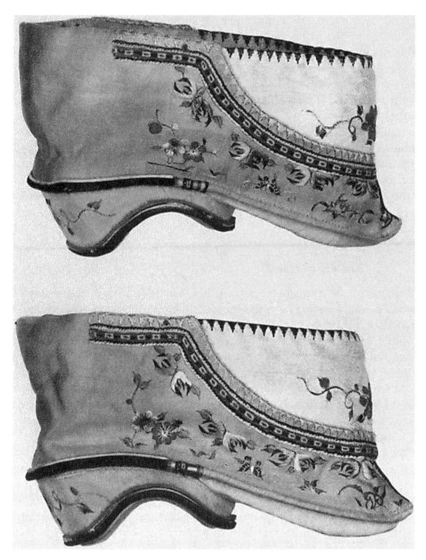

2. Embroidered shoes for bound feet. *Source:* Dorothy Ko, *Every Step a Lotus: Shoes for Bound Feet.* Berkeley: University of California Press, 2001, p. 122. Printed with permission. © Bata Shoe Museum, Toronto 2011.

could be conveniently consummated. Either way, the end was served: marriage to one man, concealment within a respectable household, and security of body and spirit in a patriline.

Securing the boundaries of the household was a constant concern. Women safely cloistered within domestic space were continually plied with services by liminal female figures whose specialties gave them access to respectable women. The so-called six grannies (*liu po*) and the three aunties (*san gu*), together with the maids employed in respectable households, formed a corps of boundary-crossing females that threatened the security of walled compounds and the purity of the women they enclosed.[4] Why? As Hongniang in Yingying's story shows us, women who could cross the boundaries of respectability made contacts in, conveyed information about, and arranged access to the world outside the inner quarters.

Sexuality and mobility

Because of the importance attached to seclusion and concealment of women, social networks in the nineteenth century were overwhelmingly homosocial: that is, men spent most of their time with other men, and women spent most of their time with other women. Women cared for children and the elderly of both sexes, but in respectable households they did so within the confines of the *guige*. Public co-mingling of the sexes was frowned upon, and women who moved publicly on the streets or in the shops, restaurants, or entertainment centers, or even on pilgrimage to temples and shrines, could be criticized or satirized as sexually compromised or available. Thus maids and actresses, as well as female shopkeepers and peddlers, announced their lower status by their presence outside concealed domestic space. Apart from a few convents and Daoist temples, where women lived together as nuns (these institutions were the subject of ribald stories and bawdy jokes), most respectable women did not belong to same-sex groups outside the home and family. There were no schools for girls outside the home. No charitable or other organizations offered membership to respectable women.[5]

---

[4] The occupations of these nine types are generally identified as follows: broker, matchmaker, shaman-healer, procuress, drug-seller, and midwife (the six) and Buddhist nun, Daoist nun, and soothsayer (the three). See Leung 1999:102–105.

[5] Exceptions to this rule in the "women's houses" of the Canton delta only underscore the regional particularity of that local culture (Stockard 1989); the same might be said for the sisterhoods pledged among women using the "women's script" (*nü shu*) in southern Hunan (Silber 1994).

By contrast, all-male organizations and networks outside the home were pervasive and essential to mobility and survival, and they were accessible, in different forms, to all classes. At the peak of the social hierarchy, men studying for the examinations attended local schools and academies where they formed bonds as *tongxue*, fellow students, united not only by their shared classroom experience but also by their shared debt to a common teacher. The examination system drew successful men from the county to the prefecture, from the prefecture to the provincial capital, and, ultimately, from the capital to the apex of the mobility ladder, the metropolitan examination halls in Beijing. At each level, men formed new *tongxue* bonds and ties to teachers or examination officials. Those who received examination degrees in the same year shared a further bond (*tongnian*, or "same year"). These "same" bonds were lifelong, forming part of the complex matrix of *guanxi* (connections) that enabled elite men to maneuver skillfully through the vast but cumbersome governmental bureaucracy.

For those unable to devote their time to education, male networks of other kinds promised security, companionship, and support. For artisans and merchants, *tongye* (same occupation) or *tongxiang* (same native place) were the bonds that grounded guilds and trade organizations, which offered travelers living space; temple worship; meals, lodging, and friendship; the familiar sound of local dialect and the familiar taste of local food; and even free burial to those who died away from home. Farmers belonged to crop-watching groups, local defense clubs, temple organizations, or lineage organizations – social networks that mobilized the connections of men in the community, sometimes across status lines. Retired scholars, or scholars whose careers had stalled at the local level, often assumed leadership roles in local community organizations for fellow clansmen, or supported a public service project such as rebuilding a shrine, constructing a new bridge, or dredging a waterway.

For men who became bare sticks, whose short and miserable lives were spent on the road or at sea, working short-term jobs or performing hard labor – as miners, as boatmen, or as heavy laborers hauling barges, building dikes and walls, and so on – secret societies afforded fellowship and protection, including common worship of a patron god and shared resources (Kelley 1982). Secret societies reached from the lowliest men at the margins up into the ranks of the local elite, whose links to brotherhoods were essential to their own security and the security of their families and property (Murray 1994). Other more marginal groups, such as pirate gangs, gave single men ways to stay alive outside family and community (Murray 1987). The spaces where men formed public bonds that joined them across regions, languages, occupations, and

kinship networks often had a tenuous – and sometimes even antagonis-
tic – relationship to the political order upheld by the central government.
It was these kinds of same-sex organizations – the secret societies – that
the leader of China's 1911 Revolution, Sun Yatsen, tried to mobilize
for his revolutionary alliance. Secret societies remained a problem for
the new Republican government and were not eliminated until after the
Communist victory in 1949.

Sexuality and government

Recognizing the family as the foundation of political and social order,
the late imperial government promoted values to keep the sex-gender
system in place. Those values centered on the twin virtues of loyalty and
fidelity. Loyalty, conceived as a male virtue, meant loyalty to the dynasty.
Loyal subjects were created by parents who raised their sons to be filial.
A respectful and obedient son, reared to pay homage to his parents in
life (through service) and in death (through veneration), made an ideal
compliant imperial subject, as we hear in the saying "Seek a loyal subject
in a filial son." For women, who left the natal family at marriage and
transferred loyalty to another line, a different virtue was called for. The
womanly virtue – the proper analogue for male loyalty – was fidelity:
the constant devotion to one husband for which every respectable young
girl was prepared from the time she lost her milk teeth. "Your husband
is like Heaven to you," she was told; a loyal minister, after all, does
not serve two rulers, and a faithful woman serves only one husband.
Widows who remarried were scorned, and the government honored with
silver and monuments women who, although widowed young, maintained their chastity until death, renouncing and, if necessary, violently
resisting remarriage.

To instill these values, the government from very earliest times stressed
the importance of positive rewards and voluntary compliance (giving
"pleasure" to the people) rather than punishment and coercion (Nylan
2001). In late imperial times, that statecraft strategy was honed to a fine
art through the promotion and cultivation of the patrilineal family system.
Government-approved editions of books illustrating womanly virtue, full
of lively illustrations and quotations, were published and widely circulated throughout the Qing period. Figure 3 shows a "chaste and obedient
wife" refusing rescue from a flood because the retainer sent by her husband to save her had arrived without the proper credentials.

Family and lineage instructions, privately printed and distributed,
echoed the values in these didactic books. At the same time, the government periodically banned the publication of books considered licentious

3. A chaste and obedient wife drowning. Illustration from the classic collection of biographies of exemplary women, first published in the Han dynasty: The "Chaste and Obedient" Zhao Zhen Jiang of Chu. *Source:* Liu Xiang, comp., *Xinbian gu lienü zhuan* (New edition of the original *Biographies of Exemplary Women*), printed 1825, *juan* 4 p. 9a.

or subversive of these womanly virtues, especially opera scripts and fiction about sexual passion. The Qing government under Manchu rule was particularly censorious, backing up its purges of private literary collections with laws that gave new definition and harsh punishment to certain kinds of sexual behavior. These and other state policies affecting the values and norms of sexuality are discussed in detail in the chapters that follow.

Late imperial transformations

The culture of the late empire drew heavily on the past for its institutions, values, and statecraft models. The classical age (the Zhou and Han periods, from the time of Confucius in the fifth century BCE through the end of the Han dynasty in 220 CE) saw the articulation of ideas about human nature, the body, and sexuality that formed the core of political theory, medical practice, and cultural norms throughout the imperial era, and well into the twentieth century. These theories, norms, and practices included not only Confucianism but also Daoism, medicine, and stories of heroes and heroines (or villains and viragos) who became legends for posterity. The middle empires of Song (960–1279) and Yuan (1279–1368) marked two significant changes in gender relations. The first was the beginning of footbinding of women – a practice traced to the fashionably ribbon-bound feet of young dancers at elite banquets in the Song period (Ebrey 1993, Ko 2001). The second was a new obsession with widow fidelity, including new honors for women who refused to remarry following the death of a spouse (Bossler 2012, Birge 2002). Bound feet and widow chastity were vital aspects of women's gendered identities in Qing times.

The wrenching historical changes of the twentieth century, a major subject of this book, did not begin until the end of the late empire, a period defined by the Ming (1368–1644) and Qing (1644–1911) dynasties. Yet even these last two dynasties represent very different historical moments in the history of gender and sexuality. The late Ming dynasty was a period when writers and readers became greatly interested in what they called "marvelous," "strange," or "unusual" behavior. One example of this new interest in performative expression was the explosion of theater – operas performed in all kinds of venues, from temple festivals to elite compounds and from the village marketplace to the official yamen. The Ming theater, and the wildly sexualized plots in late Ming novels and other fiction, reveal audiences who were quite at home with explicit and bawdy sexual excess. Not only cross-dressing and bizarre costume but also deep fascination with emotion, passion, and desire were all part of the consumerism and voyeurism nurtured in the urban print culture of the seventeenth century (Ko 1994). These ideas mixed with religious teachings that drew on Buddhism as well as Daoism and Confucianism to stress the potential for sagehood in ordinary persons. Such teachings in turn drew fresh attention to the moral worth of commoners, increased opportunities for education, and broadened the audience for both moral and ethical instruction and hedonistic consumption. The fascination with romantic love among seventeenth-century readers and viewers became a kind of cult – the cult of *qing*, roughly translated as "emotion," "passion," or, as in the following quotation, "love." In his preface to the famous opera *The Peony Pavilion* (which plays with themes from Yingying's story), the playwright Tang Xianzu summed it up this way:

Love is of source unknown, yet it grows ever deeper. The living may die of it, by its power the dead live again. Love is not love at its fullest if one who lives is unwilling to die for it, or if it cannot restore to life one who has so died. And must the love that comes in dreams necessarily be unreal? For there is no lack of dream lovers in this world. Only for those whose love must be fulfilled on the pillow and for whom affection deepens only after retirement from office, is it entirely a corporeal matter. (Ko 1994:79)

The late Ming obsession with sensual love, physical lust, and enchanting romance did not survive the Manchu conquest of 1644. The Qing dynasty, which was ruled by a non-Han people, the Manchus, supplies the historical context for the chapters that follow. So we begin with an eyewitness account of the Manchu invasion that accompanied the collapse of the Ming dynasty (1368–1644). The following record of a Han Chinese survivor's experience shows how political upheaval in the early Qing was sexualized through images of women:

The women were put in a side room wherein were two small square tables, three dressmakers, and a middle-aged woman, who was also working on some garments. She was a local person, heavily made up and gaudily dressed, who gestured, talked, and laughed smugly. Every time the soldiers ran across some good item, she would beg them for it, brazenly using her fawning charms. One of the [Manchu] soldiers at one point remarked, "When we campaigned in Korea [1627 and 1636–1637], we captured women by the tens of thousands, and not one lost her chastity. How is it that wonderful China has become so shameless?" Alas, this is why China is in chaos. Then the three soldiers stripped the women of all their wet clothes, from outer to inner wear and from head to heel, and they ordered the middle-aged woman to take measurements and make alterations so the others could change into fresh new gowns. Needless to say, the women, relentlessly forced to expose their naked bodies, felt so ashamed and awkward that they wanted to die. After the women had finished changing clothes, the soldiers cuddled them while drinking wine and eating meat, doing all sorts of things with no regard for propriety. (Struve 1993:37)

As the Manchus proclaimed their new regime, moreover, they issued aggressive new rules about bodily adornment for the conquered Han population that had a different kind of sexual meaning. They forced Chinese men to shave their foreheads and wear their hair braided into a queue, Manchu style (see Figure 4). The queue replaced the centuries-old hairstyle favored by Han Chinese from the time of the Tang dynasty (618–906), when men pulled up and pinned their hair in a topknot, sometimes covered with a cap or net. Every Han Chinese man who shaved his forehead in submission to the Manchu order, in other words, symbolically abandoned his manly determination to defend the realm and denied his cultural heritage. The emasculating impact of the queue was intensified when the Manchus banned footbinding (Manchu women did not bind their feet) and Han Chinese women defied the new rulers. The paradoxical symbolism of submissive men and resistant women was captured in a popular contemporary saying: "*nan xiang, nü buxiang*," or "men submit, women resist" (Mann 2002:437). Some stories explaining why footbinding persisted do show men as women's protectors, sacrificing their own interests in exchange for upholding the honor of their female counterparts. The Ming official Hong Chengchou (1593–1665), who was castigated for surrendering to the Manchus and who later led the Qing campaign against the southern Ming loyalist resistance, agreed to

4. Early-twentieth-century photograph of the Manchu queue. *Source:* Jonathan D. Spence and Annping Chin, *The Chinese Century: A Photographic History of the Last Hundred Years.* New York: Random House, 1996, p. 18.

shave his own forehead only on condition that the clothing and hairstyles of Chinese women be left untouched – or so the story goes.[6] In point of fact, the Manchu ban on female footbinding proved impossible to enforce, precisely because to restore peace to the empire, the Qing rulers had to permit women to remain safely concealed at home. Government campaigns to unbind feet stopped at the gates of respectable households, and within a few years the Manchu court abandoned them entirely.

Under Manchu rule, as a result of these policies, bodily comportment and clothing signaled ethnic and social identity as never before. In its heyday, the government of China's last dynasty deployed unique and contradictory images of gendered performance, captured in the queue and the bound foot. These images frame the beginnings of the twentieth century.

[6] This perhaps apocryphal story is cited by Gulik 1951:5 in the introduction to his text; it does not appear in any other account of the conquest that I have consulted. Hong's own mother was profoundly affected by his shift of allegiance, and their relationship was also the subject of many stories (Wakeman 1985: vol. 2, 764n, 924n).

The Manchus blamed the fall of the Ming emperors on sexual indulgence and moral transgression, and they aimed to set the moral order back in place. They censored books, remade fashion, and launched a kind of moral rearmament campaign in the name of strict Confucian values. These values placed the husband-wife relationship at the center of the human social order, as classical texts continually reminded the reader (Rosenlee 2006:86): "The way of husband and wife is the beginning of human relations" (*Lienü zhuan*). "The way of husband and wife cannot but be proper; it is the root of the way of ruler and minister, and father and son" (*Xun Zi*). "The way of the gentleman in its simplest element is found in the husband-wife relation" (*Zhongyong*). Chaste women – not only faithful widows, but all women who preserved their chastity in the face of threats – were a centerpiece of these new programs. Qing programs honoring faithful wives produced long lists of "virtuous women" that filled the pages of local histories and peppered the landscape with shrines and memorial arches (see Figure 5).

Not content with these normative and material rewards, the Qing rulers also introduced tough new laws to reinforce their values. In the middle of the eighteenth century, the Manchus issued a series of edicts and statutes aimed at universalizing family values and extending them to every subject in the realm. These laws promised to eliminate the distinction between respectable and pariah families, and to promote family formation among even the poorest and most marginal sectors of the population (see Chapter 3). As a result of these Qing policies, nineteenth-century China probably saw the most "democratic" dissemination of norms governing gender and sexuality of any preindustrial society. With these relentless drives to disseminate a common core of gendered values to all commoners, and to eradicate the last vestiges of social discrimination from the Qing polity, the Manchus nearly succeeded in producing a conception of "the people" that was blind to rank and birth. In turn, all commoners were held accountable to the same standards of gender performance; all were subject to the disciplines, pressures, incentives, and rewards that the government supported and sustained. This universalizing approach to government that was firmly established by the Qing emperors served well as a foundation for China's twentieth-century nation-state.

Twentieth-century transformations

From the time of the Opium War in 1842, the Qing dynasty found itself under increasing military pressure along its maritime coast: first from Western powers (England, France, the United States) and

5. Photograph of a widow arch in Huizhou, Anhui province. Photograph courtesy of Yulian Wu.

then – after 1895 – from Japan. Foreign military pressures did not immediately challenge norms governing sexuality and gender. After the Boxer Rebellion in 1900, however, when the powers were threatening to "carve up the Chinese melon," urgent reforms began that aimed to galvanize all of the energies of each individual subject. These reforms, initiated before the dynasty fell in 1911, focused on women and the family. The reforms called for an end to footbinding, and they were accompanied by a vast new campaign to bring women out of the home and into schools and workplaces, where they could contribute to the nation-strengthening effort – and become better mothers of a generation of new citizens.

If the sex-gender system of the old empire centered on concealing women, then twentieth-century reforms focused on moving women into public spaces outside the home. In the campaign to build a strong nation, women's education and women's gainful employment topped the agendas for reform and revolution. Concealment was no longer tenable, especially for the upper classes. Bound feet lost their allure as nationalist fervor, changing lifestyles, and Western fashion made them look embarrassingly backward and unconscionably crippling. By the end of the Republican era at mid-century, bound feet – the emblem of concealed sexuality – had vanished from China's cities. During the 1950s, the Communist revolution in the countryside ended footbinding for good.

But remnants of concealment, legacies of skewed sex ratios, and other aspects of the nineteenth-century family system continued to shape gender and sexuality, especially in the countryside, where state policy constantly deferred to kin-based household organization. Patrilocal marriage, for example, was still the norm, with the result that when women married out of their villages and entered adult life in a new community, they remained on the margins of public life in the contemporary countryside (Judd 1994). Although rural women were no longer concealed from view, they encountered obstacles when seeking business or political positions that would take them abroad in men's company. Bias against women, sometimes expressed as concern about the proper separation of the sexes, effectively limited the presence of rural women in off-the-farm occupations. And although rural women were considered "in charge" of the domestic sphere (*nan zhu wai, nü zhu nei*) (Judd 1994:225), the tasks that were their charge were less technologically demanding, less prestigious, and less remunerative than those available to men. Resurgent interest in identifying women as "housewives" (*jiating funü*) – a corollary of the post-Mao reform era's insistence that men and women are not, in fact, the same – only exacerbated these differences and widened the gap between male and female in the countryside. By the same token, young farm women seeking escape from the constraints of rural life by migrating to cities to work in contract or temporary labor markets faced sexual harassment and exploitation as "working sisters" (*dagongmei*) (Jacka 1997).

The rest of this book is about the transformations in gender and sexuality that accompanied the twentieth-century changes briefly outlined in this introduction. How, and to what extent, did new ideas from Japan and the West affect notions of gender and sexuality, and the performance of gender roles, in modern China? Answers to these questions are still emerging in China's rapidly changing society, and the answers vary along the rural-urban continuum and across disparate ethnic cultures.

Chapters are arranged to underscore the importance of sexuality and gender in temporal context, with the focus on changes that began in the late Qing and continue today. As readers will see, some of the biggest changes have not received from historians the attention that they deserve. Political and economic policies forcing change for "women" – such as the call to send girls out of the home to school – produced contradictions and conflict in sexuality and gender performance that affected marriage and family, the self-perception and self-confidence of individuals, and the very foundations of gender difference established in the earliest Chinese classical texts. It is these contradictions and conflicts that will be our concern in this book.

The categories of analysis we are using, gender and sexuality, are conventional tools for contemporary scholars and students of Chinese history. It is therefore important to recognize that until the twentieth century there was no word in classical *or* vernacular Chinese for "gender," "sexuality," or "sex." When the modern concept of sex was introduced to Chinese readers, translators borrowed from modern Japanese translations and redefined the term *"xing"* (性). *Xing* was a problematic choice, because the earliest meaning of the Chinese ideograph *xing* had nothing to do with sex, and none of the eight different meanings associated with the term in standard dictionaries of the late imperial period has any relation to sex either.[7] To be sure, the classical philosophers and the Qing scholars who read classical philosophy had a clear notion of sexual appetites, which they commonly referred to as *"se"* (色). The iconoclastic eighteenth-century poet Yuan Mei even insisted that sexual appetites, and the emotion and feeling that accompanied them, were the essence of human creativity. "The fundamental driving force in human society," he wrote, was "not the altruism of sages but rather gross desires such as hunger for food and sexual craving" (Schmidt 2003:60). But Yuan Mei was not thinking of sexuality either. So this book is the history of a cultural category that did not exist during most of the period of this study.

Why, then, should we insist that sexuality and gender are important categories of historical analysis? The answer to that question lies in the challenge of engaging in any kind of cross-cultural research. To avoid imposing our own assumptions on the subject of our study, we use categories of analysis that defamiliarize familiar – or seemingly

---

[7] Ruan Fangfu, in Pan 2006:15. Ruan cites the *Shuo wen jie zi*, the oldest classical dictionary, and two dictionaries of late imperial literary Chinese: *Kangxi zi dian* and *Zhonghua da zi dian*. On the introduction of "gender" as an analytical concept, see Zheng Wang 1999a.

familiar – material. If the categories don't fit, we get to ask why. If the categories do fit, we get to see difference, variation, and change over time. Either way, we are introduced to ways of being in the world unlike our own, and in the process, we see a broader range of human possibilities. In the case of this book, using gender and sexuality as categories of analysis enables us to study the cultural logic of gender and sexuality in a context different from our own; to approach changes in ideas about what is right or wrong, good or bad, pleasurable or dangerous, enticing or loathsome, and admirable or despicable, using historically specific terms defined by Chinese cultural norms and values; and to understand more clearly – from a distance, so to speak – how gender relations and notions of gendered personhood are culturally constructed. Enduring structures of Chinese culture, particularly patrilineal kinship and a state empowered to manipulate family relationships, have made gender relations and sexuality in contemporary China uniquely Chinese: intelligible only through informed historical understanding. In that sense, the study of sexuality and gender relations in a different cultural context also challenges the universalizing claims of Western modernity.

PART I

GENDER, SEXUALITY, AND THE STATE

1   Family and state: the separation of the sexes

> Boji was a widow.... Once... she found herself at night in a house that had caught fire. Those nearby cried, "Lady, flee!" Boji said, "The rule for women is that when the matron and governess are not present, they do not leave the house at night. I await the coming of the matron and governess." [The matron arrived, but the governess did not, and so] ... she continued to stay there until the fire reached her and she died.... Thus did Boji fulfill to the utmost the duty of wifehood.
>
> Liu Xiang, *Lienü zhuan* (Biographies of Exemplary Women), first century BCE, chapter 4.2 (O'Hara 1945:105).

> One year after my mother died I got a stick and a bowl and started out begging. It was the spring of the year and I was twenty-two. It was no light thing for a woman to go out of her home. That is why I put up with my old opium sot so long. But now I could not live in my house and had to come out. When I begged I begged in the parts of the city where I was not known, for I was ashamed.
>
> Ning Lao T'ai-t'ai (Pruitt 1945:62)

Boji was an aristocrat who lived before the first century CE. Ning Lao T'ai-t'ai was a working woman who came of age at the end of the Qing dynasty. Each articulates clearly a conviction that women belong at home, and that "coming out" risks shame and dishonor. To be sure, Boji was mildly ridiculed by a noted sixteenth-century scholar who found her story an example of womanly virtue taken too far (Handlin 1975:19–20). But the testimony of Ning Lao T'ai-t'ai shows that ideas about the proper separation of men and women retained their power into the twentieth century. Even village girls in North China, interviewed in the 1980s by Carma Hinton and Richard Gordon for their documentary film *Small Happiness*, believed that it was improper to be seen in public

27

with a young man unless the two were already engaged to be married (Hinton and Gordon 1984). How and why did this moral sensibility survive despite sweeping social and political change? Ning Lao T'ai-t'ai, the female servant whose life story Ida Pruitt recorded as Ning settled into old age, was married in the late nineteenth century to a drug addict. Her husband's opium supply came from foreign markets in the treaty ports that sprang up along the coast after the Opium War of 1842. As the daughter of a man whose spending habits had reduced her natal family to poverty, Ning Lao T'ai-t'ai was hardly a cultivated lady (*guixiu*). But she was reared with *guixiu* values. Her parents arranged her marriage with the proper rituals, sheltering her from the traffic in women that circulated furiously all around them. To "come out" was to risk falling into that traffic. In Ning Lao T'ai-t'ai's world, the separation of the sexes defined gender and status. Ning's world is not so far removed from the world of the young women in Long Bow Village filmed by Hinton and Gordon. The star of *Small Happiness*, a young woman who was a successful tractor driver in high school, had to give it up because it was unseemly for a woman to be out on the road overnight, as tractors were commonly used for long-distance transport. As for girls trying to find a husband, as one father explained to Gordon's camera, in Long Bow there was no way for a young man and woman to get acquainted on their own. Parents had to make arrangements for them.

The separation of the sexes

The foundational idea of the separation of the sexes, summed up in the phrase "*nan nü you bie*," was an integral part of classical Chinese thought. Ancient political theory joined the social order to an encompassing cosmological and geophysical order. As early as the Han dynasty (206 BCE–220 CE), philosophers argued that the separation of the sexes was vital to that order, indeed, that it was the foundation of heaven and earth, and of all human relationships (Hinsch 2003). In elaborate Han cosmologies, the complex web of interactions joining humans to the forces of heaven and earth was called the *Dao*, or "Way." Its energy and continual transformation came from the alternation of two great forces, *yin* and *yang*: dark and bright, shadow and sunshine, night and day, wet and dry, weak and strong, moon and sun, cold and warm – the diurnal cycle, the sequence of the seasons, and even the rise and fall of dynasties were all understood using the language of *yin* and *yang*. In this embedded and interlaced understanding of the known world, the gender categories female and male were often subsumed under or syncretized with notions

6. Hexagrams *qian* and *kun* from the *Book of Changes*.

of *yin* and *yang*. Han commentaries on the *Book of Changes*, for example, identify two hexagrams, *qian* and *kun*, as the foundational symbols of that classic, as follows: "The movements of *qian* [*yang*] create the male, and the movements of *kun* [*yin*] complete the female" (Robin Wang 2003:29). (See Figure 6.)

Male and female, in this understanding, are complementary categories. They do not exist in isolation from one another; rather, they are constantly interacting to produce the social order. Han commentaries on the *Book of Changes* also say that *yang*, representing heaven, is superior to *yin*, representing earth:

Although a yin person has excellence, he effaces it in order to attend to his sovereign's business and does not dare take credit for its success. This is the Dao of Earth, the Dao of the wife, and the Dao of the minister. The Dao of Earth has one 'make no claim for . . . success' but working on behalf of the other [*Qian* – Pure Yang, i.e., Heaven – husband, sovereign], 'he should bring about a successful conclusion' (Lynn 1994:148).

This way of thinking about hierarchical dualisms based on *yang* and *yin* played out systematically in the conceptualization of all human relationships (*renlun*), so that the bonds between ruler and subject were easily understood as "like" those of husband and wife: although the relationships were hierarchical, each relied on the other for legitimacy: they were, in the words of one scholar, "complementary pairs that complete rather than contradict one another" (Rosenlee 2006:63).

In Chinese political philosophy, this cosmological understanding of complementary-yet-hierarchical gender relations took pragmatic shape in a model of political economy based on household units. Each household comprised males and females performing complementary tasks that produced food, clothing, and shelter for their members, and revenue for the state. In the nineteenth century, this model was captured in the statecraft phrase, "men plough, women weave." Here is how it was first formulated, in the third century BCE, by the philosopher Mencius, in his famous advice book for aspiring kings:

Around the homestead with its five *mu* of land, the space beneath the walls was planted with mulberry trees, with which the women nourished silkworms, and

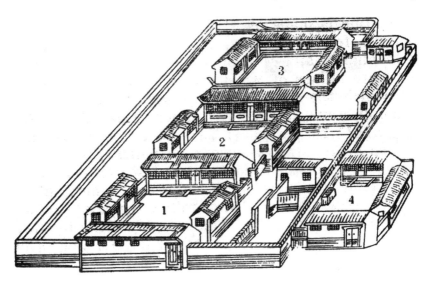

7. Drawing of the interior of a traditional Chinese house, showing the court where visitors are received (1), the domain of the master of the house (2), and the women's quarters (3). *Source:* C. A. S. Williams, *Outlines of Chinese Symbolism and Art Motives*, 3rd revised edition. New York: Dover, 1976, p. 22.

thus the old were able to have silk to wear. Each family had five brood hens and two brood sows, which were kept to their breeding seasons, and thus the old were able to have flesh to eat. The husbandmen cultivated their farms of 100 *mu*, and thus their families of eight mouths were secured against want. (Mencius VIIA.22; Legge 1983:461)

Notice that in Mencius's model, women are confined to the domestic space of the house and its gardens, while the men work outside in the fields (see Figures 7 and 8). Cloth and meat from domestic animals are women's concern; men take charge of grain production. This ancient model of a gender division of labor persisted in the nineteenth century in many parts of rural China, and you can see it still in the courtyards of Long Bow Village during the early 1980s when you watch the film *Small Happiness*.[1]

---

[1] As Yan Yunxiang has emphasized, a "common feature of the traditional Chinese house was to separate the activities of men and women, both spatially and socially, and to downplay the importance of conjugal intimacy" (Yan 2005:375). See Bray 2005 for a fuller discussion.

Mencius also had a few words to say about sexuality and the ways in which it might undermine the security of household units and the order of the *Dao*:

When a man is born his parents hope he will find a wife; when a woman is born her parents hope she will find a husband. All parents feel like this. But those who do not wait for the command of their parents or the words of a matchmaker – and instead bore holes through walls to peep at one another, and jump over fences to go off together – are despised by parents and everyone else in their state. (Mencius IIIB.3; translated by Bryan Van Norden in Robin Wang 2003:103)

Here Mencius was cautioning his audience about the chaos threatened by romantic love and sexual attraction, another concern of early philosophers. Songs in the *Classic of Poetry* celebrate sensual passion, especially the infamous Ode 95, about the rivers Zhen and Wei:

> A lady says, "Have you been to see?"
> A gentleman replied, "I have been."
> "But let us go again to see,
> Beyond the Wei,
> The ground is spacious and fit for pleasure."
> So the gentlemen and ladies
> Make sport together,
> Presenting one another with small peonies.
> (Robin Wang 2003:19, translation based on Legge 1991)

Commentators tried their best to turn such poems into warnings, but this was not easily done. Already in the earliest Chinese classical writings we hear about tensions between family duty and sexual desire.

Passion and pleasure

How was sexual passion understood in earliest Chinese philosophy? Most early philosophers were interested in human nature, and in how humans differed from animals (or not). For the most part, they regarded sexual desire as an innate physical need like hunger, thirst, and the desire for warmth and rest. All philosophers agreed that, for humans, the need to satisfy physical desire had to be tempered by social rules and rituals. Xun Zi was the most outspoken on this subject, arguing that human nature in its raw physical state was fundamentally antisocial and had to be tamed by strict education and regular ritual performances. Even Mencius, who had great confidence in the innate goodness of human

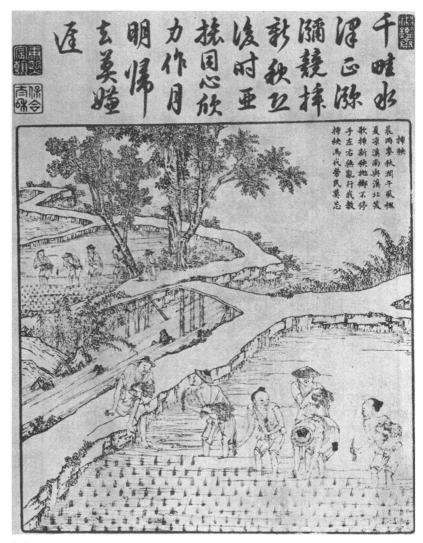

(a)

8a–b. Hortatory illustration showing women weaving inside and men sowing outside. From *Yuzhi gengzhi tu* (Imperially endorsed illustrations of ploughing and weaving), 1696. *Source:* Zhou Wu, *Zhongguo banhua shi tu lu* (Catalog of Illustrations from the History of Chinese Woodblock Printing). Shanghai: Renmin meishu chubanshe, 1988, vol. 1, pp. 276–277.

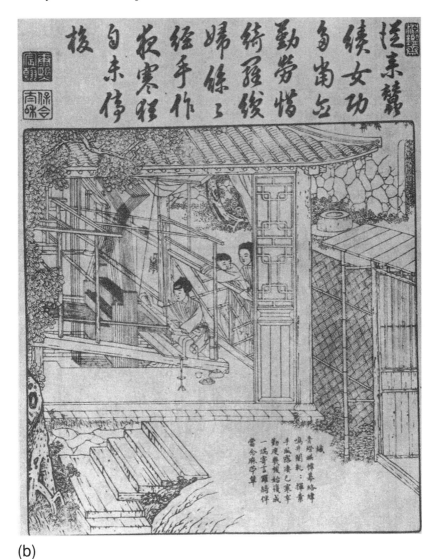

(b)

8a–b (*continued*)

nature, nonetheless insisted that "in gratifying the appetite for sex, . . . the observance of rules of propriety is more important" than meeting an individual's need (Mencius VIB.1; Legge 1983:422). Social practices that enabled people to live in harmonious order demanded that individuals deny or contain their sexual desires.

Instead of focusing on sexual desire as the site of pleasure, the early philosophers conceived of pleasure in other terms. The pleasures they fancied were ideally to be dispensed by the government (or the ruler) in the form of honors and rewards of all kinds that the people could look forward to, enjoy in the immediate experience, and remember with fondness after the fact. When considering individual pleasure, the early thinkers focused closely on the strategy of the "wise person" or "gentleman" who could discern over the long run what would ultimately supply the most pleasure and then pursue those long-term goals resolutely throughout life, avoiding frantic struggles and costly anxiety. In this view, desire (including the desire for sex) is not a problem; in fact, desire is necessary for humans to be motivated to act. Rather, the key is fulfilling desire so as to maximize pleasure and minimize anxiety and chaos in the pursuit of it. Xun Zi, for example, pointed out that a person might long to be clothed entirely in silk but would renounce that desire in the knowledge that if he spent all his money on silk he would have nothing left to live on. Similarly, he observed, a young man longing to have sex with a girl might hold back if his parents or elder brother were present because of anxiety about flouting ritual propriety (Nylan 2001:99–100). The point here is that pleasure, including sexual pleasure, was conceptualized holistically, in a context in which the ultimate goal was long-term pleasure, on many fronts and for as long as possible.

In other words, classical arguments that appear to stress sexual discipline or constraint were actually appealing directly to individual self-interest. The same appeal is made in the techniques for nurturing and prolonging life (*yangsheng*) spelled out in bamboo and silk manuscripts from the early part of the second century BCE. Enchanting visions of an elixir of immortality that could stave off aging and death (invoked in the toast *wansui*, "may you live ten thousand years!") enticed early emperors to empty their treasuries on expeditions sent searching for it (Knoblock 1988:144).

From the government's point of view, human sexuality also had a practical and positive purpose: the reproduction of subjects who would work hard to feed, clothe, and shelter themselves, and whose labor would generate surpluses that the government could tax. Recruiting men as soldiers and corvée laborers, as well as officials, gave the government a particular interest in male bodies. In a polity where the ruler held sway over myriad commoner households, gendered behavior was clearly specified. Males, socialized in patrilineal families, became filial sons and then loyal subjects. Females, reared for marriage into another patriline, became faithful wives and wise mothers. These forms of gender discipline kept the order of the *Dao*. Sprung free of the economic, emotional, and moral structures of marriage and the family, both male and female subjects became dangerously disruptive. Unmarried men were called "bare sticks" whose lack of family ties threatened stable communities with rape and robbery. Courtesans and prostitutes lured husbands and fathers and their money away from family responsibilities.

Enforcing the separation of the sexes

The imperial government did its best to control sexual transgression through a combination of coercive punishments and positive rewards. Legal punishment for rape, and severe penalties for fornication, tightened in the eighteenth century (see Chapter 3). Censorship of "licentious" religious cults and practices, opera and theater performances, and books and paintings accompanied the government's crackdown on "seditious" materials in the middle of the eighteenth century (see Chapter 8). But the government's most pervasive controls took non-coercive forms: rewards for women whose virtuous or meritorious behavior curtailed, denied, or overcame sexual desire; promotion of family-based activities such as the compilation of family instructions and genealogies; and kin-based honorific titles, which were awarded to parents and grandparents (male and female) of distinguished civil servants.

How was the imperial government able to deliver its negative and positive messages so pervasively and effectively? In Qing times, the reach of the state was deeply felt through the institutionalization of the *baojia* system, in which every household was registered, along with the names and number of adult males, in groups of ten, headed by a leader who was responsible for reporting on all of the households in his group. The duties of the members of these groups were "to watch, detect, and report any crime or criminal that might be found in the neighborhoods" (Hsiao 1960:45). Aggressive programs to expand this system in borderland and minority areas continued throughout the early nineteenth century and then waned (Hsiao 1960:51–55). But the system was used in many parts of the country to collect taxes and to carry out certain kinds of political campaigns, including opium suppression, throughout the nineteenth century. The *baojia* system was not designed to control sexuality, except where it was linked to criminal activity such as kidnapping or rape. Such a pervasive system of mutual surveillance must have had a powerful effect on people who lived in areas where the system functioned effectively, however, if only because it clearly separated members of settled communities from outsiders. The primary victims of the *baojia* system, moreover, were those excluded by it: the bare sticks (*guanggun*), or single men, who did not belong to households at all. The effect of the *baojia* was to further isolate and stigmatize these individuals as outsiders and dangerous people. In its precocious concern with counting and recording population data, China's imperial government was "seeing like a state" from its inception (James Scott 1998).

Alongside the *baojia* system, the imperial government sponsored large-scale propaganda programs in the form of public lectures promoting desirable sexual behavior. At meeting halls, temples, and marketplaces, lectures touting the virtues of family harmony were delivered as often as twice monthly in some areas. The lectures may have been less inspiring than the government hoped, but concrete rewards for virtue proved extremely effective. Shrines to honor "local worthies" included both filial sons and faithful widows, and individual families who successfully nominated a member for one of these honors could receive up to thirty silver taels to pay for the construction of a special memorial arch, and even a congratulatory gift of calligraphy written in the emperor's own hand. One reason for the Chinese state's enormous power in this morally charged arena was the absence of competing sources of authority, especially religion. Although religious beliefs figured powerfully in some aspects of sexuality and gender in the nineteenth century (Daoist *yangsheng* beliefs, for example, or Buddhist rituals of pollution and purification; see Chapter 4), no religious institution installed itself as a mediator in defining sexual behavior.

While honoring sexual behavior that comported with family norms, the government also tried to ban or limit sexual interactions outside the context of the family. Here the burdens of enforcement fell on county magistrates, the so-called father-mother officials (*fumu guan*) who were closest to the people. As a handbook for magistrates put it, warning against "rampant adultery": "Licentious customs are easily developed through the maintenance of intimate contact between the sexes. The enforcement of strict separation between males and females is the foundation of the cultivation of proper conduct" (Djang 1984:431). Mindful of imperial edicts condemning religious pilgrimages to shrines and temples (where, as the Qianlong Emperor put it, "men and women mix promiscuously, and it is impossible to tell the good from the bad" [Hsiao 1960:230]), magistrates viewed temples with deep suspicion as venues for illicit sex, often accusing nuns of acting as procuresses. Even women of prominent families, the magistrates' handbook warns, may "seek liaisons with dissipated youths in secret passages of the monasteries" (Djang 1984:608). Magistrates tried to influence the daily habits of local people in their homes, issuing periodic reminders about the proper separation of the inner and outer apartments and the segregation of sexes at mealtime

(Djang 1984:431). Local officials could mobilize the *baojia* network to help them monitor sexuality, including efforts to identify, isolate, and drive away commercial sex operations, not only in local markets and public roadways, but also, again, in private homes, because (as the handbook warns) "certain wealthy individuals and unscrupulous licentiates[2] shelter prostitution in exchange for carnal pleasure, and these shameless people are no different from pimps" (Djang 1984:500–501). Chapter 3 looks more closely at the challenges magistrates faced as they tried to control illicit sexual activity in the areas under their jurisdiction.

Despite this range of coercive and remunerative policies, the government's ability to control sexuality had limits. A magistrate might be responsible for 250,000 people in a single county, and he had many more pressing concerns. Enforcement of the limits on sexuality fell more directly to families at the household level, and to the lineage organizations to which many families belonged. Female sexuality was a focal concern of patrilineal kinship organizations, clearly delineated in the many editions of "clan rules" that guided lineage elders. Family rituals – from ancestor worship, weddings, and funerals to *rites de passage* for young men and young women entering adulthood – were central to the authority of the patriline. Male elders also had decisive control over decisions related to marriage, matters of childhood socialization and education, and leisure activities. As one genealogy put it: "Without due control, the ever-present sexual desire in both men and women could lead into adultery and violation of morality" (Liu 1959:78). Accordingly, some clan rules stipulated penalties for visiting prostitutes, for "being licentious," and for committing adultery. Punishments ranged from oral censure to corporal beatings and, in some cases, exclusion from the genealogy, the ancestral hall, or even the kinship group (Liu 1959:259). These rules and punishments focused partly on guarding the purity of the male line, of course. But equally important were other needs: to avoid costly litigation, to uphold a reputation – essential to making good marriage alliances, to keep married brothers together to forestall the fragmentation of family assets, and to secure the safety of wives, mothers, daughters, and daughters-in-law. The goal of every lineage, as one instruction book put it, was to "keep suspicion from arising so that people cannot possibly slander the family" (Liu 1959:93). A woman who was raped, or accused of adultery, became the centerpiece of public scandal that sometimes resulted in violence or even death (see Chapters 3 and 6). By contrast, a faithful widow could bring a family accolades straight from the imperial throne, and a

---

[2] Holders of the lowest degree in the civil service examination system, sometimes called the "lower gentry" because of their limited influence beyond their own localities.

well-educated and talented daughter with a pure record could attract a choice husband from a prime family.

Clan rules sought to keep women separate from men in three ways (Liu 1959: 93–96). Within the domestic sphere, all interaction with men except the husband and younger sons was prohibited. Women could not dine at the same table with men; male family members could not enter the bedroom of a young woman; male servants were not allowed inside the women's quarters. If disagreements arose between a female and a male member of a large family, the dispute had to be settled by the husband of the woman in question, acting as mediator, or – if an unmarried daughter was involved – by her father. When goods or services were brought into the house from outside, men (or female servants) attended to them. Respectable women were not to interact with female vendors, and even midwives, female fortunetellers, and nuns were blacklisted (among the menacing "six grannies" and "three aunties") in most family instruction books. Again, the threat here appears to be not so much sexuality per se as the danger of gossip about respectable women being conveyed abroad to other households. But the six grannies were often accused of luring gullible young ladies into the clutches of lecherous men – an endlessly appealing plotline for fiction writers and storytellers. Finally, of course, there were the inevitable bans on visits to temples, operas, and festival celebrations – no spring outings, no sightseeing, no visits to a friend's house, and so forth. Even the obligatory visit home to the natal family by a married woman, which properly came every three lunar months or so in many parts of China, was forbidden after her parents died.

Perhaps in recognition that these kinds of rules were extreme and could even be silly – and, moreover, that they had no basis in classical Confucian teachings – the "punishment" for women who sallied forth, or welcomed visitors, or bargained over silk thread was mild, if it was recorded at all (Liu 1959:96). Moreover, because we know that highly educated women managed to conduct lively "poet friendships" across neighborhoods and whole regions of the country, the isolation envisioned in these prescriptive texts was probably rarely achieved. For women in ordinary commoner households, moreover, there was no space to segregate for the exclusive use of women, and the demands for female labor in the household economy often took women outside the home, either to work in the fields or to earn money by some other means. Sex segregation, then, was more of a platitude than a reality in the lives of most women. But the constant references to it, in writings by officials and kinship organizations, show that monitoring the activities of sexually active women was an obsessive concern. And the messages conveyed – avoid suspicion, shun male company, stay out of gossip – clearly had their effect on women's consciousness.

For evidence of that we have only to reread the preceding words of Ning Lao T'ai-t'ai, who was so ashamed to "come out."

The crack in the wall problem: tensions between passion and arranged marriage

As clear as the boundaries separating the sexes were the tensions that continually threatened those boundaries. China's earliest philosophers acknowledged these tensions explicitly. They agreed that sexual attraction and desire were a part of human nature, innate to humans just like the desire for food and drink. They counseled restraint, stressing moderation in all things and cautioning that over-indulgence in sex could be dangerous to your health. Philosophers and physicians alike warned men that too much sexual activity could deplete their vital energy and shorten their lives. Techniques for conserving energy and prolonging life – perhaps even achieving immortality – could be learned from Daoist teachers. By practicing "inner alchemy," a man could circulate his vital breath (*qi*) through the inner channels of his body and preserve sexual vigor. In the early text *Guan Zi*, male readers studied how to concentrate vital breath so that "seminal essence," the wellspring of life energy, never dried up (Knoblock 1988:145). Techniques of inner alchemy like this were later developed for postmenopausal women as well, using texts like the *Classic of the Plain Girl* (*Su nü jing*). Although these *yangsheng* techniques were controversial, even among Daoists, they show us domains in which regulating sexual desire was part of spiritual practice and individual self-cultivation, as well as political thought and control, in earliest times.

In Figure 9 we see healthy sexual practice and long life or immortality displayed in the Daoist alchemical body, in which a man's sperm (*jing*), his vital essence (*qi*), and his spirit are harmoniously conjoined.

An eclectic text on statecraft, prepared for the First Emperor in the second century CE, offers a fine summation of these ideas:

When Heaven gave life to humans it caused them to have appetites and desires. Certain desires belong to the essential nature of humans, and those that are essential to their nature are inherently self-limiting. The sage keeps these limits in good repair to make the desires stop at the right place; this is why when he acts he does not transgress the limits belonging to his essential nature. (*Lüshi chunqiu* 2/3.1; Knoblock and Riegel 2000:84)

But of course youthful passion is not moderate, and Chinese thinkers were well aware of this big problem. When Mencius talked about

9. The Ming alchemical body. *Source:* Charlotte Furth, *A Flourishing Yin: Gender in China's Medical History, 960–1665.* Berkeley: University of California Press, 1999, p. 194. Printed with permission of the Needham Research Institute.

ordinary people in families, he was explicit in his concern about the conflict between arranged marriage (ritual propriety) and youthful passion, as we have seen. Mencius' image of lovers who peek through holes and leap over walls recurs in favorite lines from the *Classic of Poetry*: "I pray you, Mr. Zhong, do not come leaping over my wall" (Legge 1991:126; Mao Ode 76). Stories about romantic passion and desire saturate myths

10. The meeting of the Herd Boy and the Weaving Maid on the borders of the Milky Way. *Source:* C. A. S. Williams, *Outlines of Chinese Symbolism and Art Motives*, 3rd revised edition. New York: Dover, 1976, p. 372.

and legends that inspired popular festivals and paintings. The legendary Herd Boy and the Weaving Maid, for example, separated forever by a heavenly decree, can be together only one night a year, on the seventh day of the seventh month, when they cross the magpie bridge and meet in the starry skies (see Figure 10). Why were they punished? She was so love-struck that she neglected her weaving.

Fiction offered other lessons about passion and its price, as in Ying-ying's story, which supplied a kind of sex education, giving a young girl who read or heard the story the experience of vicarious romance and sexual freedom, while impressing her with the costs (Luo 2005). In the eighteenth-century novel *Dream of the Red Chamber* (*Honglou meng*), the hero and heroine read a play about Yingying, and each takes from the play his or her own message: his about the glories of love and romance, hers about the hopelessness of love and romance (Waltner 1989). Illustrations for the opera *The Peony Pavilion*, that other tale of transgressive youthful romance, show the heroine Du Liniang dreaming blissfully of a tryst with her beloved (see Figure 11).

Exemplary biographies of women, dramatically illustrated in popular books, show heroines killing themselves in an act of passion, whether threatened with rape or declaring their fidelity to the man to whom they were betrothed (Weijing Lu 2008). Stories of women's passionate death were dramatized in every venue, from plays watched by seventeenth-century peasants to short stories read in elite boudoirs, and even at local shrines, where the spirit of a woman who had killed herself was honored with incense and offerings (Carlitz 1997b). The illustration in Figure 12 shows one of the most sensational female suicides: the death of the beautiful Yu *ji*, consort of the hero Xiang Yu, a contender for the throne when the first dynasty (Qin) began to fall. The scene is set in Xiang Yu's tent, where he and his troops have been surrounded by the enemy. Trapped and doomed, Xiang Yu's spirits sink as his troops mourn their homeland in the state of Chu, and the enemy cynically performs a Chu song to heighten their sense of isolation. Xiang Yu drinks with Yu *ji* and reviews their happiness together and then in a poignant poem asks plaintively: "What is to become of you?" She replies:

> The Han army is intruding
> We are besieged on all sides;
> So depressed is your majesty,
> Why should I live any longer?
> So saying, she slits her throat.
>   (Peterson 2000:50)

How did female readers respond to these stories in the Qing period? Scholars studying legal cases, especially transcripts from criminal trials involving rape, have found that female defendants in the eighteenth century, including commoners, offered impassioned defenses of their honor that echo the passion of martyrs from fiction and myth (Theiss 2004). In the same period, we also read heartrending accounts of

11. Du Liniang dreaming of encountering Liu Mengmei in a garden. Scene from *The Peony Pavilion*, by Tang Xianzu. *Source:* Robert E. Hegel, *Reading Illustrated Fiction in Late Imperial China*. Stanford, Calif.: Stanford University Press, 1998, p. 230.

12. Yu *ji* slits her throat. *Source: Lidai mingyuan tushuo* (Illustrated Stories of Noted Women through the Ages). Preface by Lu Wenchao [1779]. Dianshizhai facsimile reprint, 1879, vol. 1, p. 20b.

parents concerned about a phenomenon known as the "faithful maiden" complex, which provoked complicated moral debates about young women's extreme devotion to a single man. A girl who declared herself a faithful maiden was one who, betrothed to a man who died before the wedding, vowed never to marry anyone else. This kind of fidelity unto death (in some cases faithful maidens did kill themselves) – or resignation to a celibate life like that of a virtuous widow – made parents distraught, caused girls to defy their parents' wishes, and upset scholars who argued about when, precisely, Confucian ritual actually sealed a betrothal agreement. For many parents, a beloved daughter's future depended not only on a satisfactory marriage but also on the good health and emotional security that were thought to accompany healthy sexual relations and bearing children (Weijing Lu 2008). So sex and passion were subjects that endlessly preoccupied young and old, male and female, and elite and commoner in late imperial times.

The pleasures and passions of sex made separating the sexes a continual challenge not only to families but also to the state. Every lineage instruction book echoes the magistrate's warning to keep women out of sight, and keep men and women separated, even within the same household. Separation of the sexes was promoted by the organization of production, which, as we have seen, favored occupational differentiation that drew males outside while keeping women inside. That these constraints focused on females in their fertile years is clear from the fact that clan rules singled out for attention women between the age of puberty and fifty. That women over fifty (and girls under twelve) were considered above suspicion (Liu 1959:93) reflects assumptions about female sexual desire, and also beliefs about longevity and sexual vitality in male and female bodies (see Chapter 4).

The expectation that women would remain "inside" or "at home" meant that respectable activities outside the home were dominated by men. Men at every level of the status hierarchy sojourned abroad: scholars to sit for civil service exams, officials to serve in their posts, merchants to distant markets, and laborers to jobs. In a society where everyone was supposed to be safely anchored in a registered household, men away from home were always at risk. The better-off educated man could count on patronage from people with influence: an employer who needed his services as a student, as a tutor for his children, as a medical specialist to treat his family's ailments, or as a scholar engaged in compilation or other research projects. Men who aspired to government office, the most prestigious occupation in the empire, sat endlessly for civil service examinations that took them away from home, first to the county and prefectural seat, then to the provincial capital, and finally – if they reached the top – to the imperial capital itself. Along the way, male scholars of all ages lodged in native-place halls or in temples, if they could not find shelter with friends or relatives. The most fortunate among them enjoyed government stipends at public or private academies, surrounded by male teachers and fellow students. Sojourning scholars, in any case, kept company almost exclusively with other men; the women of their class were, after all, secluded. The courtesans' quarters, famous for their lively appeal in major examination centers like Nanjing, gave the only respite from this male-dominated homosocial life, unless a man was lucky enough to have a relative's or friend's mother take pity on him and make him a spoiled guest. (Or unless he took a risk like the bold young scholar Zhang who wooed Yingying.)

Merchants and traders, lacking the networks and credentials of scholars, had to resort to other support systems. Route books and travel guides helped them locate the safest roads and waterways and the most reliable inns, the clothes to pack, and the dangers to avoid. Fortunate merchants from major commercial cities could often count on guilds to serve as a temporary advocate and shelter as they traveled; petty traders and itinerant artisans who were shut out of these circles had to cope with isolation and with the threats to their property and safety from the bare sticks who were also on the road. Just how vulnerable a lone trader could be is underscored in the advice books for travelers, which warned of highwaymen and river pirates, innkeepers and their guests who would rob you while you sleep, con men posing as people from the same native place, dishonest porters or boat crews, shyster pawnbrokers and money-changers, and all manner of swindles (Lufrano 1997:157–176). Although traveling men of all classes faced these kinds of difficulties, merchants and traders were more vulnerable than scholars or officials, who could more reliably count on the backing of a magistrate or a connection with someone in the local elite to help them out in the event of a crime. For the most part, the merchants' world was a male domain, especially for sojourners. Although women were involved in many kinds of commercial transactions, from operating small restaurants and shops to serving as go-betweens and agents for the hiring of female domestic labor, most sojourners understood that women they met while traveling were sexually available but possibly dangerous. Women who seduced and tricked gullible travelers out of their money were a vivid theme in guidebooks, which warned against them. Yet the saying that "the prostitute is the traveler's wife" suggests that even if guidebooks threatened torture in a Buddhist hell as punishment, brothels were a common stopover for merchant wayfarers (Lufrano 1997:101).[3]

Now we are in a position to understand better the sharp line dividing women who were cloistered in families from those who entered the market for sex. The line, once crossed, could permanently destroy a woman's reputation and, with that, the reputation of her family, including her marriageable brothers.[4] Family instruction books reflect this anxiety about making sure women stay safely in their place: "Maintain the dignity of the women's apartments," a key injunction in family instruction books, made it clear to all that secluding women was the most important way for men to maintain a family's moral integrity (Furth 1990:196). Other warnings about women in family guidebooks also show, however, that men were supposed to guard against undue influence by their wives (Furth 1990:196–197) while also resisting the lure of the pleasure quarter, a

---

[3] Who were the women in those brothels? Chapter 2 takes up the trafficking that pulled women out of the family system and into commercial sex and servitude.

[4] Chapter 3 shows how the courts treated the families of women who became involved in "disgraceful matters" (Theiss 2004).

domain that threatened their moral commitment to family obligations (Furth 1990:204–206).

Twentieth-century shifts

The pervasive awareness of sexual desire in late imperial times – the concern about its entanglements, and the heartache it caused when marriage did not lead to the fulfillment of sexual desire or at least to some kind of emotional satisfaction – sheds important light on twentieth-century history. When young people in the May Fourth era called for "free social interaction between the sexes," their longing for free mate choice and love marriage was hardly a radical new notion. Arguably it was a predictable, welcome, and culturally logical move, suddenly sanctioned by the urgent demands of nation-building. Arranged marriage had been clearly identified in late imperial culture as a source of deep pain and emotional cost for men and, especially, women, and arranged marriage depended on the separation of the sexes. Once alternative arrangements were spelled out and made available, even desirable and prestigious or fashionable, the logic of modern marriage could be explained using traditional Chinese cultural understandings of sexual desire and its importance to human emotional health and happiness.

But what about the so-called woman question of the early twentieth century? How are we to understand that question in historical context? First of all, as we have clearly seen, the category "woman" was not new to Chinese political discourse in the twentieth century. Late imperial injunctions to "separate the sexes" (*nan nü you bie*) continually referred to men and women as binary categories of persons with complementary but separate roles to play in the household and in society at large. The "inner" sphere confining women to the household, out of sight, was seen as a necessary counterpart to the "outer" sphere where men moved about freely. Other gendered terms pointed to the familial roles played by women at different points in the life cycle: hence, *nüzi* (girl, meaning unmarried woman) and *fu* (wife, or married woman). In the twentieth century, with the movement of women outside the home for school and for work, new terms displaced the old complementary phrase "*nan nü.*" Women now had their own particular role to play in the construction of the new polity, as citizens of the nation. A neologism created in Japan (*nüxing*, "female"), was joined in the late Qing period by other new words, including the term "*funü*," which became in China the widely accepted reference to women in twentieth-century political discourse. The woman question (*funü wenti*) raised by twentieth-century reformers pointed specifically to problems that arose when women moved outside the home (Barlow 1994, Rosenlee 2006:45–48). In other words, conversations about the woman question were all about the cataclysmic rupture in the late imperial sex-gender system: the end of the classical separation of the sexes that was necessary if China the nation was to be saved.

Under the rubric of the woman question, women were the object of reform and revolutionary discourses throughout the Republican era. Elite women became educators, attorneys, physicians, and professionals in many fields, including government, buoyed by the new programs designed to educate them abroad and promote their leadership at home (Zheng Wang 1999b). Women assumed a special new position in the world of commercial publishing, as foreign media and foreign role models circulated new ideas about gender and as the long-standing literary bent of upper-class women turned to new kinds of books and magazines (Hu Hsiao-chen 2004, Judge 2008, Qian 2004). Women workers, thousands of them migrants from rural areas brought into urban job markets under labor contracts, filled the light industrial factories, especially in Shanghai. Alert to the concerns of the parents of young unmarried female workers, contractors promised sex-segregated and carefully supervised dormitories, with earnings sent directly home to parents (Honig 1986), even though such promises offered questionable protection from the market for commercial sex, which expanded with the growing industrial economy and labor force. During the first decades of the twentieth century, foreign and Chinese prostitutes made Shanghai into a "paradise of adventurers" (Hershatter 1997). All of these women – new professionals, workers, prostitutes, and even housewives – became part of an emerging modern urban culture that produced new theater, new fiction, new film, and new values. The Communist revolution in 1949 closed down Shanghai's brothels and sent prostitutes into rehabilitation programs, issuing its call to all women to become productive workers who would "hold up half the sky." The call sounded just as the last generation of *guixiu* (cloistered ladies) was passing from the scene. In the early years of the People's Republic, the new government moved aggressively to eliminate vestiges of footbinding, expand marriage opportunities for poor males, promote divorce and remarriage rights for women, and eradicate the remaining foundations of the old sex-gender system based on cloistered women. But as late as 1958, many young married women in Shanghai had still not left home to go out to work: it took the coercive injunctions of the Great Leap Forward to break the grip of mothers-in-law who remained devoted to the old gender system (Mann 1994). As Gail Hershatter's interviews in rural Shaanxi have shown, in contrast, female labor in agriculture supplied the crucial surplus that made possible the success of China's rural revolution, starting in the 1950s (Hershatter 2011).[5]

The tight links between state and sexuality in late imperial times anticipated the gendered dimensions of policy-making in the contemporary People's Republic. "Campaign politics" in the Maoist period (1949–1976), for example, had clear agendas that oscillated between periods of mass mobilization ("Red" phases) and periods of economic pragmatism ("expert" phases). In peak Red phases, when the push for male-female equality was strongest, the boundaries separating the sexes were overridden by the movement of women into men's worlds of work and political activism. The Great Leap Forward (1958–1961) and the Cultural Revolution's early militant phase (1966–1969) are both classic examples. In contrast, in periods in which the expert line prevailed, women's relative disadvantages (in job training, education, political leadership, and so forth) made retreat from public life either necessary or advisable. An extreme example of the government's interest in actually restoring the separation of the sexes appeared in the post-Mao reform era during the 1990s, when reactions against Maoist policies and appeals to economic privilege were used to entice women to retreat into the home, as devoted wives and mothers of precious only children. This revival of what closely resembled Confucian womanly virtues even fed campaigns to reinvent and circulate an old Confucian-style advice book for women, the *Women's Classic* (*Nü'er jing*), in the last decade of the twentieth century.[6]

The contemporary Chinese state's intense concern with women's place in the family, the polity, and the economy is not new. Rather, it builds on centuries of government involvement in promoting a social order grounded in the gender division of labor within households. Absent the mediating influence of powerful religious institutions, the modern Chinese central government – like its predecessors – has been relatively free to manipulate the family system in directions favoring the interests of its own leadership. Moreover, because of the conflation of political values with gendered values (the links between loyalty to the state and a wife's fidelity to her spouse, for example, or between weak women and vulnerability to foreign invasion), appeals to put the nation's interests ahead of the interests of women as a group have met with ready compliance, despite the rhetoric of the woman question.

[5] The costs to rural women of going out to work in the fields are thoroughly examined in Hershatter's study.

[6] This early-twentieth-century pseudo-classic, closely modeled after didactic texts for women in circulation during the eighteenth century, includes admonitions about obedience, chastity, and demure dress and demeanor. A new edition with "fresh interpretations" was published in 1997 (Ran 1997).

2 Traffic in women and the problem of single men

> "Come," he said [to my daughter, his wife]. "This is not such bad business, having girls. Each one will sell for three hundred taels and we can live on that a long time, and then I can sell you for three hundred more if there are no more girls to sell."
>
> Ning Lao T'ai-t'ai (Pruitt 1945:168)

> Little Lu had to go to the railway station to pick up and escort home a young woman who was kidnapped into another province.... Girls are tricked into signing on to work on the coast, and then are sold as brides into poor mountain villages.
>
> Woman's Federation cadre in Sichuan (Gates 1996:8)

The late imperial social order anchored married men and women in stable family relationships, organized around the principle of separation of the sexes. But what happened to men or women who abandoned the family, or were forced out of the family, or were denied a family? When things fell apart, as they did in Ning Lao T'ai-t'ai's world at the end of the Qing dynasty, wives were rented, daughters were sold, and unattached men at the bottom of the social hierarchy banded together to survive. In other times of stress, such as the Taiping Rebellion in the mid-nineteenth century, parents put female infants to death so they could count on rearing a son who would carry on the patriline. Social disorder, then, was always encoded with sexual and gendered conflicts and tensions, ranging from female infanticide and suicide to rebellion and the collapse of dynasties.

Maintaining social order was the charge of the emperor, who, by wise governance, ensured that heaven, human society, and earth remained in harmonious accord. The ruler received a "mandate" from heaven to assume this weighty responsibility. Chaos in society and in the natural world (drought, flood, earthquake, or rebellion) signaled that heaven's mandate had been withdrawn. Free-floating sexuality not only threatened the social order; it also endangered the emperor's hold on the Mandate of Heaven. Some of this danger lurked close to the throne, as the early philosopher Han Fei Zi warned:

The ruler is easily beguiled by lovely women and charming boys, by all those who can fawn and play at love. They wait for the time when he is enjoying his ease, take advantage of the moment when he is sated with food and wine, and ask for anything they desire. . . . The ministers . . . ply them in the palace with gold and jewels and employ them to delude the ruler. (Burton Watson 1964:43)

Stories of rulers seduced by the charms of young men or women fill the history books of every dynasty. Bao Si, consort of the last ruler of the western Zhou, brought down the house of Zhou; Yang Guifei, consort of Emperor Minghuang, caused the collapse of the Tang empire; Heshen, the Manchu youth who won the favor of the Qianlong emperor, was blamed for the decline of the Qing dynasty. These stories of seduction center on two sexualized tropes: the imperial favorite (male lover) and the state-toppler (seductive woman). The phrase "cut sleeve" recalled the tale of the infatuated emperor who cut the sleeve of his royal gown rather than disturb the sleeping boy lying on his arm. A state-toppling woman was a "female disaster" (*nühuo*), as if a woman in the guise of a cyclone hit the palace and blew it apart. The cut sleeve image of the seductive boy was often sentimentalized; the disaster image of the female state-toppler was always filled with antipathy. Consider, for example, this poem from the *Classic of Poetry*:

> A clever man builds a city wall, a clever woman overthrows it;
> Beautiful is the clever woman, but she is an owl, a hooting
>   owl;
> A woman with a long tongue, she is a promoter of evil;
> Disorder is not sent down from Heaven, it is produced by
>   women;
> Those who cannot be taught or instructed are women and
>   eunuchs.
>   (Mao Ode 264; Raphals 1998:64)

The poem demonizes the Zhou consort Bao Si, and its rhetoric anticipates attacks on Mao Zedong's wife, Jiang Qing, who was pilloried as the seductive demon who had led Mao astray during the Cultural Revolution (see, for example, Terrill 1999). The sexual tensions foregrounded in the rise and fall of dynasties were continually replayed in fiction and in drama for audiences of all classes. When Yingying's lover, Scholar Zhang, for instance, finally turns against her and vilifies her as a dangerous female demon, he compares the hapless Yingying to female "demons" from the

past: Xi Shi, the beauty who became a treasonous agent in an early political intrigue, and Yang Guifei, the "precious consort" who infatuated
Emperor Xuanzong of the Tang (West and Idema 1991:99–101).

If sexual seduction was a danger to the ruler and his hold on the
Mandate, and sexual transgression figured in most narratives of dynastic decline, it was also the case that a virtuous ruler whose mandate
was secure relied on virtuous women. The Grand Historian of the Han
dynasty, Sima Qian, observed that "since antiquity, [as to both] those
who received the mandate as emperors and kings and rulers who maintained the rites and guarded correct principles, it was not only their
inner virtue that flowered, they were also helped by their wives." (*Shi ji*
49:1967; Raphals 1998:17). He attributed the rise of the Zhou house –
the model rulers of Confucius' day – to the wisdom of the mothers of
Zhou rulers, just as he blamed the Zhou queen Bao Si for the decline of
Zhou power (Raphals 1998:17). As Lisa Raphals puts it, "this double-
edged representation of women places female virtue at the heart of the
dynastic cycle" (1988:15).

In the realm known as "all under Heaven," over which emperors
presided, the need of every man for a virtuous wife was a foundation
of statecraft theory. The logic was simple: to the extent that government
could promote and expand family formation, the risk of politically unstable masses of unmarried males would be reduced. Men (and women
too) outside the family system spelled danger, to themselves as vulnerable subjects, and to the political order of the empire. These dangers were
encoded in political rhetoric that charted the rise and fall of dynasties
in three phases. Phase one was the period of conquest and consolida-
tion, when a new ruler pacified the country, claimed the Mandate of
Heaven, and reestablished a legitimate government under a new dynastic
name. The second phase was the "peak" or "flourishing" age, when the
government's efficacy reached its zenith, bringing peace and prosperity,
flourishing scholarship and markets, rising revenue, growing population,
and efficient administration of public services. This inevitably led to the
third phase, a period of "decline," when the gap between rich and poor
widened, impoverished peasants were forced off the land, tax shelters
shrank government income, and social unrest led to rebellion and the
eventual fall of the dynasty, as the cycle repeated itself (see Figure 13a).

At the local level, the dynastic cycle had its own particular manifestations. Communities were most "open" at the peak of the dynastic cycle,
when flourishing commerce, ebullient scholarship, and expanding labor
markets pulled people out of their local areas and into the empire-wide
circulation of goods and services that marked a flourishing age. When the
dynasty declined, social order broke down and markets suffered, causing

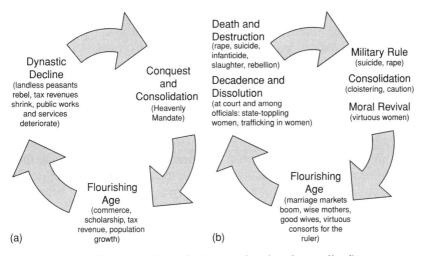

13a–b. The dynastic cycle (conventional and sexualized).

local communities to close in on themselves: literally, by arming local militias to provide the protection that the government could no longer offer and, figuratively, by withdrawing leaders from government service and engagement with the larger polity (Skinner 1971).

Analyzing the dynastic cycle using sexuality as a category of analysis reveals the gendered implications of these cyclic political changes. At the peak of the dynastic cycle, marriage markets were optimal, ritual investment was most extravagant, security was maximized, and opportunities for family formation expanded. Family values flourished in the flourishing age, as the norms celebrating cloistered women and widow chastity reached a wider audience, stable communities supported normative separation of the sexes, and sexual assault and criminal violence waned. By contrast, dynastic decline disrupted marriage markets. Poor single men caught in the marriage crunch joined rebel bands and bandit gangs. Marriageable males died in combat and marriageable females committed suicide, as threats of rape and assault rose and security broke down. The very rich bought more concubines and invested in extravagant relationships with sexually available women and men. Loyalism played powerfully in local imaginations, as people fighting for the old dynasty succumbed heroically on the battlefield defending their communities. Women who committed suicide in these moments of crisis were powerful emblems of loyalism twice over: they were faithful to the vanquished dynasty, and they were faithful to their husbands (see Figure 13b).

The fearful images of rape and suicide from the Ming-Qing transition show how the brutality of interdynastic fighting made women a primary target by breaking down the boundaries that protected cloistered ladies (*guixiu*) and making them vulnerable to predatory "bare sticks" (*guanggun*), whether marauding soldiers or bandit gangs.

In a counterpoint to the dynastic cycle, classical texts enshrined constant beliefs about marriage and the family. A son's unvarying responsibility to his parents was to marry and carry on the descent line. Government policies backed this up by promoting and supporting families, and stigmatizing unmarried men. Women too were expected to marry, for an unwed daughter had no legitimate place in the ancestral line of her natal family. Thus to be an unmarried woman was to be a person without a social or ritual identity. Unlike men, however, as we have seen, women could follow many legitimate paths to a place in the family system. The ritually correct marriage of a young cloistered woman was the most respectable path. But even an indentured maidservant expected her master to release her from service at a marriageable age so that her parents could arrange a betrothal for her; if parents were unable to do this, responsibility fell on the master himself. For parents of limited means, placing a daughter as a concubine in a well-off family was often the necessary compromise between marriage and servitude.

Concubines, who circulated in a separate channel of the marriage market, remained in the family system through contracts that joined them and their sexual services to a patriline. Such contractual arrangements, which usually involved payment, brought a concubine into a kinship unit under special conditions, usually focused on bearing sons to carry on the descent line. The sons a concubine bore to her master were coparceners in his estate, and for ritual purposes, they were treated like the sons of his wife. A fecund concubine was ritually acknowledged at her death, mourned by the sons she bore and by her husband's other sons, even though her tablet had no formal place on the ancestral altars. She might also enjoy the privilege of a posthumous title, awarded thanks to the achievements of one of her sons or grandsons. Yet she never acquired the prestige and power of a wife's status, because she entered the household on a contract, and the rituals she observed required her to bow to her husband's wife, not his parents. A concubine was, in that sense, as Rubie Watson (1991) has remarked, closer in status to a maid than to a wife. Personal maids and body servants in upper-class households were all considered sexually accessible to the master of the household or his sons, and pregnancy and the birth of a son might also elevate such a servant to a position as concubine.

Beyond these household-based systems through which women circulated lay the world of the courtesan. In late imperial times, courtesans occupied shifting ground in the traffic in women. During the late Ming, elite courtesans (*mingji*) in the southern capital of Nanjing occupied the center of a glittering literati high culture. Across the river from Nanjing's examination halls, cultivated and beautiful young women welcomed scholars to enjoy conversation, wine, and delicacies, their mutual pleasure enhanced by poetry, calligraphy, and music. Ranking these beautiful women became a favorite literati pastime. Fanciful, nostalgic notes in chapbooks recaptured encounters in the courtesan's quarter: her looks, her skill, her talent, her wit, her scent. Printed catalogs gave scores for these "ranked flowers" to guide the novice. Longtime patrons of the "kingfisher quarter" (*qing lou* or *cui guan*) made money – and gained notoriety – from their insider stories. Details of dress and makeup and ambience and conversation, with very occasional delicate allusions to a courtesan's bound feet, were eagerly passed around, first in handwritten notes and then in printed volumes. Those feet – the awareness of them, their concealment under folds of dress, and the occasional peek at an elegantly embroidered shoe – were at the heart of the courtesan's "aura" (Ko 1997b). Courtesans, in other words, appeared to be outside the world of commercial traffic, while at the same time they were victims of it, and their sexual services were almost never mentioned in the nostalgic memoirs of their patrons (see Figure 14).

The courtesan's world that flourished in the late Ming period began a long, slow decline with the Qing conquest in 1644. Female entertainers had a central place in the court life of earlier dynasties, when they were supported by the government on lists of registered households often referred to as "music households" (*yuehu*). But the Manchu government officially abolished these government-sponsored bureaus and banned female entertainment at official functions. Households registered as musicians were also encouraged to shed their pariah status in the population records and "clean up" (*qingbai*) their records by performing respectable labor over three generations. This movement to abolish pariah groups was the project of the Yongzheng Emperor, who was at least partly influenced by his Buddhist beliefs. As a result of these changes in the law, by the late eighteenth or early nineteenth centuries, female entertainers employed by the literati class retreated from the public world, working privately as courtesans on elaborate river boats or in secluded quarters where they could discreetly receive visitors. The sentimental memoirs of visits to such women mirror the sentimentality of romantic fiction, idealizing the purity and aesthetic gifts of courtesans and pitying their "miserable fate" (*bo ming*). Male patrons of female

14. A courtesan. *Source:* Zhou Wu, *Zhongguo banhua shi tu lu* (Catalog of Illustrations from the History of Chinese Woodblock Printing). Shanghai: Renmin meishu chubanshe, 1988, vol. 1, p. 39.

courtesans portray themselves as lonely men in search of an intimate relationship (*zhiji*) and occasionally as helpless patrons who cannot protect a beloved woman from the predations of lawsuits, abusive lovers, or illness. As women who worked in public entertainment, even those not formally registered as *jian* persons, courtesans were legally barred from marrying ordinary commoners. But they could aspire to a position as a concubine, and most courtesans strived to end their days as a concubine in a former patron's home.

As their star role in literati culture slowly faded, courtesans were viewed with new eyes. Government criticism had something to do with this, but equally important were broader changes in sexuality and gender relations in Qing society. Footbinding, once a practice confined to high-status entertainers and the leisured elite, became fashionable in the families of ordinary commoners, including peasants. So footbinding, the heart of the courtesan's aura, gradually lost its power as a status marker (Ko 1997b). Elite culture of the Qing dynasty was ruled by the *guixiu*, those cultivated ladies cloistered in the inner chambers. These ladies made the literary arts, especially poetry, their own domain: a way to display their learning and, at the same time, to affirm their virtue as morally upright wives, mothers, and daughters. They created and policed their own literary standards and compiled their own anthologies through their own exclusive networks of patronage and friendship, from which they conspicuously excluded courtesans (Mann 1997).

In this way the late imperial marriage market and its substrata absorbed virtually all women in a continuous stream of upward mobility, with the richest men gathering the most women about them. Those women, in turn, were stratified according to their ritual and legal relationship to the man and his patriline. Female infants and young girls were always at risk of kidnapping and sale, and naïve or unsuspecting married women whose work exposed them to outsiders were vulnerable to sexual abuse or rape. Families who could sequester their daughters, therefore, enjoyed an immense moral and practical advantage in the hungry market for brides and wives. Although marriage and concubinage always involved contractual agreements, marriage was designed to emphasize the mutual exchange of ritual obligations and material wealth between the families arranging the marriage. Ideally, this exchange was to be perfectly balanced, as suggested by the phrase "matching doors" (*men dang hu dui*), used to characterize a well-matched couple from families of comparable status and means. Dowry, in any case, almost always exceeded the value of bridal gifts or wealth conveyed from the groom's family to the bride's. A bride was not for sale; she stood apart from the traffic in women, dignified by ritual and by her parents' investment in her dowry. Her curtained bridal sedan, preceded by musicians and followed by a parade of servants carrying lacquer chests, announced this to the world. The staging of a bridal procession was also titillating: What did she look like? How much money did her family have? What kind of reception awaited her? Onlookers could speculate freely. If the bride's parade through the streets was a "public" appearance, her concealment in a sedan chair and her subsequent disappearance into the *guige* of her marital family were continuing signs of her protected status and her security as a woman who was not at risk from traffickers. This dynamic sense of women's vulnerability to trafficking, and the pressure of bare sticks on the security of settled families, tightened the close relationship between the government's investments in social control and order-keeping and the stability of the family system.

For a dynasty in decline, the relative scarcity of women accompanied a growing traffic in women and their sexual and reproductive services that operated at many levels of society, from prostitution to the marriage market (Gronewold 1982). In good times brides were sequestered from the traffic in women by their status as ritual wives and mothers, and by dowry, leaving concubines, courtesans and prostitutes, and maids to circulate. But even wives could be rented, pawned, or sold by desperate husbands in the grip of poverty or a crisis that threatened survival (Sommer 2005; Rubie Watson 1991). The same "hypergynous" pattern in the Chinese marriage market that prevailed in the best of times gave rise to the infamous "marriage crunch," when, at the nadir of the dynastic cycle, millions of men were left without a spouse. Bare sticks rarely threatened at the peak of a dynastic cycle, when prosperity helped to lower the sex ratio (by reducing economic pressures that fed female infanticide) and raise the rate of marriage in lower-income families (by enabling parents to accumulate bride-price and dowry for their children). But as the history of the Qing dynasty shows, when social, economic, and demographic pressures increased, the cumulative rage of young unmarried men pressed to the margins of settled communities helped to drive the dynasty to its collapse (Kuhn 1990).

Twentieth-century shifts in markets for women

As Chapters 4 and 8 show, even in Qing times there were good reasons for men to limit their sexual relationships with courtesans and focus instead on shared appreciation for music, poetry, and other aesthetic pursuits, both in the interest of male health and in the pursuit of a satisfying emotional life. Medical advice books, fiction, and drama of the period all celebrated this kind of heterosexual pleasure, which in the Qing was concentrated in the courtesans' quarters of the Lower Yangzi region, especially Suzhou, Nanjing, Yangzhou, and Hangzhou. The late-eighteenth-century poet Yuan Mei, and other cognoscenti, drew a sharp line between the ethereal Lower Yangzi courtesan and her counterparts in the southeast coastal port of Canton, whom he dismissed as vulgar and polluted. Yuan Mei's disdain pointed to the emerging commercial sex market in ports of foreign trade along the coast, which exploded with the signing of the treaties ending the Opium Wars of the mid-century. An early sign of the dangers signaled by this new sex market appears in a novel published and circulated in 1835, in which Canton was identified as the place where you could contract the "foreign disease" known as *yangmei chuang* or *meidu* (syphilis) through a *yangmei ji*, or prostitute who carried it (Martin Huang 2003:92).[1] Commercial sex markets catering to foreigners began in Canton and then, after 1860, centered on Shanghai, the "brothel of Asia" (Henriot 2001:6). Prostitution in nineteenth-century Shanghai grew along with the diversity and scale of its population, expanding to serve workers and businessmen, both Chinese and foreign. Some of the old elite courtesan culture survived there into the early twentieth century, with its limited sexual intimacy and its focus on entertainment (especially music), parlor games, and sophisticated banter (Henriot 2001: 52–55; Hershatter 1997:109–116). Sexual relationships in these courtesans' quarters resembled a kind of serial monogamy in which a male customer was expected to devote himself to only one courtesan for at least a four-month season (Hershatter 1997:135). Such limited sexual access was compatible with Daoist beliefs about men's health and also with concern for exclusive sexual access to female partners. But as the market became more commercialized, limits on sexual access broke down, and many prostitutes began making excuses to stave off or limit demands by customers (Henriot 2001:54). The shifting place of the courtesan at the end of the Qing was emblematic of other changes in the hypergynous sex-gender system that came with the end of the imperial era.

The traffic in women and twentieth-century revolutions

In 1911 the new Republic of China was founded and the dynastic cycle came to an end. "New women" entered the emerging public sphere, through education and employment. They would replace courtesans and prostitutes in the intimate spheres of sexual life. They were celebrated as ideal partners in the new "small family" based on monogamous conjugal love. Seeking independent personhood and freedom from arranged marriage, the new woman set herself clearly apart from women who offered sexual services for sale. Her consciousness, her education, and her values

---

[1] The phrase "*yangmei chuang*" (literally, "bayberry sores") refers to the red fruits that the sores resemble (Leung 2009:45–46).

marked her as "modern." What passed unremarked, with the appearance of the new woman, was a corollary: the end of polygamy for men (McMahon 2010). Managing male sexuality in this new era posed new social and political, as well as medical and ethical, questions.

Throughout the Republican period, meanwhile, constant warfare – among warlord armies and between contending factions in civil war – kept women vulnerable to trafficking, rape, and assault. Diana Lary has called rape "the greatest terror" facing ordinary people who survived the decades of fighting after 1911 (2001:107). Records – sometimes couched in euphemisms because of the shame attached to sexual assault – show not only how women suffered abandonment and the loss of spouses and fathers in war, but also how they lacked protection from predatory soldiers (Lary 2001:107–108, McCord 2001:23). Some have claimed that Communist troops were well disciplined and that the threat of rape in areas occupied by the Red Army was significantly reduced, a sign of the party's recognition of the overwhelming importance of female honor in Chinese communities. For example, Judith Stacey's otherwise critical analysis of the Communist revolution's impact on women nonetheless suggested that "the Red Army earned a well-deserved reputation for exemplary sexual restraint, in no small part because of the seriousness with which this was demanded by the party. Army regulations treated violation of women as a criminal offense, and the army engaged in conscious efforts to absorb the sexual energies of its soldiers" (1983:187).[2]

The Chinese Communist Party's commitment to "equality" for men and women entailed an assault on the sex-gender system with other far-reaching implications for the traffic in women. That same commitment also strengthened heteronormative structures based on the late imperial family system. The Communist government, like its forerunners, continued to view the family as the foundation of social order. As one scholar has argued, to the rural male population that formed the base of the Communists' successful revolution, the main message of sex-gender reform was, in effect, the promise of a wife for every peasant: a broader and more equitable redistribution of scarce women (Stacey 1983:174, 190, 250, 258). By reducing the numbers of single men at the bottom of the social hierarchy, and by enhancing family formation and reproductive success for the entire population, the great hope of the revolution's rural supporters was that everyone – not just the rich – would "get children." Ending concubinage, ending female servitude, ending commercial sex markets,

---

[2] However, Stacey notes evidence of a double standard where officers were concerned (1983:187).

and promoting widow remarriage all served to reverse the hypergynous flow of women and soften the marriage crunch. The transformation of class structures that accompanied the revolution, therefore, was as much a gendered process as a political and social one. Its goal, however, was not necessarily to promote male-female equality. Its goal was to shore up family-based production and secure social order by anchoring every person in a stable family unit subject to registration and control by the government. The papercut in Figure 15 (originally printed in vivid red) celebrates the party's commitment to families.

Reformers in the Communist government after 1949 made the commercial traffic in women an early target in campaigns attacking bourgeois and feudal customs. One of their first successes abolished prostitution in major cities, especially Shanghai (Hershatter 1992). Meanwhile, expressions of individual sexual desire and performance were suppressed in the early decades of the 1950s and 1960s, as the Chinese Communist Party (CCP) focused on its economic goals and on raising productivity by pushing women into labor outside the home. Cyclic political campaigns modulated these programs. In the Great Leap Forward (1958–1960), for example, divisions between family units were overridden in many rural areas, and co-mingling of the sexes in work at all levels of the society was common. In a memorable scene from a documentary film, a female informant recalls working to exhaustion in the local steel smelter all day and collapsing into bed one night, only to discover on awakening that she had slept in the men's tent. (Not a problem, she tells the camera: we were all too exhausted to care [Ambrica Productions 1994].) During the Cultural Revolution, by contrast, when so many young urban women and men were sent alone or in small groups to remote villages, young women found ways to pass along reports of rape and assault, both by co-workers and by party cadres who used sexual favors to grant access to perquisites such as visits home. The central government was forced at one point to issue a classified document warning about sexual violence against women, according to a conversation between Harriet Evans and Pan Suiming, although no documentation of this warning has been found (Evans 1995:364n12). These concerns about sexual violence and abuse contrast with the parallel interest of Chinese writers and filmmakers in exploring the erotics of the Cultural Revolution era (Larson 1999). Meanwhile, the post-Mao era brought sex markets back with a flourish. Prostitution returned, and even the central government's "strike hard" campaigns against prostitution faced resistance from local governments eager for its profitable business. As one scholar observed, the official "post-1949 understanding of the causes of prostitution [that

15. "Honor to the Families of the Defenders of the People." Paper-cut, Hebei province. *Source: Folk Arts of New China.* Peking: Foreign Languages Press, 1954, pl. 22.

it is a product of capitalist exploitation and therefore will disappear in socialism], combined with the emphasis accorded to social stability . . . , has meant that social problems like prostitution are considered to be social diseases" (Heqing Zhang 2006:156). The government has found it difficult to find a new language for tackling these issues in the era of "socialism with Chinese characteristics."

Trafficking in women and the one-child policy

The most intractable problem in the CCP government's long-term strategy of anchoring people in families was an unintended consequence of the reform era's one-child family policy. The policy, initiated in 1979, created enormous conflict between government officials and families striving for a son to carry on the descent line. The first decades of enforcement of the policy resulted in skewed sex ratios that have been widely reported in parts of rural China, where ratios as high as 119:100, 126:100, or still higher appear in census data. Such skewed ratios can only be produced by some form of sex selection, either through infanticide or neglect of female newborns or with the use of ultrasound scans permitting sex-selective abortion. Informants told a researcher in central China during the 1990s that almost every couple whose firstborn child was a girl tried to get access to ultrasound readings for the sex of the second, preferably at a private clinic where information on the sex of the fetus was more likely to be available, and 84 percent of rural women surveyed knew about ultrasound technology. Even though its use for sex selection was illegal, ultrasound scanning was available at public hospitals for twenty-five to thirty yuan (about three to four dollars) or at private clinics for about twice that amount (Junhong Chu 2001). Pregnant women arriving in county seats from the countryside were greeted at the bus stations by tricycle-pedaling hired workers who offered them rides to abortion clinics with access to ultrasound technology. Prescriptions for ensuring the birth of a boy were still in circulation, based on old medical texts that identify herbs for changing a female fetus into a male fetus during the early months of pregnancy (Junhong Chu 2001:272). This strong preference for dealing with the problem of sex selection before the birth, rather than afterward, avoided "the crime of killing life" that informants deplored (Junhong Chu 2001:278n11).

Instead of improving the status of women by increasing their value to the family system, skewed sex ratios exacerbated by new technologies increased the traffic in women in rural China, as would-be brides from rural areas "married up" into urban areas and criminal gangs kidnapped and sold scarce women on the underground marriage market.[3] Families

---

[3] The one-child policy and skewed sex ratios are now causing problems in nuptiality for males. Never-married males in China aged twenty to forty-four outnumber females in the same age group by as much as two to one. Data are difficult to find, but 1997 figures from Guangdong already showed that in the population aged fifteen and above, never-married males numbered 7.244 million, and females, 5.445 million; for Hebei in the same year, there were 5.122 million never-married males over the age of fifteen, compared with 3.706 million never-married females in the same age cohort. See www.unescap.org/esid/

planning to marry off a son had to start saving and strategizing for a bride as soon as the son was born, often by recourse to purchasing agents who located women in poorer parts of the southwest (Yunnan and Sichuan in particular) and acted as intermediaries between their families and the bride-takers (Junhong Chu 2001:277).

Meanwhile, the traffic in women to work as prostitutes revived with the commercial economy, with traffickers using strategies ranging from outright abduction to purchase from parents desperate for the cash (Henriot 2001:199–200). Contemporary critics of prostitution in China's post-Mao reform era often focus their attention on the "extreme individualism and nihilism" introduced into China along with Western notions of sexual liberation, arguing that these problems have resurfaced in the guise of loveless marriages and rising individual incomes, feeding new sex markets. Critics also note, however, that in the reform era, prostitution constituted one of the few arenas in which women could get ahead in the commercial economy – especially young female immigrants from the countryside (Hershatter 1997:373–375).

The postsocialist traffic in women has given unprecedented commercial value to the nubile bodies of rural women who come to the city seeking work. As many of them quickly learn, it is hardly worth it to take a respectable but low-paying job as a maid when the likelihood of rape by an employer is so high. One young bar hostess put it this way: "Dalian men try to cheat both our bodies and emotions. Without spending a cent, they get what they want from us." The only way to avoid being "tricked, used, and abandoned," said another, is to protect yourself by making sure you get enough money for the sex you sell to men (Zheng 2009:220). Prostitutes in Dalian perform to please their clients: they are demure virgins for young men and unruly whores for older sophisticates. They stage their bodies erotically to maximize the income they earn. Yet offstage, like prostitutes in Shanghai's courtrooms before 1949, bar hostesses in the post-Mao era present themselves primarily as filial daughters serving their parents. They see doing sex work as a rational choice: it earns the highest return on the capital they have to invest (Zheng 2009:147–171).[4]

psis/population/database/chinadata/guangdong.htm   and   www.unescap.org/esid/psis/population/database/chinadata/hebei.htm.

[4] See also Margery Wolf (1972:208) on the problem of young women sent out to work as prostitutes in 1960s Taiwan. Wolf noted that if such a girl "behaves herself in the village" where her parents live, she is regarded as "particularly filial," having "paid her debt to her parents more completely than other young women." But parents must observe careful limits on their demands, Wolf added, in order to avoid being thought greedy or abusive. Zheng's analysis reveals similar contradictions and complexities.

Young prostitutes working in the city of Dalian, in other words, have commodified romance, intimacy, and sex. They present themselves as rural migrants who choose the highest-paying job available to them, using the most valuable resource they have: their bodies. As one explained: "So many men are waiting in line. I am still young and have my capital [*ziben*]. How can I give it [away] without any remuneration?" (Zheng 2009:222). Tiantian Zheng, the anthropologist who studied the Dalian bar hostesses, has this to say of their self-presentation:

By allowing their bodies to be sexually fragmented and erotically staged for marketing, [karaoke bar] hostesses refuse the state's attempt to regulate rural women's promiscuous and transgressive sexuality and to control them for purely reproductive purposes. By flaunting their hypersexualized bodies, hostesses intend to employ the hegemonic portrayal of rural women as the exotic and erotic Other for their individual profit. (2009: 216)

Whether commercial capitalism offers young women a haven preferable to state control is a question Zheng does not address.

The resurgence of rural trafficking in women and the specter of whole villages made up of bare sticks unable to find wives have caused demographers and social scientists to write with alarm of a growing threat to social order. As the *Washington Post* reported in an article on similar patterns in India:

We have already seen in China the resurrection of evils such as the kidnapping and selling of women to provide brides for those who can pay the fee. Scarcity of women leads to a situation in which men with advantages – money, skills, education – will marry, but men without such advantages – poor, unskilled, illiterate – will not. A permanent subclass of bare branches from the lowest socioeconomic classes is created. In China and India, for example, by the year 2020 bare branches will make up 12 to 15 percent of the young adult male population. Should the leaders of these nations be worried? The answer is yes. Throughout history, bare branches in East and South Asia have played a role in aggravating societal instability, violent crime and gang formation. (Hudson and Den Boer 2004:B07).

Trafficking in women, in sum, did not end with the marriage crunch of the dynastic cycle. It continues in rural China because of the "missing" girls in the marriage market due to the one-child policy's pressures on peasant households strategizing to maximize their male labor force and secure their descent lines. Trafficking endures in urban China with the incessant flow of young women into commercial sex markets, in which their bodies can now be turned into capital.

3 Sexuality and gender relations in politics and law

To be chaste is very difficult and painful, favored by no one, of profit to no one, of no service to the state or society, and of no value at all to posterity. It has lost its vigor and has no reason to exist.

> Lu Xun, 1918 (Pao Tao 1991:118)

Of late the new reformers have suggested the so-called new ethics. They denounce filial piety on the ground that children are borne by parents only because of their sexual passion.... They also regard lustful women and disloyal ministers in history as good people.
Lin Shu, letter to Cai Yuanpei, 1919 (Tse-tsung Chow 1960:69)

Today, there are still those who regard marriage problems as "personal affairs." This viewpoint is mistaken.... Now we have to publicize the Marriage Law and have public trials to convince people that marriage problems are not just personal matters and everyone should care.
Women's Federation report on the 1951 Marriage Law (Diamant 2000:45)

During the New Culture Movement (1915–1919), China's urban intellectuals rejected the Confucian family values espoused by the late imperial government. But the system they challenged was deeply rooted in local custom and lineage power. The Qing government had created an informal system of control that minimized reliance on punitive legal sanctions to maintain the family-based social order. In addition, as we have seen, the late imperial state stressed positive rewards and transformation through education, rather than coercion, to enforce its policies. The imperial government's exceptional success in spreading its messages internalized gender values, especially in women, who were honored for widow fidelity and even for martyrdom in resisting rape or asserting their sexual purity. Court records show individual women testifying to their deep commitment to chastity, not only as a matter of family honor but also as a personal individual responsibility, to the point where a woman would take her own life to express her moral conviction (Theiss 2004).

The Republican government after 1911 took steps to create new laws that would loosen the control of lineage elders and local custom over the lives of women. As women moved into new arenas outside the home – for work, education, and leisure – the government began to draft legislation to support these new social roles. The Marriage Law of 1930 was only the first step in a long process of dismantling the local structures that sustained old family values. When the post-1949 Communist government attacked lineage organizations and local customs, it removed powerful local sources of authority that had enforced the imperial state's messages at the local level. The People's Republic of China (PRC) government also issued two major revisions of the existing Marriage Law (in 1950 and again in 1980) that significantly changed the position of women in the family system. In the PRC legal code, the conjugal monogamous bond between husband and wife became the fulcrum of social relationships, overriding the intergenerational hierarchies that had dominated family life (Evans 1997:121). Those legal changes made it possible for women seeking divorce, free mate choice, remarriage, or (in the case of the 1980 law) child support to appeal to the government to uphold their claims. At the same time, because the present government continues to bolster the family system by promoting universal marriage, the language of current law holds all women to the expectation that they will marry (or remarry) and bear at least one child. Law, in other words, has been a crucial part of the apparatus enforcing and supporting norms governing gender and sexuality from late imperial times to the present.

Law and sex in late imperial thought

The school of political thought that prevailed in Qing times was based on writings by Mencius and his followers. This school took for granted the innate potential for goodness in human nature and stressed the wisdom (and the low cost and efficiency) of building public policy to cultivate and reward that innate potential, with market incentives as well as redistributive programs (Rowe 2001, Wong 1997). The Qing government, to be sure, had a vigorous legal system backed by horrific punishments. But the government also developed to a high art an elaborate system of positive rewards and sanctions, including education, honors, public ceremonies, and what can only be called propaganda campaigns, in support of its policies. The success of these measures relied largely on indirect means: they reached their audience through the family system. In other words, the Qing government, more than any previous imperial state, supported, expanded, and gave legal force to a family system that internalized the values the government wanted to promote through child socialization and adult gratification.[1] This strategy was viewed as greatly superior to any attempt to enforce the same behavior through law and punishment.

Universal marriage and residence in a household based on this family system was the government's goal for all of the "people," and that goal was aggressively promoted after the Manchus consolidated their power. The most effective steps in expanding universal marriage were taken by the Yongzheng Emperor (1723–1735) and reinforced in laws and sanctions developed in the subsequent Qianlong reign (1736–1796). Matthew Sommer has argued that these policies enabled the government to shift the criteria for judging sexual conduct from *status* to *gender*. That is, *all* women, not only respectable women identified as *liang*, were held to the same standards of chastity. *All* men, not only free commoners, were expected to attach themselves to households in settled communities, preferably by marriage. Qing law showed remarkable concern for ensuring access to marriage for even the most marginal people. We have already seen, for instance, that whereas masters had sexual access to servants, a master was also responsible for seeing to it that a female servant was properly married while she was still at a marriageable age. Magistrates were enjoined to enforce this law in the courtroom (Djang 1984:609–610). Moreover, under Qing law, even incarcerated criminals were permitted conjugal visits once or twice a month, if the criminal had no heir and his wife was still of childbearing age. As the seventeenth-century magistrate Huang Liuhong put it, "This is a humane practice

---

[1] Although it has been argued that a Foucauldian form of governmentality did not begin in China until the founding of the PRC (Greenhalgh and Winckler 2005: esp. 320–327), this book shows that many aspects of Foucauldian governmentality are readily visible in Qing times, particularly in modes of self-discipline and habits of labor and consumption that in the long run served the interests of the state and its commitment to social order. These were all instilled successfully through the family with the government's support. As Susan Greenhalgh has observed, in shifting its focus from family to population, the present government has introduced problems of control that the late imperial government successfully minimized (Greenhalgh and Winckler 2005:321).

permitted by the law and is aimed at producing an heir for the criminal so that his family line will not be broken" (Djang 1984:410).

The Qing law's tolerance for a male master's sexual relationship with a female servant underscores a broader principle: all laws were applied contingently, based on the gender, status, and family relationship of the parties in each case. Where ordinary commoners were concerned, sex outside marriage for males or females was illegal.[2] Rape was punishable by death; the penalty for adultery by mutual consent was flogging. As Magistrate Huang Liuhong explained it, "Sexual desire is universal and no one is immune from it. Only by observing the principles of propriety can a cultivated person refrain from indulging in it." Social gatherings and secluded places, in Huang's view, invited flirtation and "carnal knowledge." Nevertheless, he opined, with a trace of Mencian empathy, "If harsh laws are applied to such offenders, many young and beautiful lovers will have to forfeit their lives. Therefore when the ancients enacted the law, they considered human feelings." By contrast, the penalty for rape was heavier than for any other sex offense because (again in Huang's words) "when a sexual act is forced on a woman, an innocent and chaste person suffers violence and dishonor under duress. The death penalty imposed on the rapist is a means of acclaiming the virtue of chastity and discouraging debauchery of womanhood. The heavy penalty is not designed simply to punish those who use force to satisfy their animal desire" (Djang 1984:437–438).

Avoiding rape charges – not only for men, but especially for women – was a paramount concern of every respectable household, even as defense against such charges became increasingly difficult for women as a result of changes in Qing law. Immediately following the Manchu conquest and the establishment of the Qing empire in 1644, the government issued a new law that made it extremely difficult for a woman who was raped to defend herself in the courts. The law established rigorous requirements for proof that she had been coerced, including witnesses who saw the rape or heard her cries for help, bruises and lacerations on her body, and torn clothing (Ng 1987:58). These new provisions squelched lawsuits protesting the violent conquest, but they also were part of a broader program to promote strict standards and rewards for female chastity. By adding negative legal sanctions to positive normative and monetary rewards, the government heightened the importance of female seclusion and greatly expanded awareness of the need to keep women safely out of sight. The new laws further increased the risks for women who for economic

---

[2] See Djang 1984:431–443 for instructions to magistrates on adultery and its various forms (translations here slightly adapted).

or other reasons had to move and work outside the home or court-
yard, while raising the stakes in female chastity among the population at
large.

The "disgraceful matters" chronicled in Qing legal archives show how
high these stakes were. If a woman survived a rape, any case that went to
court was likely to find her guilty of "illicit intercourse by mutual consent"
because (in the legal reasoning favored by Manchu law) her assailant
could not have consummated his attack unless she had stopped struggling
(Djang 1984:441–443, Ng 1987:61). As one nineteenth-century critic
pointed out sarcastically, the only sure way for an assaulted woman to
defend her reputation was to die – fighting off her attacker, or by suicide
(Ng 1987:63–64). Penalties for a convicted rapist, on the other hand,
were dire. The mildest punishment was death by strangulation, and the
prospects for conviction were enhanced if the victim's prior reputation
was impeccably pure. If she was known to be an "innocent and chaste
person," this would help her case in the courts, provided that other
factors (family and local politics, for example) also worked in her favor
(Ng 1987:65, Theiss 2004). Gang rape was punished more severely than
rape by individuals, and the rape of a known "chaste woman" more
severely than the rape of a prostitute. So class as well as gender figured
heavily in decisions involving rape charges, making sequestered women
the most protected and vagrant single men the most vulnerable.

In Qing times concerns about sex outside marriage did not adversely
affect the daily lives of most ordinary commoners, as long as they
avoided lawsuits. For families who could afford it, bringing in concubines
for men's sexual pleasure or procreation continued. Courtesans' quarters flourished. Consensual sex went unheeded unless a family member decided to litigate, because any accusation about sexual miscon-
duct posed a great risk to the alleged victim as well as the perpetrator
(Theiss 2004). Homosexual relationships were well known at all levels
of male society. Literati patrons of comely young boys and actors wrote
about their lovers and bragged about their beauty. Crews on sailing ves-
sels (Murray 1992), and workers in fields, mines, and protoindustries,
shared beds and (if we may judge by anecdotal evidence from lawsuits)
sexual intimacy. Rape laws, meanwhile, focused on heterosexual acts. As
Matthew Sommer (2000:131) observes, "the judiciary was highly skep-
tical that a man could be raped at all," even in cases involving juveniles,
because the assumption was that even a boy would be strong enough
to resist forcible rape (2000:134–135). Not until 1740 did the Qing
government formulate a substatute on male rape, departing from the
informal sanctions developed in court cases before that time, mainly by
analogy with cases of heterosexual rape (Meijer 1985). The trigger for

adding bans on homosexual rape to the formal Qing code is unclear, but Sommer (2000) attributes rising concern about homosexual and heterosexual rape to the fear of those vagrant rogue males ("evil rascals" or "bare sticks") who were stereotyped as sexual predators in legislation and in the popular imagination during the eighteenth century. The 1740 statute criminalized all male homosexual acts, including consensual sex between adults or between an adult and a boy (Ng 1987:67). Where one of the parties was underage, as in the many cases of boys age ten to twelve who had sex with a teacher, and where "consent" might be ambiguous, extensive discussion and review yielded different and sometimes contradictory judgments, because the model for trying cases involving homosexual rape was derived from the protocols governing heterosexual rape (Meijer 1985). Laws alone do not remake social practice, of course, especially when sexual activity is concerned, because of shared interests in keeping sex secret, whether for protection or honor. If we are to judge by the cases that did enter court records, wife-renting was widely practiced in parts of rural China, prostitution flourished in towns and cities all over the empire, and sex between men remained common, not only in monasteries and schools but also in the labor force at large.

The law's focus on penetration as the defining sexual act left sexual activity between women beyond its scope. Although female homosexuality was largely ignored by writers and observers, because it did not involve the phallic penetration that posed legal and medical problems (see the following and also Chapter 7), fiction and erotica supply evidence for sexual as well as emotional intimacy between women (see Chapter 8). Homosexual and erotic bonds between women are evident in the "women's script" of southern Hunan, in the girls' houses in the Canton delta, in poetry and song lyrics, and in some prose works as well. That these often highly visible practices attracted neither opprobrium nor legal sanction tells us something very important about sexuality in the Qing period. Concerns about sexuality focused almost exclusively on protecting female chastity and containing male intercourse. The law did not allude to health concerns about semen preservation, nor to ritual concerns about pure patrilineal descent lines, even though both must have been on the minds of the officials who wrote these laws. The overt and overriding concern of laws themselves was to preserve *and* expand the parameters of respectability that defined good people (*liang min*) and set them apart from pariahs (*jian min*). To be good (*liang*) connoted sexual purity, meaning that sexual activity was confined to marriage. Respectable men were not to have intercourse with prostitutes, nor were they to penetrate other men. To do so was to pollute and stigmatize their sex partners and, by implication, to violate the boundaries of respectability that secured their own status.[3] The magistrate Huang Liuhong emphasized repeatedly the need for strict separation between males and females to prevent "licentious customs" from creating new cases for his courtroom (Djang 1984:431). His long list of breaches of the line between the sexes shows how impossible task his task was.

Matthew Sommer (2000:10) has suggested that late imperial anxieties about female chastity were coupled with anxiety about "vulnerable masculinity" during this era. He believes that the pressure on women to be chaste wives and devoted mothers was coupled with new pressures on men to perform as husbands and fathers. Most importantly, he has argued, the result of eighteenth-century law and rewards systems was "to extend a uniform standard of sexual morality and criminal liability to all. . . . Previously tolerated spaces for extramarital sexual intercourse were eliminated from the law, and the imperial center mandated that local officials intensify their surveillance of sexual behavior and gender roles" (Sommer 2000:10–11). Both male and female commoners, in this new regime, were held to strict new standards of gender performance, leaving new deviants as targets: bare sticks (*guanggun*), homosexual rapists, pimps, and wayward husbands. In particular, hitherto legally recognized prostitutes were now pressured to move into respectable status as ordinary commoners, and penetrated males were singled out as a group whose lowly status was indelibly stigmatized (Sommer 2000:12).

The cumulative results of these pressures can be felt in the eighteenth-century legal cases analyzed by Janet Theiss, whose findings point to the deep internalizing of chastity norms by women who became victims of rape. The resulting new identities did not necessarily contribute to social order, because each family member had a different stake in the sexual behavior of relatives. But for young women growing up in the eighteenth century, a pervasive awareness of sex as danger, and exposure to view as risk, was almost unavoidable in respectable families. Shame from involvement in a "disgraceful matter" (*chou shi*) made some young women kill themselves when assaulted, or even when flirted with, by a stranger. (See Chapter 6 on suicide.) At the same time, competing images of female sexuality showed women either as weak, fickle, and in need of control (Djang, cited in Theiss 2004:184), or as sexual objects who could be rented for income (Sommer 2005). Court cases from the eighteenth century involving spousal violence in which a husband killed his wife

---

[3] As Kathryn Bernhardt puts it, "abetting the other woman in her crime of fornication," for example in the case of a husband having sex with another man's wife (Bernhardt 1994:208).

commonly describe the wife as a shrew. But the judgments rendered by presiding magistrates show that a woman who was out of control was also judged to be the product of a husband who was incapable of exercising appropriate moral authority. In fact, the palpable disdain displayed by Qing judges toward husbands who could not control their wives has led Janet Theiss (2007) to argue that male self-mastery (*zhu*) or containment, and not the virtue of women, was seen as the key to social order in the family.

Early-twentieth-century shifts

During the late Qing reforms at the end of the dynasty, a movement to Westernize Chinese law proposed decriminalizing sexual activity by unmarried women and widows. The result was vociferous debate and a resounding affirmation of the importance of old values to nation-building: citizens must owe their first loyalty to the family and state, not to themselves as individuals. Alison Sau-chu Yeung sums it up this way: "Reformers had to demonstrate that their proposals would not threaten the moral and economic centrality of family, and Western legal principles had to be altered to fit this requirement" (Yeung 2003:320).

The reforms following the revolution of 1911 were similarly slow to change the laws on gender and sexuality. Two major efforts at rewriting the old Qing code foundered, faced with opposition to any changes that privileged the individual over the family (Bernhardt 1999:75). Not until 1929–1930 was a new civil code promulgated, and even then changes in most laws were minimal. Many of these changes simply spelled out "rights" more explicitly than the Qing code had done, without altering the basic intent or provisions of the old code. Special provisions of the new code did, however, explicitly address questions about women, notably the status within the family of concubines and widows, whose position was problematic in light of the new discourses on gender equality and monogamy that affected the attitudes of lawmakers. Divorce was also significantly reframed in the new Republican law.

Concubines were legal under the Qing, but (as one scholar puts it) a concubine's "position was not very closely regulated in the old law" (van der Valk 1939:23). Ming and early Qing law had stipulated that a male commoner was permitted to take a concubine for the purpose of having a son, but not until he had reached the age of forty and then only if he had no sons. In 1740, the new legislation on sexual behavior that included the criminalization of male rape struck this law from the books, lifting legal constraints on concubinage entirely (van der Sprenkel

1962:15).[4] Even in the new laws promulgated in 1930, the problem of what to do about concubines was completely sidestepped, despite the fact that the intent of these laws was to promote monogamy and free mate choice (Bernhardt 1994:210). Judges, confronting contradictions in the courtroom, concluded that a concubine did not enjoy any of the formal legal protections of a wife, and therefore her status had to be understood in a context outside the Marriage Law. At the same time, court rulings show a gradual acceptance of concubines as "family members," and even recognition that a concubine who had reached the age of a legal adult should be free to leave the family at any time of her choosing (Bernhardt 1994:210–211). By contrast, the family head who wished to expel a concubine had to show good cause in the courts, and to offer support in the form of alimony or other payments if it were shown that she would suffer hardship as a result. In this respect, Republican law strengthened the protections for women who were sold as concubines. These new protections came with a caveat: a wife could not expel a concubine for any reason. She was stuck with her husband's choice(s), and her only recourse if she wished to escape was divorce or legal separation (Bernhardt 1994:212–213).

Perhaps the law's benign treatment of concubines was due to the influence of the relatively small proportion of well-off Chinese families who could afford a concubine at all. Sidney Gamble's (1954) survey of Ding county found concubinage in less than 1 percent of families surveyed.[5] As Sybille van der Sprenkel observes, "If we consider Chinese society as a whole, concubinage was not as common as one would suppose from reading novels and biographies that depict upper-class life. Expense was one obvious deterrent" (1962:15). John Lossing Buck's survey of Chinese farm families in the 1930s showed that concubines made up only 0.2 percent of family members (Rubie Watson 1991:237).[6] Noting the relatively higher incidence of concubines even among poor families in

---

[4] *Qinding Da Qing huidian shili* 1899: *juan* 756 p.4a. The note about punishments for improperly installing a concubine as a wife, or making a wife a concubine, or other infractions of the proper seniority of wife to concubine adds the following: "The original statute also stated that an ordinary commoner who reached the age of 40 without having a son could at that point only take a concubine. Those who violate this regulation are subject to 40 blows with the bamboo rod. . . . In the fifth year of the Qianlong reign the emperor ordered this provision expunged from the statutes."

[5] Gamble's largest sample was 5,255 families (1954:38); the survey was conducted between 1926 and 1936. Gamble's results also showed that the figure was considerably higher for families holding more than 100 *mu* of land: one in eighteen.

[6] Again, class and income figure in these statistics. For instance, in a survey conducted at roughly the same time, 11.4 percent of high school and college students reported a concubine in the family (Olga Lang, cited in Rubie Watson 1991:237).

certain rural communities in South China, anthropologist Rubie Watson has opined that concubinage may have been linked to the need for female labor in some local economies (1991:238).

By contrast with this sketchy treatment of concubines, China's Republican divorce laws were among the most liberal in the world. In Qing civil law, a man who decided to divorce his wife had seven reasons to choose from: barrenness, wanton conduct, neglect of his parents, loquacity, theft, jealousy, and chronic illness. In the Qing a woman's only protection against these "seven reasons for expelling a wife" (*qi chu*) were the so-called *san buchu* (three reasons for not expelling her): if she had observed three years of mourning for his parents, if she had stuck by him through adversity, or if she had no natal home to which she could return (Philip Huang 2001:164). Chinese law in the 1930s, patterned after laws in Germany and Switzerland, provided ten grounds for women to seek divorce, as well as procedures for "no-fault" divorce that minimized time and expense to both parties (Bernhardt 1994). Although the new avenues for divorce opened up by Republican law drew unprecedented numbers of women to court, social stigma, expense, economic concerns, and other factors unaffected by changes in the law (such as the difficulty of remarrying) continued to make it difficult for most women to take advantage of legal options. Even in Shanghai, the divorce rate overall remained remarkably low – less than one divorce for every 1,000 persons in the 1920s and 1930s (Bernhardt 1994:301n1). Meanwhile, widows continued to suffer from the Confucian stigma attached to remarriage, which was never challenged in Republican legal reforms. Chaste widowhood remained the norm for respectable women. Because the reforms were designed to bolster the authority of the young against their parents, moreover, widows were left with virtually no protection for their claims to hold property in behalf of a surviving heir (a foundational principle in Qing law).

Republican law of the 1930s transformed the court's views of women by treating them as equal persons with "natural rights." But the law's new emphasis on women's individual rights had unintended negative consequences for many women. In a single stroke, the law removed certain protections for women in Qing civil law, including protection for widows resisting remarriage or for wives sold into prostitution (Bernhardt 1999:47–100). The new laws presumed that as a free and independent agent, a woman could stand up for herself in such situations and simply say no. Given the structures of power and custom that remained in place in most parts of the country, this presumption proved largely unfounded. In a sweeping comparison of changes in the law from Qing to Republican times, Philip C. C. Huang identified certain cases of "women's new autonomy in marriage decisions": for example, a twenty-one-year-old schoolteacher who sued her father for betrothing her to a policeman and won an annulment through mediators. But Huang also observed that such women were "more likely to be from the cities and large towns than from villages and hamlets . . . and to be more financially independent than the majority of women" (Huang 2001:198–199).

Sexuality, politics, and the law in the People's Republic of China

The most important laws affecting gender and sexuality in the PRC have been the Marriage Laws, beginning with the Marriage Law of 1950 and continuing with the 1980 law that was rewritten to accommodate the post-Mao reforms, especially by stressing the obligation of children to care for aging parents, as the state sector and its benefits began to shrink. Both laws were publicized with aggressive government campaigns to encourage people to take advantage of them. Both aimed to improve the status of women. Note, however, that laws addressing gender relations, particularly laws pertaining to women, appeared only in this form: as laws concerning *the family*. In other words, women's rights under these laws were defined exclusively in the context of marriage and reproduction.

The Marriage Law of 1950 stressed the conjugal bond as the core relationship in the new socialist society, echoing the Confucian classics' reference to the foundations of the imperial polity. Accordingly, the 1950 law focused on marriage reform. The 1950 Marriage Law banned bigamy and concubinage and drew a distinction between the two: a case in which a man married another woman without divorcing his wife (bigamy) was distinguished from one in which a man brought sexual partners into his family in addition to his wife (concubinage). In general, the law and court cases enforcing the law strongly supported strict monogamy and, as in the Qing code, strongly opposed sexual relations outside of marriage. The main goal was to end arranged marriage; the key was to eradicate "feudal" thinking (Evans 1995:361–362, Meijer 1971:92–97). At the same time, publicity surrounding the law and its dissemination through schools, women's organizations, and popular culture stressed that monogamous marriage was – as a 1959 newspaper article put it – "dictated not only by the physiological difference between the sexes, but also by the perpetuation of the race" (Evans 1995:362). In this way the law linked monogamous marriage to the wife's fertility and made her obligation to bear children its primary purpose. Women were cautioned not to postpone marriage, not to "refuse to see their husbands," and not to devote too much time to education (Evans 1995:262). By the same token, the 1950 law firmly opposed free love and dealt cautiously with divorce because of the social conflicts and economic difficulties that accompanied it. Lower-level cadres who were in charge of enforcing the new laws were themselves often prone to what the party called "feudal" views, as illustrated in a case reported in *Renmin ribao* in 1950 (Meijer 1971:117). The case involved a seventeen-year-old girl who was betrothed to a butcher when she was fourteen but who fell in love with a twenty-four-year-old party member when she joined the New Democratic Youth Corps. She and her lover were both expelled from their party organizations when their affair was discovered, but when they took their case to the local government bureau to ask for permission to cancel the betrothal and marry, the magistrate in charge humiliated the girl and permitted his constables to make jokes about her in her presence. The girl killed herself by drinking kerosene, and the magistrate was disciplined for his "backward" thinking.

Local conflicts of this sort involving the implementation of the law led villagers, abetted by disdainful local cadres, to dismiss it as the "women's law" or even "divorce law" (Meijer 1971:125). This situation caused deep distress at the higher levels of the party. By 1953, in a concession to such resistance, the government had moved to an emphasis on building marital happiness and harmony, making divorce more difficult and focusing more on education and mediation to keep faltering marriages together (Meijer 1971:130–132). Still, the Marriage Law's provisions for divorce did have a wide impact. Neil Diamant (2000) shows that divorce laws touched off different kinds of controversy in rural as opposed to urban areas. In cities, the party complained of "chaos" in sexual relationships: out-of-wedlock pregnancies, homosexual relations, and passionate affairs in the workplace (2000:191–198); in rural areas, peasants who embarrassed party urbanites with their frank discussions of sex became instantly adept at manipulating the new laws to achieve their own ends (2000:228ff.).

The 1950 Marriage Law was enforced in the context of the Maoist policies that centered on work units (*danwei*) in the cities and on collectives in the countryside. By contrast, the 1980 Marriage Law was designed for the post-Mao reform era, when work units and collectives steadily lost political, social, and economic significance (Palmer 1995). In that sense, the post-Mao reform government sought to reinvent the tight relationship between state and family that prevailed in the Qing era. Like its predecessors in the twentieth century, the 1980 Marriage Law focused on the conjugal bond, but with increased attention to emotional and sexual satisfaction and fulfillment. In fact, the 1980 law was interpreted in the courts to mean that an "inability to carry out sexual intercourse" constituted grounds for divorce. At the same time, even though the focus of reform-era laws was heterosexual marriage, significant change in legislation affecting the rights of homosexuals began in 1997, when the law criminalizing "hooliganism" – a Marxist code reference to male homosexuality – was abolished (see Chapter 7).

Current laws and their supporting regulations have gone very far to set standards for responsibilities within the family beyond the confines of marriage, including parental obligations to instruct, discipline, and protect their children; children's obligation to care for elderly parents; and guidelines for the inheritance of property. Although illegitimate children are acknowledged as full participants in society, in practice household registration has been denied to children born outside of wedlock (Palmer 1995:113–114). The 1980 Marriage Law aimed further to shape domestic roles in accordance with state priorities in economic development. While constructing husband and wife as equal partners who enjoy "equal status in the home," and the wife as a person with activities that extend beyond motherhood (Evans 1997:121), the law's emphasis on emotional and sexual satisfaction in marriage provided a context for women's retreat from the workforce into the home in urban areas. This in turn conflicted with other aspects of the law aimed at curbing population growth. For example, the law raised the legal age of marriage to twenty-two years for males and twenty years for women and encouraged delayed childbirth, whereas data show that most women conceive a child in the first year of marriage (Woo 2001:312). Moreover, the pressures on rural women resulting from the competing demands of family (wanting more sons) and the one-child policy (limiting births to one or at most two children) produced the problems discussed earlier, such as the skewed sex ratio caused by the two million or more "missing" girls in the cohort of marriageable young people.

Other tensions in the family system that reform-era law tried to address arose from what one scholar has called the "commodification of the feminine." Rural women, increasingly valuable in the labor market, migrated out of their native localities, not only for labor but also for marriage, while at the same time urban women retreated "from the public workplace to the private space of home and hearth" (Woo 2001:315). The result of both of these trends was to isolate women from the community and natal family structures that once buffered pressures on them. In 1995 the government took note of these problems by passing the Women's Rights Law (*Funü quanli baozhang fa*) giving women whose legal rights had been violated formal recourse, by directly petitioning either the relevant administrative unit, the Women's Federation (*fulian*), or the courts (Woo 2001:318).

The relationship between current family law and the political economy of the reform era, in sum, is contradictory. As Michael Palmer (1995) pointed out, the government's reliance on stable family units to maintain and enforce social order was at odds with many of the current law's provisions, which promote freedom of divorce, limits on family size, and emotional and sexual satisfaction. These tensions continue to show up in generational and spatial differences that separate youth from their elders and rural residents from their urban counterparts.

PART II

GENDER, SEXUALITY, AND THE BODY

4 The body in medicine, art, and sport

Chinese elite males in the seventeenth century regarded foot-binding in three ways: as an expression of Chinese *wen* civility, as a marker of ethnic boundaries separating Han from Manchu, and as an ornament or embellishment of the body.

Dorothy Ko (1997a:10)

[In Chinese art] . . . the typical Chinese rock, with its convoluted, foraminate, complexly textured form, might well stand as a culturally quintessential Chinese body. The classical image of the Western tradition is the Apollo or the Venus. The classical image of the Chinese tradition is the rock.

John Hay (1994:68)

Watching *Fen-Ma Liuming in Tokyo* . . . , the audience must first certainly be struck by the incongruity of Fen-Ma Liuming's lovely made-up "feminine" face and long silky black hair with a fully nude "masculine" body. Yet Fen-Ma Liuming is neither homosexual, hermaphrodite, transvestite, nor androgyne. This creature's face and body exude conflicting images of traditional gender categories, blurring the boundaries between "male" and "female." One of the purposes of this boundary blurring is to provoke questions about the validity of our knowledge of what constitutes gender and delimits a person.

Maranatha Ivanova (1999:203)

Historical views of the body in Chinese medicine and art prefigure the complex bodily images that confounded early Western observers of Chinese culture, challenged the aspirations of modern reformers, and inspire contemporary artists. On the one hand, the decoupling of sexual bodies and sin in China's classical tradition made the unclothed physical body inconsequential, even trivial, as a site of virtue, morality, or beauty.[1] Ideas about sinful bodies – particularly notions of homophobia and heteronormativity – that informed modern sexological discourses raised confusing questions for China's twentieth-century youth. Was it modern to wear shorts to play basketball? Was it modern to scorn homoerotic theater culture? Was it modern to hire nude models in art academies? Embroidered shoes were enticingly beautiful, even elegant, but not so the stunted bare foot. Tight-fitting *qipao* dresses were supposed to be quintessentially Chinese, but did they have to be slit thigh-high? Settling these confusing questions about the body entailed conflict, but also a good deal of wit and humor, precisely (or, if only) because it was difficult to take nude bodies that seriously. They were not all that important.

Contemporary notions of the body in Chinese culture have been profoundly shaped by early ideas about nude bodies and their meanings. In this chapter, the late imperial practice of footbinding, the aesthetics of the nude body in Western art, and the modern physical culture of global sports serve as arenas for exploring the meanings of [in]significant physical bodies. The bound foot in late imperial culture, as we have seen, signaled refinement through concealment in embroidered shoes. China's classical painters, for their part, ignored the nude body, fastening their attention on the cultural and aesthetic significance of clothing. Late imperial physical culture promoted exercises to maintain sexual vitality, balance, and circulation, but not muscular development or physical strength. These distinctive views of the physical body in late imperial times made China's twentieth-century entry into the world of modern fashion, nude art exhibits, and Olympic sports a dramatic and unsteady one – even as what came to be called traditional Chinese medicine (TCM) attracted a growing body of patients and practitioners worldwide.

The chapter begins with classical ideas about the body as the site for cultivating sexual health and longevity. Confucian, Daoist, and Buddhist beliefs all shaped these discourses on the body in late imperial times. When Western notions of embodiment, including obstetrics and gynecology, introduced new technologies of reproduction and concepts of physical fitness in the twentieth century, the results within medical discourses, and also beyond, were complicated. After considering the medical body, the chapter turns briefly to art and finally to sports, showing how China's contemporary bio-state has extended its reach into

---

[1] Faces were observable parts of the *clothed* body that could be judged for virtue and/or beauty, by fortunetellers, matchmakers, and prognosticators of other sorts. Thus founding emperors displayed auspicious facial features that attracted the Mandate of Heaven.

16. Silk chart from Mawangdui (168 BCE) showing forty-four figures engaged in therapeutic exercises known as *daoyin* (guiding and pulling) – part of the process of self-cultivation or nurturing life (*yangsheng*). *Source:* Vivienne Lo, "Healing and Medicine: Self-Cultivation." In *China: Empire and Civilization*, edited by Edward L. Shaughnessy. New York: Oxford University Press, 2005, p. 158.

physical culture by promoting national sports and defining fitness and "disability."

The body in late imperial medicine

Evidence from tombs at Mawangdui in Changsha, Hunan, dating from at least 168 BCE, includes seven manuscripts on the art of "nurturing life" (*yangsheng*). Among the paintings in the tombs is the illustration depicted in Figure 16, showing a lively exercise routine. The Mawangdui texts are the earliest extant prototype of the sex manuals that came into widespread use after the end of the Han period. They take a rhetorical form that was common at the time, with an interlocutor (usually portrayed as a ruler) questioning a teacher and receiving explicit and detailed instruction from a master. Donald Harper, who has studied these texts closely, observes that unlike later texts (and unlike similar sex manuals from Greece and Rome), the teacher in these earliest texts was male, not female (the Immaculate Maid and the Dark Maid, two later female authorities, appeared only after the third century), and the object of the instruction was not sexual pleasure but sexual practice to promote health

告子曰：“食色，性也。”

17. Original text: "The need for food and sex is innate to human nature" (Gao Zi to Mencius). From Mencius 6A.4.

and long life (Harper 1987:548n19). As Harper explains it: "A fundamental premise of ancient Chinese physical cultivation philosophy was that the path to physical and spiritual perfection did not lie in repressing the natural appetite for sex, and that it could be put to good effect through cultivation. What was important was that one learn how to cultivate the appetite" (1987:592). This need to learn how to have healthy sex was distinguished from breathing and eating, which did not require learning from birth. Thus lust (se 色) "injures" life, whereas eating "assists" it. Ideas about healthy sex also appeared in debates among the "hundred schools" in the third century BCE. In the classical text recording the teachings of the philosopher Mencius (Mencius 6A.4), we watch Mencius engage his disciple Gao Zi in a conversation about human nature. Specifically, the conversation tries to establish what is "innate" and what is "acquired" – it is a conversation about nature and nurture. To illustrate what he means by "innate" instead of "external" or "socially acquired," Gao Zi cites appetites for food and sex (食色) as "human nature" (性) and therefore "innate" (內) (see Figure 17). (Their conversation moves quickly on to ask whether ritual propriety or a sense of humanity is also innate to humans, as opposed to animals – a more contentious subject.)

Gao Zi's words summarize a widely accepted understanding of human nature in early Chinese thought: sexual appetites are as "natural" to humans as appetites for food and drink. These ancient ideas about bodily health produced particular modes of sexual performance and beliefs about sexual difference that came to define "civilization" as it was understood in the Chinese empire. Indeed, these very conceptions of sexual performance and difference were not fundamentally challenged until the twentieth century, and in the twentieth century they deeply influenced approaches to modern sexuality.

Early philosophical ideas about men's health, evident in Han dynasty texts, developed alongside notions of gender difference that were conceptualized and apprehended using the binary yin and yang (variously understood as the interactive cosmological forces that produced the diurnal cycle and the succession of the seasons: dark and light, moist and dry, moon and sun, yielding and force, and correspondingly, in a sexual idiom, female and male). The cosmos was understood to be connected to the human body by the circulation of energy or vital breath (qi). In the

case of corporeal humans, this energy was channeled from point to vital
point in the body. Health or illness was defined in terms of the relative
balance of *yin* and *yang*. Female bodies were marked by a surfeit of *yin*
(associated with darkness, wetness, yielding, and cold), but female *yin*
ebbed and flowed with the menstrual cycle. So in women's medicine,
which developed later during the Song dynasty, prepubescent girls and
postmenopausal women were seen as androgynous persons whose balance of *yin* and *yang* was very much like that of a male of the same age.
As Charlotte Furth (1988:1) has pointed out, this kind of cosmological
thinking "made sexual difference a relative and flexible bipolarity in natural philosophy" – not, in other words, the embodied binary so familiar
to contemporary Westerners (see also Furth 1999, Raphals 1998, Rosenlee 2006:66). At the same time, medical texts and philosophical treatises
were clear about the binary distinction between male (*nan*) and female
(*nü*). Sexual intercourse between a man and a woman produced the sons
who carried on each patriline, and the division of labor between males
and females sustained every household. Infants whose genitalia were
indeterminate or ambiguous were regarded as "human anomalies" in the
medical literature (Furth 1988). It was the *yin* essence of the female that
early sex manuals identified as part of the key to male longevity. A male
in sexual intercourse aimed to absorb as much of the female's *yin* essence
as possible, while preserving and building up his own *yang* energy, preferably by bringing her to orgasm while refraining from ejaculation himself
and either withdrawing without ejaculating or, preferably, "returning the
semen" (*huan jing*) by pressing on the urethra between the scrotum and
the anus. Daoists believed that from there the semen could be circulated
back up through the spinal cord and into the brain as a restorative.[2]

Early medical texts, in sum, taught that healthy sex was the key to long
life. As Joseph Needham observed: "The mutual benefit of sexual union,
analogized with that of Yin and Yang, heaven and earth, was essential and
undeniable; celibacy was dangerous and inadmissible" (1983:185–186).
Rather than repressing the natural appetite for sex, each person must
learn how to cultivate it for his or her own benefit. The student practicing
yangsheng techniques learned to balance the cosmological forces of *yin*
and *yang*, which circulated through the human body as energy or vital
breath (*qi*). Females were understood to release *yin* in orgasm, and sexual
manuals of the late imperial period gave men detailed instructions on
how to bring a woman to orgasm. Along with recipes for facilitating and
sustaining erections and other *yangsheng* techniques are also found two

---

[2] In fact, the semen was diverted by pressure into the bladder and voided with the urine;
see Needham 1956:149–150.

ways to make a paste called "protector of the palace" (*shou gong*) that could be applied such that when a woman had intercourse, the mark left by the paste would disappear (Harper 1987:557–558n41). Techniques to monitor women's sexual activity thus reveal an interest in reserving the beneficial essence of particular women to enhance the health of particular men. Good health, in other words, depended on healthy sex: frequent causes of illness included "excessive or immoderate behavior, usually sexual relations after drinking wine" or in a state of extreme emotion such as anger (Raphals 1998:177n38).

When the goal of sex was to conceive a child, medical prescriptions changed. Male reproductive fluids (*jing* 精) released during intercourse were understood to combine with female Blood (*xue* 血) to create an embryo that partook of pure *qi*.[3] The sex of that embryo was determined by the timing and conditions surrounding the moment of conception. Later texts gave very explicit instructions for intercourse, identifying days following the end of a woman's menstrual cycle and even the hours of the day that were most conducive to successful conception. In this formative construction of sexuality, men's healthy need for sexual intercourse with women was a foundation of the sex-gender system. We also see the primary motivation for protecting women from sex before marriage and for seeking out first-time intercourse with a virgin: it was considered the most beneficial for the health of the penetrating male. This was a sex-gender system that attached no value at all to monasticism or any other form of institutionalized celibacy.[4]

If early *yangsheng* texts focused on male bodies, what about women?[5] We have to wait until the eleventh and twelfth centuries, and a new genre called "women's medicine," for medical theories about a gendered body. Women's medicine took "Blood as the leader" in female health. Doctors' case studies in these new texts explained how to regulate the menstrual cycle and how to care for pregnant and postpartum mothers. Blood and milk were explained as a common substance: Blood otherwise shed in menstruation was retained during pregnancy to nurture the fetus *in utero*, becoming milk to feed the baby after birth. The focus on Blood as the

---

[3] Blood is capitalized here to stress that it refers not only to blood but also to the *yin* counterpart of male *qi*, the vital life-force of women. See Yi-Li Wu 2010:24 et passim.

[4] As Joan Cadden, historian of science and medicine in medieval Europe, points out (personal communication, May 2008). Monastic celibacy was one of the most controversial aspects of Buddhism after its introduction into China.

[5] Harper (1987:585) says that early techniques of sexual cultivation for women (*yang yin,*) are preserved in the Japanese text *Ishimpō* 28.6a (see Tamba et al. 1970). Chen Yu-shih's Daoist reading of the Han instructional text *Nü jie* (c. 106 CE) by Ban Zhao proposes that the text actually was a guide to preserving life, even though it is usually interpreted as a Confucian prescription for women's obedience and submission to male authority (Chen 1996).

leader led doctors to prescribe herbs and tonics to replenish the vital energies lost in regular menstruation, childbirth, and breastfeeding. Irregular
menstrual periods were signs of poor health, and intercourse during
menstruation was strictly tabooed as polluting to men and dangerous to
women. Couples who wanted to conceive timed intercourse according
to the menstrual cycle, waiting four days after the end of a period to
optimize chances of having a son. In other words, the field of women's
medicine tied women's health and their sexuality not to long life but to
reproductive success. Only after their reproductive years did women turn
to female regimens of "inner alchemy." Guides for female sexual health
composed by Daoist practitioners – the heirs of the *yangsheng* exercisers
in the Mawangdui tomb painting – taught postmenopausal women how
to transcend the stage of sexual fertility and reproduction by converting
Blood to *qi*, or *yang* energy, like that of men (Needham 1983:239–240).[6]

Joseph Needham and other scholars have contrasted Daoist teachings
on the salutary effects of sexual intercourse, properly managed, with the
transcendent orientation of Buddhist teachings, in which (in Needham's
words) "sex was no natural or beautiful thing, but only a device of Māra
the Tempter," that bound humans to the material world of illusion and
suffering (1983:218). Buddhist teachings forced Confucian philosophers
to take the physical body seriously, posing questions about perception –
how do we hear or smell or see physical objects outside the body? – and
proposing that the body and its sensations, including both pleasure and

---

[6] *Nü zong shuang xiu bao fa* (A Precious Raft of Salvation for Women Daoists Practising
the Double Regeneration of the Primary Vitalities) was recorded in verses by a Daoist
abbot at the end of the eighteenth century (Needham approximates the date as 1795).
According to Needham, "double" in this text refers to *yang* and *yin*: "nature and life-
span, true lead and true mercury, the two operations, in fact, which a single person
could carry out within his or her own body." For a male, this would mean "transmuting
the *qi*" (*lian qi*) by "not letting the degenerated *jing* escape, then he can precipitate the
enchymoma and lengthen his days," as another contemporary text explains it. For a
female, this would require "transmuting the form" (*lian xing*) "by not letting the grosser
part of the blood leak out, then she can escape death and enter into life." As Needham
observes, "The parallel between semen and menstrual blood was thus complete, for both
contained, or were, the raw material, if skilfully [sic] transmuted, of an enchymoma in a
deathless body" (1983: 237–238). For a woman, the goal was to "convert red into white,"
by changing menstrual blood into *qi* and then circulating the *qi* up and down through the
body ("irrigating the brain with nectar" was the phrase used in the late imperial period).
Note that in the case of women, "rejuvenation" meant becoming a young boy, not a young
girl. The term "enchymoma" is a neologism coined by Needham (1983: 27–28) to refer
to an elixir of immortality that is "prepared by physiological, not chemical, methods, out
of physiological constituents already in the body" (27). The "elixir within," or *nei dan*,
points to juices or fluids (blood, saliva, or semen, for example) used to rejuvenate and
restore youth. They must be accumulated, preserved, and circulated through breathing
and other exercises. See Figure 18.

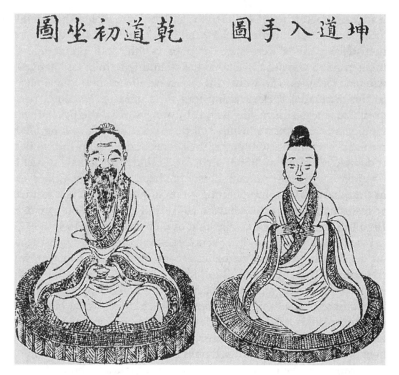

18. A couple practicing quiet sitting. Note the different hand positions for men and women. This is the foundation for a transcendent state of bliss that is achieved without awareness or effort. Catherine Despeux and Livia Kohn, *Women in Daoism*. Cambridge, Mass.: Three Pines Press, 2003, p. 216.

pain, were the cause of delusion that had to be transcended by extinguishing bodily awareness and desire. Buddhist beliefs about the physical body attached new notions of "virginity" to existing ideas about female purity and fidelity and exhorted believers to "conquer" or "overcome" physical sensations including sexual desires or appetites. The emphasis on Blood as the leader in women's medicine, moreover, found negative expression in Buddhist beliefs about the polluting nature of female blood and the enduring suffering of women who gave birth to children. And Buddhist beliefs promoting self-immolation as an expression of pure belief flew in the face of Confucian convictions that the body is a gift from one's parents and should be protected from injury at all costs (see Chapter 6).[7]

---

[7] In the *Classic of Filial Piety* (Xiao jing), memorized by every child as part of early education, Confucius explains this to his disciple Zeng Zi.

Influenced by Buddhist thought, later Neo-Confucian beliefs sometimes undermined – or outright rejected – the sex-for-health regimens of Daoism and traditional medicine. In late imperial Confucianism, the strict injunction to "watch oneself when alone" produced agonized self-criticism and introspection among men struggling to master their sexual desires. Sexual desire now had to be suppressed and restrained; sexual intercourse was strictly for the moral purpose of having children. Even the seventeenth-century school of Confucian thought that condemned the suppression of sexual desire and affirmed the morality of the human body ran into trouble with practitioners. Li Gong, the school's founder, who insisted that corporeal feelings and passions were "manifestations of 'the inherent moral propensity of man'" and that sexual union between husband and wife was "the fountainhead of all social relationships" (Ko 1996:68), also kept a diary in which he ruthlessly examined his own sexual thoughts and behavior every single day. Li Gong was unable to escape the sense that his moral self and his desiring self were at war with each other (Ko 1996). Li Gong's dilemma reminds us that a cultivated person in China's late empire embraced certain assumptions about human sexuality: containment for men, concealment for women. These assumptions were heteronormative: healthy sex was heterosexual sex. They embodied the familiar double standard: wives had only one sexual partner, whereas their husbands could have many. Norms of containment nonetheless criticized men who over-indulged in sex, whereas norms of concealment privileged wives over other women.

Li Gong's moral struggles were, in a sense, built into the hypergynous family system, in which upper-class men took concubines, as well as maids and courtesans, to bed, and the rules of Confucian patriliny made all male offspring of a man's sexual unions the ritual sons of his wife. Tensions generated by these competing sexual demands and opportunities produced the hierarchies that separated wives from other sexually active women, as we have seen. The same tensions shaped everything from domestic scenes portrayed in painting (in which upper-class men might be surrounded by women, but only female servants or entertainers, never their wives) to fashion (in which the seclusion of women was quite compatible with the spread of footbinding).

Erotica from the seventeenth century endlessly played on the tensions and contradictions generated by the imperatives of containment and concealment, as shown in the huge commercial stash of pornographic mini-sculpture, painting, how-to sex manuals for newlyweds, and other material that sinologists Robert van Gulik, Howard Levy, and others faithfully collected.

In sum, two sets of ideas about having sex circulated in the Qing period. One came out of the literature of Daoism and *yin-yang* thought. These ideas stressed the importance of *coitus reservatus* and the role of sex in improving health and prolonging life. The other (complementary) set of ideas came from the very strict interpretations of post-Buddhist Confucianism that managed sexual desire as a mode of moral self-discipline. The legacy of these two sets of ideas about sexuality was powerful. It stressed – as we have seen – containment for men (preservation of semen, careful calculation in reproductive success, elaborate taboos and schedules for timing sexual intercourse, etc.) and seclusion for women (wives and concubines should remain inside and concealed from view, protecting and preserving their sexual energies for the continuation of the patriline). These same discourses on sexuality also touched off explosions of fantasy in fiction and drama exploring sexual love and sexual desire, especially for young men and women (see Chapter 8).

Change in the twentieth century

Sex and the medical body

New ideas about scientific bodies and health, new interest in nude bodies in art, and new notions of physical culture and sport together transformed late Qing conceptions of the body for both males and females. The most invasive and sweeping change came in response to the sexed binary model of male and female bodies that framed Western medicine and its hygienic social Darwinist language. To what extent this sweeping change affected sexual behavior, and beliefs about gender and sexuality, is the subject of ongoing research. Demographers have shown, for example, that fertility rates in "traditional" Chinese societies were relatively low, and that the same patterns of low fertility continued into the twentieth century, long before the one-child policy began in 1979. Couples in contemporary China have intercourse less often and produce fewer children than their counterparts elsewhere. This pattern of constrained fertility is now understood to arise from a combination of factors with deep roots in late imperial Chinese sexual culture, including – but not limited to – concerns about the negative effects of too much sex on male health. Other factors (in addition to childrearing customs such as prolonged breastfeeding) are those familiar to readers of this book: "sex segregation, premarital chastity as a female virtue, and a lack of premarital sexual experience for females; norms of behavior that restrain spousal intimacy, both within and outside the household; a male-centered sexuality that assigns the wife a passive role in sexual matters; the impossibility of divorce, and the assumption that sexuality within marriage is primarily for procreation" (Lavely 2007:294–295). Demographer William Lavely has noted that Mao Zedong in his later years studied and practiced Daoist sexual techniques to protect his vital energies, and that sex education manuals, although careful to debunk Daoist beliefs, still stress the importance of moderation and the conditions under which intercourse should be avoided, including after bathing (Lavely 2007:300–301). As a twenty-five-year-old married male intellectual interviewed by William Jankowiak in 1983 put it: "On your wedding night you can have sex a lot. But afterward you should only have sex once a week. Otherwise you will lose your strength" (Jankowiak 1993:232). (This view, incidentally, did not stand the test of time: the same informant, later divorced, abandoned it.) In other words, historical beliefs about sexuality have continued to shape beliefs and behavior in "modern" marriage.

Women had their own concerns in the twentieth-century world of modern marriage. As early as the 1920s, articles in the lively urban press described "an ever-increasing chorus of women avowing to live single [in reaction against oppression by men].... Celibacy may not be desirable in itself, but in China it is a good index to the abhorrence which women entertain towards married life" (Croll 1978:88, citing an article titled "The Awakening of Chinese Women and Celibacy" and observations in Seton 1924:235–236). While interviewing women who entered professional life in the 1930s and 1940s, Zheng Wang took note of their general ambivalence about heterosexual love and marriage. For all of her informants, sexual relationships and marriage posed enormous problems in the new society in which they could pursue professional careers and socialize freely with men (Zheng Wang 1999b). Modern fashion, for instance, required that a wife take her husband's surname, a compromise that one informant found so abhorrent that she refused to marry at all (Zheng Wang 1999b:263–264). Gossip followed a woman's every affair, marriage, and divorce, to devastating effect (Zheng Wang 1999b:169–170, 183–184, 306–307). The appeal of romantic love and freedom to choose a mate, under these circumstances, was far greater for men than for many women.

Ideas about sexuality that hark back to the early philosophers linger on in twentieth-century discourses. In 1922 the male editor of the *Women's Journal* composed an article on love declaiming that

the human race has two basic desires, for food and for sexuality. The two desires are at the center of all social customs, norms, morality, law, and institutions.... Therefore, hunger and love are the basis of all social problems. All entangled struggles in society originated in these basic desires. Socialism is a fundamental solution to the hunger problem; and "freedom-to-loveism" is a fundamental solution to the love problem.... Freedom to love (*lian'ai ziyou*) is a start in solving women's problems as well as an end in solving women's problems. (Zheng Wang 1999b:88)

Here we see classical ideas about sex or sexuality conflated with a notion of love that is presented as modern and liberating (Zheng Wang 1999b:87–89).

In other beliefs about the body we can identify the legacy of traditional Chinese medicine, especially from the notion of Blood as the leader, as anthropologist Emily Martin Ahern discovered in her fieldwork in rural Taiwan during the 1960s. In Ahern's analysis, the premenopausal woman's menstrual blood was a source of both power and danger (Ahern 1975). The pollution of blood removed rural women from participation in ancestral rites, nor were they permitted to celebrate the festivals for high powerful gods. Instead, women presided over the rites honoring "dirty, low spirits and ghosts" such as the privy goddess (Ahern 1975:206). A filial son could rescue his mother from eternal punishment in the afterlife, a consequence of her polluted state, through a ritual that saved her from drowning in the underworld's bloody pond by "breaking the blood bowl" (Ahern 1975:214, Seaman 1981). The stigma attached to menstrual blood persisted in popular culture through much of the century in Taiwan (Cordia Ming-Yeuk Chu 1980). Men could suffer severe illness and even die from the poisonous *yin* absorbed during intercourse with a menstruating woman, and the woman herself might suffer irreparable damage to her cycle or even her reproductive future if she violated this taboo. This was the case despite the recognition that menstrual blood also nourished the fetus and, after birth, flowed upward to become milk (blood becomes the "bone and flesh" of the baby) (Ahern 1975:196, Cordia Ming-Yeuk Chu 1980:41). Ahern proposed that the "dangerous power of menstrual blood" was another way of pointing to a married woman's power to build a "uterine family" of her own offspring who were emotionally bonded to her. These uterine bonds threatened the solidarity of grand families composed of brothers and their wives and offspring (Wolf 1972).

In the People's Republic of China (PRC), conversations about menstruation have displayed continued contradictions, confusing the protection of women's interests and the problem of women's weaknesses (Evans 1997:65–70). The post-1949 government sponsored extensive education programs for adolescent girls that explained menstruation as a "normal" bodily process essential to health. But concern about women's exposure to cold during the menstrual cycle is evident in contemporary Chinese labor law, which forbids assigning menstruating female workers to "work at high altitudes, in places with low temperatures, or in cold water" (Woo

1994:281). Under the one-child family policy after 1980, menstruation acquired new salience as party officials began to monitor fertility and enforce birth quotas. In the 1990s, as women workers steadily lost their jobs with employers under fire to show a profit, managers could justifiably complain that women workers' special needs and benefits associated with menstruation and pregnancy threatened their business success.

The body in art

Western conceptions of a biological organic body with a physique and musculature, and Western artists' fascination with the aesthetics of the nude body, directly challenged fundamental premises of Chinese art. Chinese artists and sculptors were famously uninterested in nude bodies before the twentieth century. Why? Partly because of the medical conceptions of the body that we have just examined. In medicine the body's boundaries – the skin as surface – were seen as permeable to the larger circulation of cosmic energy that surrounded it (Kuriyama 1994:36–38). Moreover, in the medical understanding, physical bodies themselves held no particular individual interest. What made people distinctive, interesting, and culturally significant was not their bodies, but their clothes. The *clothed* body signaled gender, age, ethnicity, and status. Chinese portrait artists were meticulous in recording the details of clothing, especially the markers of official rank associated with decorations on embroidered garments for men and women. Students today can decode a Chinese genre painting from the late imperial period by marking status and gender according to the dress of the crowds displayed in the streets of Suzhou or Kaifeng. Who could tell anything worth knowing from looking at a nude body? The lack of interest in the nude in late imperial pictorial art may explain the curiously low level of titillation in nineteenth-century Chinese erotica featuring undressed women and men (Cahill 2010). It also helps us to understand the utter fascination of tiny embroidered shoes concealing bound feet. As Dorothy Ko has shown so well, once the bound foot was X-rayed, its "aura" was destroyed, for its only appeal lay in the mystification of the body it concealed (Ko 2005).

In the twentieth century art world, the relative absence of nudes in Chinese painting has sometimes been chalked up to prudishness or, more recently, government censorship. Concerns about nudity surfaced powerfully, for example, when Chinese painters and sculptors began to recruit nude models for their work in the 1980s, although nude bodies have become more visible in commercial advertising since the 1990s, especially in foreign advertising. An exhibit of paintings of nudes at the Beijing Art Gallery in 1989 was sufficiently shocking to stir debate and

19. Zhang Huan (b. 1965). "To Add One Meter to an Anonymous Mountain." Performance piece (photograph), 1995. Performance at Miaofeng Mountain, Beijing, May 22, 1995. Source: Gao Minglu, ed. *New China Art: Inside Out.* San Francisco Museum of Modern Art and Asia Society Galleries, New York; publ. Berkeley: University of California Press, 1998, pl. 49. Printed with the permission of the artist.

provoke embarrassment, even while record crowds of 10,000 people a day jammed the gallery for more than two weeks, paying up to half a day's working wage for a ticket. As *New York Times* reporter Nicholas Kristof observed, writing on the last day of the show (January 9, 1989), five of the paintings in the exhibit had already been replaced before the show closed, due to pressure from models who had posed for the artists in the exhibit. Two models engaged lawyers and planned to sue the gallery because the artists had left their faces recognizable: "Many of the models apparently had been too embarrassed to tell family members, even their spouses, about their jobs" (Kristof 1989:A4). Fifteen years later, nude models were still difficult to hire: one artist estimated that there were no more than twenty working in all of Shanghai, according to a *Shanghai Star* report published in 2004 ("Nude Modeling: Business or Art?").

The contested place of the nude figure in Chinese art has given China's contemporary artists an opportunity to layer the human body with multiple meanings. Consider the performance piece by Zhang Huan titled "To Add One Meter to an Anonymous Mountain," depicted in Figure 19.

The title cues us that Zhang is using bodies to play on (or play against) the painterly iconography of the rock. Compare Zhang's piece with a classical landscape by the early Qing painter Shitao (1640–1718), shown in Figure 20. Mount Lu is the famous subject of countless late imperial landscape paintings, which commonly feature one or more tiny human figures wandering amid towering peaks and cascading waterways. Zhang Huan's performance piece inverts the point of classical art forms that suborned and erased the human figure and exalted famous rock formations. We can barely see his "anonymous" mountain, and its sole point of interest is the pile of naked bodies that fills the frame. Here Zhang's transgressive use of nude bodies can only be understood in its multiple meanings if we understand the history of the body in Chinese art.

The body in sport

In sport Western models of the muscular body transformed the arenas in which physical strength was displayed and admired, for both men and women. Physical strength in late imperial times was cultivated through martial arts (*wushu*) that stressed control of energy and balance along with physical dexterity. Toward the end of the Qing dynasty, however, especially during the Boxer Rebellion (1900), indigenous martial arts acquired a subversive flavor and *wushu* was discredited among the educated elite. At the turn of the twentieth century, therefore, there was no vocabulary in classical Chinese, and no legitimate cultural practice in late imperial society, that might have supplied a comfortable home for the athletics and sports introduced into China first by missionary schools and then by educators in Japan (Brownell 1995).

This makes it all the more striking that competitive sports for both men and women instantly tapped the energies of patriotic young people eager to defend China's position in the world of competing nations. Competitive athletics drew their appeal not from any indigenous traditions in medicine or martial arts but rather from the modern language of social Darwinism. China's urban leaders, and the students in China's new schools, saw their country as a weak nation struggling against powerful rivals for survival. Sports competitions became an immediate venue for developing and displaying the strong citizens who would save the Chinese nation. As Denise Gimpel (2006) has pointed out, at a time when Western women's entry into sports was being vigorously contested, early-twentieth-century Chinese women plunged enthusiastically into athletic training and physical education in Beijing and Shanghai. New schools for girls introduced physical education as part of their curriculum; sports teams promoted women's basketball, swimming, track, and volleyball.

20. Shitao (1641–c. 1717). "The Waterfall on Mount Lu." Hanging
scroll. Ink and light colors on silk (w. 24 in.). *Source:* James Cahill,
Chinese Painting. Geneva, Switzerland: Albert Skira, 1960, p. 183.

For both male and female athletes, developing the body for physical exercise demanded (or offered) a wholly new conception of the embodied self and of the body politic as well. In classical thought, as we have seen, the filial child who was bound to care for aging parents (or parents-in-law) must tend carefully to his or her body, avoiding risk and injury to ensure a long and healthy life. Athletic competition challenged this and other gendered meanings of the body. Long fingernails, a hallmark of the leisured elite; the queue, which imposed severe constraints on the speed and skill of male athletes; the bound foot (no explanation necessary); and the long gowns favored by upper-class men and women – all had to go when the time came to run, jump, kick, and tackle. In the first National Games held in Beijing in 1910, the high jumper Sun Baoxin was disqualified twice because although his body cleared the bar in record-breaking leaps, his queue – coiled up on the back of his neck – came loose, caught, and dislodged the bar on the way down. A Chinese historian describes the scene: "In that moment, people's hearts became indignant, their revolutionary spirit welled up, and they longed to eradicate the customs that the Qing imperial court forcefully imposed on people" (Wang Zhenya 1987:136, quoted in Brownell 1995:42). Backward bodies spelled backward government and weak citizens, bringing an immediate end to those gendered markers of the Manchu conquest: the queue and the bound foot.

Dressing for athletic competitions put Chinese women and men into new clothes (see Chapter 5) that exposed limbs and body shape directly to the public gaze. This sparked controversy about the public display of the body, which persisted throughout the century. In bodybuilding, for example, as China entered global competitions in the post-Mao era, women were expected to wear bikinis – long associated with decadent sexual mores in Western culture and disdained by Chinese female athletes. Discomfort about nudity ran high among the female athletes that Susan Brownell interviewed in her fieldwork during the 1980s (Brownell 1995:270–277). And yet female athletes became a centerpiece of contemporary Chinese sport, sweeping gold medals in the Olympic Games in Beijing in 2008. Their success was not necessarily a measure of liberation, because women have remained low on the hierarchy of coaching and sports administration, as well as other professional ladders. Instead, the success of China's contemporary female athletes has multiple causes: "the long-standing involvement of women in martial arts, the general regard for sport as a low-class activity, the rural background of many sportswomen, and the influence of Confucian ideology in inculcating such traits in women as obedience, sacrifice, discipline, humility and respect in regard to men" (Riordan and Dong 1996:151–152) – and, of course, the Maoist ideal of equal opportunity for women:

There is an absence in China of a number of deep-seated prejudices with regard to sexuality that have been common in Western historical development, centred on the notion that sport is a "male preserve." Chinese women are thereby challenging cultural assumptions about behaviour being directly related to biological make-up, and demonstrating that many of the male and female characteristics long taken for granted by the dominant ideology of Western society are determined by social custom rather than by genetics. That does not mean that the Chinese believe that the ability of male runners to run faster than female runners has no genetic component. Rather, there is a firm conviction that women's biological disadvantage in physical performance may be compensated for by socially-conditioned superior abilities of hard work, discipline and stamina. (Riordan and Dong 1996:151)

Able and disabled bodies

The discourses of biomedicine, social Darwinism, and global athletics combined to celebrate the strength and masculinity/virility of the active body in twentieth-century China.[8] These discourses framed reform-era conversations about "quality" (suzhi) and "disability." At the end of the 1980s, thanks in part to the leadership of Deng Xiaoping's son Deng Pufang – himself disabled as a result of violence during the Cultural Revolution – about fifty million disabled persons achieved social recognition as a "special population" represented by their own party organization, the China Disabled Persons' Federation. The government tried to monitor and control this group of potentially disruptive claimants on government services in a time-honored fashion: through programs promoting heteronormative marriage for all persons classified as disabled. These programs had roots in persistent beliefs about bodily health, in lingering eugenicist attitudes suggesting that disabled men are not "real men" (nanzihan), and in other traditional views of male self-worth, potency, and occupational legitimacy – all of which depended on access to women and placement in a conjugal unit (Kohrman 2005:179–180).

The difference between the pre-twentieth-century and twentieth-century discourses on sexuality and gender was the new view of sexuality as a "natural biological phenomenon" subject to scientific explanation and analysis (Evans 1995:360). State policies on sex and gender could

---

[8] As Matthew Kohrman puts it, this is the body "that can halt China's 'withering' and instead promote a racially powerful nation-state . . . , the body that can realize Mao's dream of 'continuous revolution' . . . , the body that can leap, whether through collective or individual action, to the forefront of industrialized modernity" (Kohrman 2005:183).

claim the full power of modern science in their prescriptions and regulations for men and women, males and females, newly conceived as a
sexed binary instead of the "relative and flexible bipolarity" based on *yin*
and *yang* that shaped old understandings of embodied gender difference
(Barlow 1994, Evans 1995). This makes it even more striking that the
introduction of modern science made barely a dent in many old ideas
about gender and sexuality. James Edwards (1976:88), studying sexology
in the late Maoist era, stressed what he called "the lingering influence
of 'old society' sexual beliefs." These beliefs included the view that men
must be more careful than women about healthy sex to protect their
limited *yang* essence. Taboo days when sex was dangerous or ill advised
and certain hours of the day that were optimal for sex (e.g., 10 PM to
midnight) – all were identified in sex manuals published between 1951
and 1976. The message of these manuals counseled moderation in sexual activity. Readers were told to have sex once or twice a week at most;
to avoid sex during menstruation, pregnancy, and illness; and to limit
sex with advancing age. The same pamphlets cautioned women not to
pressure their husbands to have sex too often, lest they deplete the supply
of semen, making it harder to get pregnant. Similarly, men were warned
that masturbation was strongly associated with maladies that followed
depletion of *yang* essence. Women too were strongly cautioned against
masturbation in some handbooks (Edwards 1976:96–97).

Sex education in the post-Mao era, especially from the 1990s, reaf-
firmed presumptions that heterosexual activity was "natural" and "legitimate" (Evans 1995:366), and more open attitudes toward sex and sex
education were encouraged. Still, taboos on masturbation and on sex
during menstruation persisted, alongside the belief that sexuality should
be "controlled in the interests of social morality and order" and that the
purpose of healthy sexual intercourse is reproduction (Evans 1995:366–
367). In fact, as Harriet Evans has emphasized (1995, 1997), all of the
scientific discourses of the post-1949 government reiterated the unalter-
able link between female bodies and reproduction. Marriage and motherhood remained the prefigured destiny of women subject to the control
of the Chinese government, and on terms dictated by the state's birth-
planning administration, despite the relatively recent attention to female
sexual pleasure and the apparent tolerance of homosexuality. Notions of
sexual behavior and sexual practice, closely linked to the social roles pre-
scribed for males and females, also showed surprising continuity from the
1950s through the 1990s. Masturbation was condemned, in almost the
same language, in sexology handbooks published in 1955 and in 1986 –
in both cases the handbooks warned that masturbation compromised
fertility and good health (Evans 1995:360). Early 1950s publications on

sex education, in fact, were the only materials available to sex educators looking to reopen information about sexual practices for men and women in the 1980s reform era. A single rupture in this relatively constant discourse on sexuality occurred in the years from the Great Leap Forward (1958–1961) through the Cultural Revolution (1966–1976), when public policy declared sexual matters including love and marriage to be private matters that had to be suborned to the cause of the revolution and the interests of society as a whole. During that period, men and women were offered "no advice" on these subjects (Evans 1995:364–365, quoting an anonymous source).

In this way beliefs from the imperial past continued to freight changing conceptions of the body in Chinese cultures. Concern for the importance of preserving semen, for example, informed the diagnosis and treatment of patients in Taiwan into the 1980s, especially those diagnosed with a malady called "vital or kidney deficiency" (*shen kui*). Kidney deficiency, attributed to insufficient reserves of vital male essence (*jing*), caused severe illness with symptoms ranging from impotence to dizziness, insomnia, and acute anxiety (Wen and Wang 1980). Persistent concerns about sexual vitality also surfaced in recurrent waves of panic reported by Han Chinese in South China and some overseas Chinese communities, fed by fear that the sex organs (male penis, female breast and nipples) would disappear into the body. The last major such report was in 1984–1985, from Hainan Island and the Leizhou Peninsula. These panics, called *suoyang* or *koro*, were blamed on fox spirits that possessed their victims and pulled the sex organs inward. Family and friends had to apply force to pull in the opposite direction and use exorcism and special potions to counteract the powerful spirit's grip (Sheung-Tak Cheng 1997:62).[9] The fears of these communities point to a persistent link between ideas about sexual vitality and life itself, a legacy of the earliest notions of the classical Chinese medical body.

[9] Nocturnal emission in these communities was thought to represent sex with a fox spirit in a dream.

5   The body adorned, displayed, concealed, and altered

The dynasty has gone and there is no new one; the teeth of the dragon have dropped out. Hair, part of the body given us by our ancestors, is cut, even by women.

Ning Lao T'ai-t'ai (Pruitt 1945:245)

I was guilty of wearing a bright red woolen top and black skirt. To make matters worse, I had tied a silk scarf around my neck. . . . Women had just started to unbutton Mao's straitjacket and slip into more colorful and fashionable attire.

Lijia Zhang (2008:194)

The body unadorned may have been meaningless, but things that covered and decorated the body were crucial markers of civilization and social hierarchy in late imperial times. Clothing, hairstyle, shoes, and badges – these gave the physical body its significance. The absence of proper adornment signaled savagery, barbarism, and backwardness. As Dorothy Ko (1997a:12) observed, commenting on late imperial culture: "Correct attire – headdress, dress, and shoes – was the quintessential expression of civility, culture, and humanity." Every dynasty issued new regulations to stipulate how officials should display their status through costume, and which colors were reserved for the exclusive use of the imperial family. Medallions on official gowns blazed the status of the wearer down to his level in the nine-rank bureaucratic system, and the number of claws on a gown's embroidered dragons signaled the wearer's degree of distance from the emperor himself (see Figure 21).

The "modern girl" of the twentieth century, sauntering along the street in Shanghai, proclaimed her distance from her backward country cousins and her membership in the modern world with her "natural" feet, her bobbed hair, and her tight-fitting, high-slit skirts (Figure 22). And women in post-1949 China dressed, up or down, in fashion constrained by the current political line.

21. Man's outer coat with embroidered rank badge. *Source:* Verity
Wilson, *Chinese Dress*. New York: Weatherhill Press, for The Victoria
and Albert Museum, 1986, p. 26.

If clothing and bodily adornment displayed a person's social, cultural,
and political identity, bodily comportment (action, work) was supposed
to correspond. Work was a visible sign of moral worth, and work roles
were universally assigned by status and gender (see Chapter 1). In Qing
times, all respectable women worked with their hands, ideally spinning,
weaving, embroidering, or tending silkworms in a display of their virtue.
They dressed to suit: a maid's functional clothing was adapted for the
physical effort that her job demanded; her mistress wore silken garments
whose sleeves would never be splashed or stained, because her proper
work was embroidery. Men laboring in field or shop worked "with their
hands," as Mencius put it, displaying their own position a notch below
the governing-class elite, whose long fingernails showed that they labored
only "with their minds," studying, teaching, or serving in office. In Confucian thought, the relationship between moral worth and action was
captured in the cryptic phrase "knowledge and action are one." That is
to say, a person *is* what he or she *does*. In this understanding of the individual, there was no transcendent "self" or immutable individual identity.
Only roles, played appropriately or not, gave evidence of an individual's
moral worth, social standing, political status, level of civility, and so forth.

22. Modern girls in new hairstyles and shoes, with *qipao* cut in the latest fashionable style. *Source:* Jonathan D. Spence and Annping Chin, *The Chinese Century: A Photographic History of the Last Hundred Years.* New York: Random House, 1996, p. 111.

In other words, each person was expected to perform according to the situation in which she found herself, and dress accordingly.

Dress and adornment in the Qing period

The top fashion-setters in the seventeenth century were courtesans whose "aura" derived from the mystification of concealment surrounding the bound foot: "The practice of concealing raw flesh with cloth can be interpreted as a female expression of *wen* culture, a form of female bodily inscription or 'writing.' Indeed, in the blue-building [courtesans' quarters] accounts, footbinding was presented as one of the many cultural achievements of the courtesan, on par with her command of lyrics and painting" (Ko 1997b:96). When the Ming dynasty fell to the Manchus, as we have seen, Han Chinese men were forced to shave their foreheads and grow a long braid (queue), Manchu style, as a public sign of their submission. Han Chinese women were also ordered to unbind their feet. The first policy was in place within a decade; the second was never enforced. Fashioning of the body, then, carried powerful messages, heightened at the moment of dynastic transition or in encounters with the Other. At the time of the Manchu conquest, a Han Chinese woman's bound foot – the emblem of women's oppression to twentieth-century reformers – was instead associated with loyalism, resistance, and even ethnic identity.

Such gendered paradoxes lace the modern history of Chinese fashion. The first step in detecting these paradoxes is to recognize that little of the fashion associated with dress and adornment in Qing times was purely Han Chinese. The second step is to recognize that the political and cultural meanings of fashion changed over time. The male queue, for example, began as a symbol of treason – disloyalty to the Ming and capitulation to a barbarian invader. That was in the decades following the Manchu conquest of 1644. By the time of the Taiping Rebellion in the middle of the nineteenth century, the queue had become a symbol of honor and loyalty to the Qing throne, and the Taiping rebels – who refused to shave their foreheads – were disdainfully labeled "long-hairs" by disgusted Han Chinese officials. Then during the revolution of 1911, the queue served to dramatize the most powerful gesture of Chinese patriotism: cutting the queue became the visible and irrevocable pledge of support for overthrowing the emperor. The queue embodied all of these powerful symbolic meanings in part because of its visibility: men, after all, worked and moved about in the public domain. Still, the seclusion of women and the concealment of bound feet did not lessen the powerful meaning of women's fashion in the Qing period. During the Taiping Rebellion, for example, the rebels – who were Hakka and did not practice footbinding – decreed an end to footbinding in the areas they conquered. Resistance to the forcible *unbinding* of women's feet then became one of the rallying cries of the Taiping pacification campaign, which mobilized local defense forces and official troops to stamp out the rebellion.

Gendered female fashion conveyed ethnic messages, Han or Manchu, in the urban centers of Qing life. Manchu women admired the delicate

23. Manchu ladies' shoes. *Source:* Tcheng-Ki Tong and John Henry Gray, *The Chinese Empire, Past and Present.* Chicago: Rand McNally, 1900, opposite p. 177.

swaying gait of Han Chinese women with their bound feet, so they created the same illusion by wearing regular shoes atop tiny platforms (see Figure 23).

Han Chinese women fancied jackets with wide sleeves that were much admired and copied by Manchu ladies (see Finnane 2008:55ff. for examples). Local styles dictated everything from hair dressing to fabric cut, led by fashion centers in Yangzhou and Suzhou during the eighteenth and nineteenth centuries, with their "five-terrace sleeve" jackets and "hundred-pleat skirts." Even the Qianlong Emperor became an arbiter of female fashion: he commissioned paintings of Yangzhou beauties to adorn his private quarters (Cahill 1996). As the eighteenth-century chronicler Li Dou put it, "Clothes worn in Yangzhou are always in the newest style" (Finnane 2008:55). Describing fashionable women, observers focused not on the fit of garments but on fabric – color, texture, design, thread, weave, and pattern (Finnane 2008:55–56). The beauty of a garment often lay in the elaborately embroidered trimmings and acces-sories rather than in the finished gown they embellished. Embroidery's value was greatly increased if the wearer herself produced it: embroidered accessories, including pouches and small purses, collars and sleeve cuffs, trimmings and bindings, and shoes, were all part of the endless stitchery projects that kept women of the upper classes continually busy, and that also supplied the arena for boundless creativity and variability in fashion.

If notions of feminine beauty fastened on the figure of young ladies from Yangzhou or Suzhou, ideas of masculine beauty or handsomeness were more complicated. The sinologist Robert van Gulik argued that ideals of masculinity shifted after the Qing conquest, as Han Chinese men self-consciously cultivated a scholarly persona in opposition to the martial arts favored by the Manchus. Contemporary scholar Kam Louie has turned this argument around, suggesting that a "delicate" mascu-line style served as a protective strategy, enabling Han Chinese to keep their positions of power without being perceived as a threat to Manchu hegemony (Louie 1991:180–181, citing Gulik 2003 [1974]:296). The "ideal man" of mid-Qing fiction was Jia Baoyu, hero of *Dream of the Red Chamber*, and beautiful men like him appear across literary genres, from the "flower guides" that ranked the comeliness of boy actors in the Peking opera to the hundreds of *caizi jiaren* (gifted youth and virtuous maiden) tales that sold well in every bookshop (Cuncun Wu 2003). In other words, and for many reasons, in Qing times a young man at either end of the social hierarchy, from the bottom (actors) to the top (scholars), strived for features resembling those of a beautiful woman: pale lustrous skin like jade, a slim body that "barely supported the clothes," fingers like sprouts of spring bamboo, vermilion lips, a gentle gaze, and a tender air (Cuncun Wu 2003:22–23). For the young scholar hero of popular novels, this kind of beauty represented extreme refinement and augured future success; for the young actor in the theater, beauty was the ticket to star-dom as a *hua dan* (female impersonator). Elite admirers of Jia Baoyu saw in him their own manly ideal: the capacity to rise above worldly social conventions and practical concerns, and to dedicate himself to purity and aesthetic pursuits. The beauty of boy actors signaled pleasure, and their admirers celebrated accordingly, praising them as carefree, clever, or fragrant.

These seemingly "feminized" ideals of male beauty were not considered androgynous. That is, ideas of "male" and "female" remained perfectly clear and distinct, as when male actors were commanded to dress up as females (Cuncun Wu 2003:35), or when actresses portrayed men on the Yue opera stage (Jiang 2009). Male ideals were products of the male imagination, which celebrated and performed them. Playing on these images of male beauty, fiction writers in the eighteenth century pushed the boundaries of the erotic expression of male desire. The "chaste romances" of a scholar and a beauty contrasted with novels featuring relationships between a man and many women – up to a hundred, in one case – whose sexual encounters were described in explicit and vivid detail (McMahon 1995). Subtle displacements (squeezing a bound foot, for instance, or having an unmarried couple meet publicly while she is disguised as a man) used suggestions about the body, rather than explicit description, to convey erotic meanings (McMahon 1995:127–128). Some writers filled their stories with graphic details of anal, oral, and hetero- and homosexual encounters – to tremendous comic effect in the best work by the great seventeenth-century satirist Li Yu. The delicate male beauty, then, could embody notions of sexual vitality from traditional Chinese medicine, while at the same time suggestively transgressing the norms of sexual economy and containment.

Eunuchs and other disfigured bodies

In the Qing period, as in the Ming, castrated males served as eunuchs at the imperial court, entrusted to move about in close contact with palace women. Although palace eunuchs performed hundreds of menial chores, certain prestigious positions were also reserved for eunuchs. Lamaist priests who served the spiritual needs of palace women were required to be eunuchs, for example, as were actors who performed at court and also the attendants at the emperor's bedchamber, who were charged with recording his sexual intercourse with each woman summoned to his bed (Stent 1877:173–175). These eunuchs, powerful though many became, were harshly stigmatized. In the Qing period they were blamed for the collapse of the Ming and vilified as unfilial sons who could not produce heirs for their own descent lines. Potent derogatory images of eunuchs at the court portray them as "paranoid, petty, . . . peevish, vindictive, and capable of quick and ruthless decisions. . . . Above all, [the eunuch] always stood by his autocrat employer like a faithful dog and would come to the defense of his emperor even when the emperor flouted . . . the wishes of the people by acts of tyranny" (Tsai 1996:5). The physical changes that accompanied castration, including loss of facial hair, wrinkled skin, soft body fat, high voice, and so forth, increased the contempt of observers and political critics alike (Tsai 1996:4). Because any mutilation of the body was an extreme form of unfilial behavior, the court periodically issued decrees banning self-castration. Nevertheless, self-castration remained a painful avenue of upward mobility and employment for thousands of impoverished men. Eunuchs who castrated themselves (or were castrated by their parents) for service at the Qing court came mainly from one prefecture south of the capital. Of such men it was said that they had "left the family" (*chu jia*), the same phrase used of men who entered the priesthood or a monastery (Stent 1877:181). The agonizingly crude surgery was either self-inflicted or performed at the court in a special quarter by "knifers," as they were called by Carter Stent, a medical doctor residing in Beijing who published several studies of eunuchs. Penis and testicles were preserved after being removed, as evidence for the surgery and as necessary to a proper burial when the eunuch died. Stent blamed the practice of self-castration on polygamy, which left so many men without the prospect of marriage and offspring (Stent 1877:183). He too was cognizant of the surplus of unmarried men in the population at large, and of their desperate need for a social niche where they could survive in safety. The presence of eunuchs and the practice of self-castration, in other words, underscore the vulnerability of single males and the dangers they faced in the sex-gender system of the late empire.

To nineteenth-century foreigners, the presence of eunuchs at the Chinese court was a sign of the "Oriental despotism" that reigned there. In Stent's words: "eunuchs are only to be found in eastern despotic countries, the enlightening influence of Christianity preventing such unnatural proceedings being practiced in the countries of those who profess it" (Stent 1877:143).[1] Moreover, the presence of eunuchs was also taken as a measure of the low status of women, whose husbands or masters believed that they were so wayward that their lust could not be contained around sexually active men. Eunuchs were a favorite target of Meiji Japanese critics eager to ridicule China's backwardness and to valorize their own Westernizing reforms begun in 1868. For Japanese intellectuals, the presence of eunuchs in China was – like footbinding – telling evidence of Chinese barbarism. The fact that Japan had never embraced either the Chinese custom of footbinding or the courtly use of eunuchs

---

[1] Stent knew better, of course, because he quoted sources identifying castration as a practice in Christian countries, including Italy, where it was performed to preserve the soprano voices of boys for opera and the theater (Stent 1877:145).

24. The exemplary woman Gaoxing of Liang. Widowed very young and daughter of a wealthy family, Gaoxing declined all offers of remarriage until she was finally approached by the king himself, whose emissary is shown here offering her gold. This scene shows her ultimate gesture of renunciation: she is cutting off her nose to deface her appearance so the king will know that she has rejected him utterly by making herself undesirable. She also makes the point that she would have committed suicide, but she has children to rear, and she must remain alive to look out for them. *Source:* http://www.east-asian-history.net/textbooks/PM-China/graphics/Ch11/01.htm.

was likewise taken as evidence of Japan's predisposition to enlightenment (Mitamura 1970:16).[2]

In Qing times footbinding, as we have seen, was not considered a form of bodily mutilation, but rather one of bodily enhancement. However, mutilation of the female body did enter the discourses of elite women and of popular culture in two kinds of narratives. One was the (officially forbidden) practice of *gegu*, or cutting the flesh of the thigh, to make a medicinal broth to cure an ailing parent or in-law. The second, much dramatized form of bodily mutilation appeared in stories about exemplary women who cut off an ear or a nose to proclaim their honor. By disfiguring her face, the only part of the body visible to a suitor or matchmaker, the virtuous faithful widow publicly declared her refusal to remarry and removed herself permanently from the marriage market (see Figure 24).

[2] Although eunuchs were found in most kingdoms on the empire's borderlands, including Korea, the Japanese court never recruited castrated men to service. See Tsai 1996:14–17.

25. Hua Mulan. *Source:* Xiyuan waishi [pseud.], *Xiuxiang gujin xiannü zhuan* (Lavishly Illustrated Biographies of Resourceful Women, Past and Present). Pref. dated 1908, vol. 1, n.p. 135.

Mutilation of the body, even in the name of virtue, was nonetheless controversial in late imperial times. Were such acts admirable or reckless? Did they defile the body that was supposed to remain inviolate as a gift from one's parents? Debates about *gegu*, and even the occasional complaint about footbinding and its painful costs, point to notions of the body and its integrity that served to support later movements for physical fitness and beauty culture, especially for women.

Cross-dressing and girls who want to be boys

Cross-dressing in late imperial culture was not experienced as transgressive. A woman who dressed up like a soldier was expected to behave like a soldier, and to return to her womanly ways the minute she took off her costume, just like Hua Mulan (see Figure 25).

Moreover, a male actor playing the part of a female on stage was considered able to capture the essence of his character's speech and action even better than an actress could. Habits of role performance fed the fantasies that filled fiction, drama, and memoir – especially fantasies of girls who wished they were boys, and parents who treated a daughter like a son. These habits of role performance supplied a cultural script enabling Chinese women – and men – to shift nimbly into the many new roles created in the twentieth-century reforms and revolutions.

Unlike eunuchs, who were stigmatized as males who had taken on womanly characteristics, women who dressed up and acted like men were celebrated as heroines. The epic tale of Mulan is the most famous example: a cross-dressed heroine who goes off to fight like a man for the country. But women warriors fill Chinese history books, New Year pictures, and woodblock illustrations. They were favorite subjects of women writers, especially poets, and they appear constantly in memoirs written by twentieth-century Chinese women, as well as in the famous fiction of Chinese-American writer Maxine Hong Kingston (1976). The common standards for "beauty" or comeliness used to judge male and female bodies made it easier for girls to pass as boys simply by putting on boys' clothing. After all, elite men and women shared a common physical culture based on reading, writing, and other literati pursuits. Sword dancing by women was known to the great classical poet Du Fu (712–770), who wrote a poem about a female sword dancer named Lady Gongsun, and sword dancing remains popular in female exercise clubs today, as an early morning stroll through China's urban parks will show you.

No one can ignore the countless Qing stories of a girl who wants to be a boy and a father who rears his daughter like a son – educating her like a boy, dressing her like a boy, and giving her a boy's name (on dressing girls as boys, see Yu-ning Li 1992:109–110). As a young girl, Ning Lao T'ai-t'ai ran and jumped and climbed trees with boys, driving her own mother to distraction. Biographies of twentieth-century Chinese women recall fondly their days as tomboys and even more appreciatively the connivance of doting fathers (Croll 1995:38–40, Finnane 2008:87–92, see also Zheng Wang 1999b:148, 225, 261). Female warriors of the past captured a sense of moral courage and physical daring that animated twentieth-century revolutionaries as well as their genteel forebears (Louise Edwards 1995, Mann 2010, Pei-yi Wu 2002). Leading revolutionary women (Qiu Jin, Xie Bingying) flaunted their masculine personae by dressing as men, practicing martial arts, or joining the army.

Dressing like a man and going off to a successful career of study and official service as a man was a grand theme for heroines in late imperial women's writing, especially in the *tanci* (plucking rhymes) favored by

Qing women during the decades from 1840 to 1895, which Hu Siao-chen has earmarked as a particular new stage in writing women's consciousness that she calls the "early late Qing era."[3] The female writer Hou Zhi used the *tanci* genre to criticize the notion "to be without talent is virtue in a woman," for example. In one of the most famous *tanci*, *Zai sheng yuan* (begun by Chen Duansheng [1751–1796?] and completed by Liang Desheng [1771–1847]), the heroine dresses as a man, wins high honors in the examinations, and becomes a prime minister. Female dramatists – Wang Yun (late eighteenth–early nineteenth centuries) is one of the most famous – also used the theme of cross-dressing and disguise to imagine life as a man and simultaneously reflect on the frustrations of female roles. Here are the opening lines from Wang Yun's play titled *Fanhua meng* (Dreams of Glory), first published in 1778. The lines take the form of a song-lyric (*ci*) set to the tune *Zhegu tian*, translated by Kathryn Lowry as follows:

> Buried deep in the boudoir for more than a decade
> I can earn neither honor nor immortality.
> In my studies, I always envied Ban Chao's determination
>   [he cast aside his brush and became a military leader],
> And raised my glass, reciting the verses of Li Bo.
> I harbor a bold spirit
> Ready to soar the skies,
> But the achievements of Mulan and Chonggu
>   [both cross-dressed as men to achieve their goals] are not
>   in my lot.
> Nor am I destined for the Jade Hall and Golden Steed [halls
>   in the Hanlin Academy]
> I prefer to unfold my heart's desires in dreams.
>   (Chang and Saussy 1999:532)

Finally, as Louise Edwards has noted, women warriors served as "moral mirrors for society"; they shamed men into action with their deep loyalty and devotion to patriarchal authority, and they grew especially powerful in periods of social decline and disorder (1995:244–245). As Edwards puts it: "Women would not dress as men and perform manly deeds were it not for the fact that there was some major disharmony within the broad social fabric of China" (1995:247).

[3] Yu-ning Li, "Historical Roots of Changes in Women's Status in Modern Times," in Li 1992:108–110; Xiaozhen Hu (Hu Siao-chen) 2001:330n7. On the "heroic" style in plucking rhymes favored by female writers from Shen Shanbao to Qiu Jin, see Xiaorong Li 2005, especially her discussion of "resentment about gender restrictions" (pp. 26–35).

Judith Zeitlin, surveying images of cross-dressed women in literature, comments that what she calls "dislocations" in gender changed their meaning during the Ming and Qing periods. Whereas in earlier texts a cross-dressed woman might represent something evil or demonic, by the late seventeenth century a woman dressed as a man, for war or for school, was admirable, even "heroic," as long as she returned to her original female state in the end (Zeitlin 1993:118–119). More to the point, Zeitlin notes that "because [in cross-dressing] attention is shifted away from any innate biological sexual differences, altering one's sexual identity becomes as simple as changing one's hat and clothes" (1993:120). In any case, the true proof of feminine sexuality lay not in the genitalia but in the bound foot (1993:125). Sufen Sophia Lai (1999), in a similar vein, has argued that women in cross-dressed roles did not always act exactly like men. Narratives about women warriors, for example, rarely described battle scenes and bloodshed; poets liked to place these heroines in beautiful vistas or in vivid seasons. Their virtues were filial piety and loyalty, not martial heroism or courage. In the Ming plays by Xu Wei celebrating Mulan and also Huang Chonggu (who dressed up like a boy to sit for the exams and took first place), we see not rebels but female exemplars who always return to their proper place at the end of the story. The Qing novel *Tales of Boy and Girl Heroes* (*Ernü yingxiong zhuan*) featured a woman warrior who conformed to standards of virtue: she avenged her father's wrongful death, arranged a marriage for a man whose father was also wrongly accused, and eventually married the same man herself. Finally, as far back as the Tang dynasty, we find fictional images of female martial arts heroines who did not bother to cross-dress; who jumped, walked on walls, flew through the air, and fought better than men; and who, in the end, inevitably chose their own husbands.

By contrast with the history of women's gendered and transgendered performance, relatively little historical research has analyzed men's cultures and masculinities. Kam Louie, whose work has been most influential, has used the polarity of *wen* (literary) and *wu* (martial) to survey ideas of masculinity over time. He points out that *wen* and *wu* as distinctive qualities defining masculinity served also to draw boundaries between male and female, because although a woman could cross-dress and step outside her gender role to perform in either sphere, *wen* and *wu* were not accessible as female attributes, but only by impersonation of a man. Moreover, Louie argues, *wen* and *wu* were viewed as quintessentially Chinese attributes, characteristic only of those who had been acculturated by Chinese civilization. Foreigners and males in minority groups could not display these attributes. For *wen*, the inspiration was Confucius; for *wu*,

Guan Yu, the god of war in folk religion (Louie 2002:12–13). *Wu* males rejected women and contained their sexual desires; *wen* males more than fulfilled their sexual obligations to women (Louie 2002:19). In other words, martial heroes disdained the company of women, whereas refined men of letters consorted comfortably with them.

The confusions produced by cross-dressing, with a woman dressed as a man, or a man dressed as a woman, were elegantly captured in a play about impersonation and identity by Wu Zao (Volpp 2001b). In this early-nineteenth-century drama, one of the few surviving plays written by a woman, the heroine of the play addresses a portrait of herself garbed as a male scholar and elaborates her dilemma: she is a woman whose talent is not recognized in the world. The poems and images she invokes to express her anguish are all composed by men, and as a character she reads from a long poem by Qu Yuan (fl. 300 BCE), "Encountering Sorrow," in which the poet laments that his talent is not recognized in his time. This was the crux of the identity crisis of male and female writers in the nineteenth century: neither felt that society paid them their due, all felt marginalized and misrecognized in the cultural climate of the day. The posture in Wu Zao's work, however, was hardly a "feminine" or "masculine" posture. Instead, it was a transgendered sensibility for which sexed clothing (the "cap of manhood" instead of a "feminine coiffure," as Zeitlin puts it [1993:120]) supplied a kind of coding suited to the speaker. At the same time, the confusions in Wu Zao's work were not perfectly symmetrical. For one thing, the male actor dressed as a woman who played the part of the heroine did not participate in the ruse. He *was* a female, acting (in his perfect beauty) the ideal instead of performing the real (as a female would have to do). These ideas about the *hua dan* are part of the theory of what Tao-Ching Hsu calls "dramatic illusion" that informs all of classical Chinese opera. Movement, costume, masks, voice, and gesture perform the story and capture the audience (Hsu 1985:93–175). In this context, an actor trained to perform female roles to perfection captures female beauty in its ideal form, from delicate gestures to the gentle swaying of a body walking on bound feet. An actress playing a female part would have no advantage over the *hua dan* and indeed could perhaps be an inferior performer if her acting relied – even inadvertently – on her "real" gender identity. Artifice, in this theory, is more perfect than "reality."

Ideal notions of beauty could also turn this notion of artifice around to privilege the male body, because, as some writers pointed out, men did not adorn or reshape their bodies to conceal imperfection. Therefore a beautiful boy was exactly that: beautiful and untouched by rouge, powder, or bound feet, and free of menstrual blood and the debilitating after-effects of childbirth. A girl who appeared to be beautiful, in contrast, might simply be cleverly made up, and her beauty, such as it was, would be at best ephemeral (Volpp 1994:119–120).

Wu Zao's play helps us to see how the fascination with cross-dressing – with men donning women's clothes (in the theater, in fiction, and, sometimes, in the circles of male lovers where boys amused or accommodated their patrons by dressing and making up as women) and women donning men's (mainly as woman warriors but sometimes as students or even as officials) – permeated theories of dramatic illusion governing the theater. In their purest form, these theories suggested that all biological females were "cross-dressed," disguised with rouge and powder and transformed by footbinding and ear piercing (Volpp 1994:120). The eighteenth-century novel *Flowers in a Mirror* played with that idea by introducing its male hero into a "country of women" where he was transformed into a woman – and suffered excruciating pain – in the enthusiastic hands of a queen's female court. These fluid gender boundaries, displayed in notions of body and dress in creative writing, capture a sex-gender system that was erased by Western sexological discourse.

From concealment to exposure in the twentieth century

As we have seen, women's clothing and adornment conveyed powerful political and cultural meanings in the Qing period, if only because Chinese women bound their feet. Missionary criticism of footbinding in the final decades of the nineteenth century grew sharp but made little impact. Chinese criticism of footbinding as backward and crippling to the future of the country began only after 1895, when China's weakness became so glaringly apparent in the aftermath of the Sino-Japanese war. Almost at once, Shanghai's foreign fashions began to turn Qing trendsetters into embarrassments (Finnane 2008:52–67). Footbinding was impossible to tolerate once the new fashions required of a "modern girl" swept the marketplace. Courtesans were praised for their slender waists instead of their tiny feet (Hershatter 1997:84), while the more patriotic among them began wearing trousers in the five colors of the new national flag (Henriot 2001:50). During the 1920s shorter hemlines on skirts and trousers, hose, and leather shoes with heels all demanded a natural foot. In the interim, many women who decided to unbind their feet (or to rear daughters with natural feet) resorted to Manchu shoes that faked the look of bound feet when the occasion called for it (Finnane 1996:108).

Late Qing novels fixated on the chaotic renegotiation of dress and deportment that accompanied the transition to modern or "enlightened" (*wenming*) costume. As Paola Zamperini puts it:

Nineteenth- and early twentieth-century stories are full of details about clothes, accessories, and activities that . . . define the images of people. . . . One can get lost in trying to keep track of the making, buying, changing, tearing, sewing, and washing of clothes; the braiding, oiling, cutting, and attaching of queues; the putting up, letting down, pulling out, arranging and styling of hair and elaborate hairdos; and all the rings, earrings, head-ornaments, watches, shoes, hats, socks and stockings, purses, bags and satchels that are bought, sold, bartered, stolen, hidden, offered, coveted, in order to adorn, blemish, embellish, cover, disguise, or enhance the different body parts and extremities of characters. (Zamperini 2001a:196ff.)

By the mid-1920s, new fashion had conquered the cities, and after 1925, in the patriotic fervor of the May Thirtieth Movement, the *qipao* (or *cheongsam*) had become the dress of choice for the emerging female middle class in major cities (Shanghai, Tianjin, Canton, and Hankou). The *qipao*'s appeal to nationally conscious women lay in the fact that of all their fashion choices, the *qipao* most closely resembled the one-piece long gown favored by nationalistic young men at that time. As an androgynous (*not* sexy) garment, the *qipao* was an emblem of women's commitment to fight for the country alongside their brothers. Women who cut their hair short also spoke of their wish to fight and study alongside their male peers (Finnane 1996:111–115). In the 1930s, the *qipao* was feminized and sexualized as "the female dress of Guomindang China" (Finnane 1996:121) during the New Life Movement's emphasis on good wives and wise mothers, and urban women of all classes sported *qipao* to set themselves self-consciously apart from the backward women of the countryside who still wore loose pants and padded jackets.

Before the twentieth century, equivalence between the sexes was often imagined, performed, and celebrated in the guise of girls dressing up like boys, women disguised as men, and daughters treated like sons. As we have seen, this kind of slippage was grounded in notions of the body that, while gendered, were also malleable with the life cycle (prepubescent girls and postmenopausal women were very like their male counterparts). The slippage between boy and girl, male and female, was further eased by long-standing convictions about human nature elaborated in certain kinds of Neo-Confucian thought, such that all persons – regardless of sex and gender – were understood to share a common potential for moral development, including learning. Finally, the disinterest in bodily strength so evident in classical writing about the body, and the fascination with disciplined bodily and mental energies (accessible to all humans regardless of physical strength), meant that male bodies never managed to dominate the normative discourse as they did in eighteenth- and nineteenth-century Euro–North American medicine and natural science. What Western writers often decried as the "effeminate" appearance of elite Chinese men was also a leveling factor in the social and physical relation of the sexes in early twentieth-century China. At the same time, Western notions of masculinity stigmatized Chinese men as weak and inferior.

The emergence of martial heroism in the revolutionary struggles of the early Republic, and the eclipse of the intellectual as a paragon of political and moral leadership while warlords rose to power, shifted the ground for gendered bodies. The Republican government's new elite was a military elite. Even though some revolutionary women embraced military culture, the "new woman" and her fashion statements came to define gender difference in urban China during the 1920s and 1930s. The boyish look of early revolutionary women's clothing, which favored straight lines, flat breasts, slim-fitting high-collared jackets, and narrowly cut trousers, gave way by the 1930s to the long, body-hugging *qipao* adorned with flowers and cut to reveal at least some length of leg. These new fashions, featured in calendar art, advertisements, and pictorial magazines, meant new bobbed hairstyles and high-heeled shoes. In a sense, the social and cultural contradictions of the new Republic were played out in fashion. The need for strong athletic women to build the nation, the concern for sexual propriety in the New Life Movement, and the demands of "buying Chinese products" as war with Japan threatened, influenced what women wore and kept women's fashion in the arena of political performance (Finnane 2008, Gerth 2003). This long history of cross-dressing and transgressive gender performance in China puts the Communist Party's call for gender "equality" in a new light.

"Men and women are the same": gender sameness and difference in the Mao and post-Mao years

During the Maoist period (1949–1976), striking shifts underscore the importance of clothing to the national project. Whereas the early years following the 1949 Revolution promoted colorful clothing as a means of emphasizing the new government's ability to provide for its citizens, by the late 1950s colorful diversity was displaced by a citizen's uniform: the Mao suit. Modeled after military uniforms, the Mao suit at first permitted individual variation in color, style, and accessory that signaled difference. Like the red scarves adorning the necks of schoolchildren who had been inducted as "Young Pioneers," the Mao suit stigmatized those who could not or chose not to wear it. During the 1960s, especially during the Cultural Revolution, the Mao suit became obligatory for both men and women, feeding the global media's representations of the Chinese as a "sea of blue ants." The gendered implications of same-sex clothing carried particular significance for women. Colorful tops and fashionable accessories were increasingly tagged "bourgeois," effeminate emblems of consumerism and flirtation with capitalist desires. The drab conformity of the Mao suit, by contrast, became the emblem of female emancipation (Tina Mai Chen 2001). The Communist leaders of the Maoist era used costume to position their subjects as submissive and loyal. Instead of stressing difference to highlight gender roles, same-sex clothing dramatized the party's commitment to gender equality.

The post-Mao reform era flooded Chinese markets with foreign imports and fashions appealing to both men and women. In addition, new trends in female fashion were celebrated for revealing more of the feminine body, in swimsuits, low-cut garments, and frilly blouses and dresses suited to the new model of the wife and mother who makes home pleasant and appealing for her working husband. New wave women's writings at the turn of the twenty-first century went further, introducing a genre called *shenti xiezuo*, or "body writing," described this way by Sheldon Lu:

Writing with one's body, or writing about one's body, is the self-styled, self-advertised strategy among these women writers. Exposing the body, its private parts, private sensations, and private thoughts, constitutes the substance of such novels. Writing about female sexuality by "beautiful women writers" is the vogue today. What is showcased here is the politics of the body – namely, biopolitics, to use Michel Foucault's term. On the one hand, this is the politics of liberation and excess in the Chinese experience of modernity, an existential condition that has rarely existed, especially for women and women writers. On the other hand, the phenomenon also bespeaks the logic of cultural commercialization, in other words, the self-packaging of the body for media effects. By posing as sexual, young, beautiful, amoral, rebellious, and anti-intellectual, the female writer dreams of creating a media reaction and becoming a celebrity. (Lu 2007:54)

In the world of global consumer culture, young people in China's cities looked very much like young urbanites anywhere in the world, in tune with the fashion statements of their peers in Tokyo's Shibuya and Harajuku. At the same time, many urban women responded to revivalist trends, such as the Korean move to bring back historical costumes, as a statement of "long lost pride" in Chinese civilization (Finnane 2008:289). Bodily adornment, in sum, has remained a key arena for fashioning the national and global citizen.

6 Abandoning the body: female suicide and female infanticide

Her body is pure, her heart is settled, and moral principles are upheld.
Growing up, she obeyed her parents' original instruction.
Following their original instructions, she guarded against her own feelings.
"Not violating [parents' wishes]" means not breaching moral principles.
The words of her betrothal came from her parents.
Bringing no blemish to her body and no disgrace to her parents,
The key to upholding her will is determination.
She would die if her will was taken away; if it prevailed, she would live.
Because her will could not be taken away, she took her life.

Poem by a faithful maiden in praise of a faithful
maiden's suicide, Qing dynasty, eighteenth century
(Weijing Lu 2008:148)

One day I was called in to show my goods to a family where the daughter was to be married. I saw her. She was not beautiful, but was well grown and pleasant to look upon. A month later I heard that she was dead. She had taken opium. Her family had sold her to a wealthy man of the town for a concubine.

Ning Lao T'ai-t'ai (Pruitt 1945:182)

Miss Zhao Wujie, of Nanyang Street, Changsha, was engaged to marry Wu Fenglin, of Ganziyuan, on November 14, 1919. As a matter of course the match had been arranged by her parents and the matchmaker. Although Miss Zhao had had only the brief ritual encounters with the fiancé, she disliked him intensely and was unwilling to marry him. Her parents refused to undo the match and to postpone the wedding date. On the day of the wedding as Miss Zhao was being raised aloft in the bridal chair to be delivered to the home of the groom, she drew out a dagger which she had previously concealed in the chair and slit her throat.

Zhou Shizhao, "My Recollections of Chairman Mao in Changsha before and after the May Fourth Movement" (Witke 1967:128; Romanization modified)

Death is a powerful theme in late imperial stories of Chinese women, especially young women on the cusp of marriage. The famous seventeenth-century opera *The Peony Pavilion* celebrates the triumph of love over death, as the beautiful young maiden Du Liniang dies of passion denied but returns to life, restored by her lover's devotion. *The Peony Pavilion* dwells on the relationship between passion and death by playing directly to the audience's fascination with the "purity of young girls" and its complications. Liniang's distraught mother and father argue about what caused her death: her mother believes (correctly) that Liniang died from suppressed passion; the father cannot imagine his daughter feeling physical desire for a man and is shocked by his wife's convictions (Idema 2003). Liniang's parents remind us that stories about the death of young women were always laced with beliefs about sexuality: especially repressed sexual desire and its lethal consequences. In the play *The Western Wing*, a dramatization of the old tale of Yingying, West and Idema make the following observation about the heroine, whom they call Oriole (translating her Chinese name into English):

Oriole's duty to her mother operates not in the realm of love and compassion but within the abused relationship of authority and filial response. The tension that develops between the filial devotion of the proper child and the demands and needs of sexual and emotional fulfillment exploits this boundary between feeling and duty to the fullest.... It is most effective because the allure and sexuality normally presented in characters of romantic abandonment are displayed instead in the true and innocent longing of a young girl of good family. Except for those moments when she realizes the effect of her beauty, Oriole's sexuality seems to be a mystery to her, something almost unconscious. Its charms are apparent to everyone else. (1991:106)

Plots in late imperial fiction embroider these themes of young women caught between the demands of sexual purity, the longings of sexual desire, and the realities of sexual abuse. Suicide is often the result. One of the most poignant examples is the phenomenon of the "faithful maiden," which became widely known in the eighteenth century. A faithful maiden, as we have seen, was a young woman who pledged eternal fidelity to her betrothed and maintained that fidelity even if he died before the wedding. For such a young woman, there were options other than death, but none were happy ones: she might be betrothed to another, or she might pledge lifelong celibacy. In the latter case, the most common solution was to move in with the family of her deceased fiancé, where she would live a life of isolation and marginalization. For many young women, it seems, a second betrothal was morally reprehensible, and a lifetime of celibacy unbearable – hence the decision to commit suicide.

The faithful maiden's anguish caused heart-wrenching arguments among parents who wanted their daughters to be happy, and it aroused heated debates among scholars who could not determine whether such young women were morally correct or pathologically misled by their moral instruction (Weijing Lu 2008). In both cases, arranged marriage was a target of criticism and concern. For the faithful maiden, commitment to arranged marriage was the driving force in moral decisions about life and death. For parents, arranged marriage became a burden and a risk that they had to assume on their daughters' behalf. For scholars, the questions were: When is a couple actually married in a ritual sense? How far must we expect a woman to go in affirming her fidelity to one husband? And what of the daughter whose arranged marriage proved so unhappy that she died? (Such cases were also widely known.) What of the young woman whose parents decided not to arrange a marriage for her and instead sold her as a concubine or worse? She might kill herself to express her *wish* for a proper arranged marriage. In other words, contradictory patterns of suicide show that in late imperial times arranged marriage was not necessarily viewed as a threat to a young woman's future happiness or security. Later, in the aftermath of the New Culture Movement and the violent critique of arranged marriage by young people seeking freedom to choose their own mates, young girls would kill themselves to *resist* arranged marriage. But that was a twentieth-century shift (see the following discussion). Whatever its cause, in late imperial times a woman's suicide was generally understood to be a deliberate display of protest, even a moral decision, carried out in the most dramatic way possible. High rates of female suicide remain characteristic of Chinese culture. At the same time, the reasons why women killed themselves have changed over time.

How are these persistent patterns of female suicide to be explained? Scholars point first to the male-centered family system, especially patrilocal marriage (the removal of young women from the supporting structures of the natal home at marriage) and son preference (the devaluing of female children) (Wolf 1975). Certain Buddhist beliefs bolstered misogynistic views of women and their worth, especially the Buddhist rituals dramatizing the "blood bowl" that pollutes all women because of menstruation and prevents them from escaping the endless round of birth and death unless they are rescued by a son who "breaks the blood bowl" for them (Seaman 1981). Buddhist devotions of self-mutilation (dipping the fingers in wax and lighting them afire, for example) display the conviction that bodies are part of the material physical world that stands in the way of enlightenment (Mann 1997:195–197). Biographies of Buddhist masters testify to the power of auto-cremation (burning the body) to move the heavens; devout rulers, inspired by their example, set themselves afire to bring rain, or to end a famine. Beyond these efficacious acts of self-destruction, self-immolation in some schools of Buddhism was seen as a path to becoming a Buddha – a way of "abandoning the body" (*she shen*) in preparation for receiving a new form (*shou shen*) in the next life (Benn 2007). Buddhist beliefs that scorned or trivialized the body talked back to Confucian convictions that the body is a gift from one's parents and should remain inviolate. Moreover, beliefs in reincarnation and in karmic retribution from Buddhism syncretized with other popular religious beliefs in ghosts and spirits, especially fears of hungry ghosts: a person who died in anger, isolation, or despair would return to take ghostly revenge on those who made her suffer. Anthropologists think these beliefs figured in many female suicides declaring innocence or protesting injustice (Wolf 1975).

The melodramas surrounding female suicide, and the stories that circulated to describe and explain it, were continually replayed in opera and fiction, and in biographies of exemplary women found in the standard histories. County histories devoted whole chapters to lists of women who had martyred themselves by committing suicide to preserve their "fidelity" or "purity." Some of these martyrs were widows protesting pressure to remarry; others were wives or daughters resisting rape. Some suicides were by women who believed, correctly or not, that their reputation for sexual purity had been compromised, even by circumstances beyond their control, as we saw in Chapter 3. During the Manchu conquest, entire households of women whose menfolk served the Ming hung themselves or threw themselves into wells to profess their own loyalty and escape sexual assault, and their stories continued to circulate long after Ming loyalism had faded. For victims of rape or attempted assault, shame and disgrace for the woman and her family combined with the law's strict standards to make suicide the only way to redeem a woman's honor. Anything less suggested consent to the sexual encounter.

Tales of suicidal women, written with a Confucian moral message, carried powerful sexual overtones and invited voyeuristic curiosity. In southeast coastal Fujian, to cite an extreme example, "platform suicides" drew crowds of spectators during the Qing period (T'ien 1988) (see Figure 26).

Young faithful maidens were particular targets of incessant gossip and speculation: How did they cope with sexual frustration? Would a lack of healthy sexual intercourse and childbearing make them ill? And, above all, were they actually virgins? Weijing Lu (2008) discovered that following the suicide of one such maiden, prurient investigators insisted on a forensic examination to confirm her virginity.

How did a young woman internalize the conviction that she must kill herself? Reports of collective suicide by young women who had pledged sisterhood suggest that suicide might have become part of girls' youth culture in certain localities. Collective suicide pacts were known in the Canton delta during the nineteenth century, for example (Stockard 1989:118–121), and collective suicide by young women defending their chastity was a theme in classical biographies of exemplary women, such as this "Story of the Three Wang Girls," recorded by the early-nineteenth-century female anthologist Wanyan Yun Zhu:

The three Wang girls were from Jintan [Jiangsu province]. Two were the daughters of Wang Chanjin. One was the daughter of Wang Yi. They lived by the shores of Changtang Lake. At the end of the Ming during an army mutiny they fled into the marshes near the lake to hide. When the rebels found out where the girls were hiding, they made a raft and poled out, pulling the three up onto the raft. The three girls joined hands back-to-back, with their arms tightly intertwined. When the raft reached a place where the current was running swiftly, they suddenly began rocking their bodies and pounding their feet, and the raft capsized, throwing everyone into the water. All drowned. The next day the rebel corpses floated to the surface, but there was no sign of the three girls' bodies. Over a month later, when the rebels had dispersed, the two families came to the spot looking for the girls' corpses. Only then did the bodies appear, with the hands and arms still linked as they had been in life. Fathers and mothers wept, and grasping the girls' hands, freed them at last. They were buried in a gravemound by the lake. The tree that grew there later had three branches, all intertwined. (Mann 2005:609)

Most acts of female suicide, however, were individual and isolated. Weijing Lu has argued that young women in respectable families were reared with a powerful sense of what she calls "honor-bound duty" (yi), which impelled them to hold themselves to standards of propriety that made living unbearable in the face of a lapse or failure.[1] Young girls who killed themselves when a fiancé died before the wedding often did so

[1] Lu 2008; yi is also translated as "self-respect" – see Riegel 1997:154.

4. Betrothed maiden hanging herself.

26. A faithful maiden's platform suicide. *Source:* Tian Rukang [T'ien Ju-k'ang], *Male Anxiety and Female Chastity: A Comparative Study of Chinese Ethical Values in Ming-Ch'ing Times. Toung Pao* Monograph Number XIV. Leiden: E. J. Brill, 1988, illustration 4.

despite the anguished opposition of loving parents, not to mention the condemnation of prominent leaders, to fulfill the lifetime singular commitment to one husband that was their honor-bound duty. These suicides, like those described by Janet Theiss in cases involving rape, appear to represent a kind of moral will that, whatever its gendered psychological complexities, was recognized as legitimate for both men and women in Chinese moral philosophy. Mencius articulated its principles when he observed that an individual may choose death to preserve his or her self-respect, simply because self-respect is more important than survival (see Mencius 6A.10 on self-control; also Riegel [1997:154], discussing early views of human nature). Female martyrs who displayed this moral will won imperial honors and local accolades. Similarly, suicidal heroines in literature were portrayed as "passionate agents of free will" determined to stamp their love or vengeful hatred in historical memory (Zamperini 2001b:78).

Women who died violently by their own hand were nevertheless controversial. Qing statecraft officials had their hands full trying to manage the passion for suicide and sought to curb it and even stigmatize it to decouple notions of virtue and violent death. The Yongzheng Emperor was one of the most vocal on the subject, accusing widows who killed themselves of taking the easy way out of a difficult life, and abandoning their responsibilities to care for in-laws and heirs (Theiss 2001:55–56). Although shrines and arches celebrated the martyrdom of women who died to keep their names pure, the ghosts of such women were known to be dangerous, capable of taking revenge on any person who drove a woman to suicide. Wolfram Eberhard's survey of 1,600 traditional short stories showed that the majority of female suicides in those stories were judged honorable because they were performed as an expression of loyalty to the dynasty or to a husband. But he also found a large number of cases in which the woman who killed herself did so out of shame for unknowingly or unintentionally violating a moral precept, or because she found herself caught in an irresolvable moral dilemma (Eberhard 1967:95–105). He concluded that sinful or immoral acts were "punishable" even if they were "not done on purpose or knowingly," because a woman who realized she had done something immoral unintentionally would kill herself in anticipation of the shame she might suffer in the eyes of others (1967:89).

High rates of suicide among Chinese women in the nineteenth century have obviously been scrutinized and explained from many perspectives. But why did those rates remain high in the twentieth century, under very different conditions?

Twentieth-century shifts

Female suicide

No longer celebrated or romanticized as an expression of loyalty, fidelity, or honor, suicide in the twentieth century was seen as an act of despair, just the way Ning Lao T'ai-t'ai saw the suicide of the daughter sold as a concubine. In the Republic of China before 1949, women's suicide was recast as part of the larger critique of the old family system and of arranged marriage. For many women in the early twentieth century, suicide protested the very conditions of marriage that late imperial womanly virtue celebrated. As Weijing Lu put it,

In the May Fourth discourse, the misery of arranged marriage was the focal point of the denunciation of the Confucian family system, and the image of a young woman killing herself to escape such a marriage became a heroic sacrifice in the face of women's victimization.... [By contrast in Qing times] faithful maidens desperately fought their parents to *defend* [italics mine] arrangements that the parents made in the first place. (Lu 2008:10)

Whereas suicide protesting arranged marriage was virtually unknown during the nineteenth century, in the twentieth century the very fact of arranged marriage became a condition that for many young women was too hopeless to contemplate.[2]

Radical young people in the 1920s – the May Fourth generation obsessed with "the woman question" – viewed female suicide as one of the most odious signs of their society's backwardness. Years before he became a leader of the Communist revolution, Mao Zedong wrote nine articles decrying the suicide of "Miss Zhao," who killed herself en route to an arranged marriage. These articles, written for a male audience and pitched as a "case study" illustrating larger principles and problems, may have been inspired by Mao's own experience. As a young man he rejected the marriage his parents planned for him and ran away from home. He later married for love a woman whose own father was a progressive critic of the traditional family system (Witke 1967). Mao's friends in his school years, moreover, included women who attended the newly created girls' schools, and women participated in the first political organizations he joined, because the area around Changsha, Hunan – Mao's home, and the site of Miss Zhao's suicide – was also ahead of most of the rest of the country in promoting women's education and advancement. In a diatribe

[2] See Lu 2008 for examples of young women's extreme passionate commitment to arranged marriage in the eighteenth century. Lu argues that even the preparation of a young girl's dowry could inspire her to imagine an ideal match.

published in a Hunan newspaper in November 1919, Mao attributed Miss Zhao's suicide to "the rotten marriage system, the benighted social system, thought which could not be independent and love which could not be free" (Witke 1967:137–138). In other words, the whole society (or, in Mao's words), the environment, caused Miss Zhao's suicide.

A different, widely publicized suicide in Shanghai in 1922 shows the rapidly shifting context in which women took their lives. The suicide of Xi Shangzhen, a "new woman" employed as a secretary in the editorial office of a professional journal, sparked a media controversy that touched off a wide-ranging debate on the social problems caused by modernization. Xi was viewed as the epitome of success in the new era: an educated professional with a promising career, safely removed from the pressures of the old family system that had produced suicide at such high rates in the old society. People blamed Xi's suicide on the stock market (she lost a lot of money) and on her employer, who was charged with mismanaging her investments. Xi was also cast, however, as the victim of lecherous attacks by her exploitative boss. Elegies mourning her death resembled the elegies for chaste women martyrs of the past. Writers asked, Who drove her to this? The answer was her employer, but not simply her employer as an individual. Public opinion in the press condemned her employer's perfidious character *and* linked it to the capitalist system that rewarded his greed (Goodman 2005). Xi's case shows how women's suicide was continually reinterpreted as a response to changing social, economic, and political pressures during the twentieth century.

Evidence from colonial Taiwan during the first half of the twentieth century revealed suicide rates among Chinese women that were the highest in the world at the time. Analyzing data collected from 1905–1940, Margery Wolf (1975) showed that Chinese female suicide rates were exceptionally high by comparison with rates in other countries. Wolf also noticed that female suicides in Taiwan tended to cluster at certain vulnerable points in the female life cycle. The first big cluster was suicide by young newly married women, who killed themselves in the years immediately after marriage and before childbirth. A second cluster of high rates of female suicide appeared among middle-aged mothers-in-law. The latter group, Wolf proposed, were middle-aged women who found themselves bereft of comforts they had been reared to expect from their married sons. Wolf concluded that whereas isolation and even abuse caused young brides to commit suicide, for middle-aged women the causes of suicide arose from the changing conditions of family life. Shifting authority in the family had begun to disempower middle-aged women as mothers-in-law, as sons and daughters-in-law developed new independence from family obligations. The rewards of advancing age were replaced by neglect or even increased responsibility for household chores or child care (Wolf 1975).

As the leader of the People's Republic founded in 1949, Mao Zedong was confident that the new society would eliminate the tensions and erase the despair that drove women to suicide. But contrary to expectation, improved conditions in Chinese women's lives since the Communist revolution in 1949 did not prevent high rates of female suicide. Newspapers carried regular reports of female suicide in the countryside, where pesticides were preferred to hanging or drowning as the expedient way to end an unhappy life. A recent study showed China accounting for 56 percent of all female suicides worldwide, with only 21 percent of the world's population (Lee and Kleinman 2003:292). More than 20 percent of all female suicides were by women from fifteen to thirty-five years of age, and rural suicide rates were three times those of rates in cities (Phillips et al. 2002, cited in Lee and Kleinman 2003:292–293).

New conditions in the post-Mao reform era have now complicated the circumstances that made women hopeless in earlier times. One is rural-urban migration, which is pulling youthful talent out of the countryside into cities. Most migrant labor is male, resulting in what some economists have called the "feminization" of rural agriculture. A woman left behind to care for children and the elderly, without access to help from an emigrant spouse or son, and lacking the means to support herself and her dependent family members on the land, may view suicide as a way to protest and also to escape her harsh fate. Women also use the threat of suicide to pursue alternatives and empower themselves, seeking control over the choice of a husband, pursuing the option of divorce, rejecting the unreasonable demands of in-laws, or criticizing the negligence of their own children (Lee and Kleinman 2003). In a modern short story, writer Ye Weilin described a different scenario: a contemporary suicide pact among five young women determined never to marry, with a plot reminiscent of the suicide pacts in the nineteenth-century Canton delta ("Five Girls and One Rope"; Louie 1991:176).

Accounts of women's suicide by writers past and present raise questions, as Katherine Carlitz puts it, about "power, gender, and the appropriation of women's voices" (Carlitz 2005:461). What is the interest of male writers in decrying or celebrating female suicide? What determines whether a female martyr has been cast as a paragon of virtue or as a victim of oppression? Scholars continue to debate the motivation of suicidal women in China, which encompasses possibilities of individual agency, moral autonomy, false consciousness, and revenge.

Female infanticide

In late imperial times, couples making decisions about their offspring were likely to aim for at least two sons. The reason for this was simple: the top priority of every married couple was continuing the patriline, and only a son could carry on the family's ancestral descent line. Sex ratios at birth, then – despite the constant demand for women in the marriage market – were skewed in favor of males. Skewed sex ratios were not necessarily the result of female infanticide; neglect of baby girls was common in families in which medical care, food, and other nurturing focused on sons first if the family had limited means (Croll 2000). Concerns about female infanticide surfaced periodically in late imperial edicts, which forbade it. Female infanticide was also condemned from time to time by local officials, and criticism of infanticide filled the writings of missionaries and reformers in the late nineteenth century. Most of these condemnatory documents attributed female infanticide to economic hardship and, to a lesser degree, local custom.

Improved health care and expanding economic opportunities for women changed demographic behavior among Chinese families through-out most of the twentieth century. The 1950 Marriage Law explicitly banned female infanticide, while fertility rose and mortality fell (Bernice Lee 1981). Then the one-child family policy (begun in 1979) and the subsequent campaigns to enforce the one-child limit provoked a resurgence of female infanticide. The causes were immediately apparent, and they appeared almost exclusively in rural areas. In cities where married women lived in public housing apart from their mothers-in-law, reproductive decisions strongly favored fewer children, especially because shopping, cooking, washing, and child care arrangements fell to already hard-pressed working mothers who were employed outside the home. Meanwhile, pension plans available to urban workers made it unnecessary for many couples to rear sons for support in old age. Daughter-only families in cities were therefore quite acceptable, and even preferred by some couples, who were quick to note that daughters often supplied more emotional satisfaction and companionship than sons. In the countryside, by contrast, reproductive decision making took place in an entirely different context. First of all, the new economic policies after 1980, which permitted households to contract for land and farm it themselves, placed a sudden new premium on family farm labor, that is, male labor (because females married out of the natal family). Second, housing in rural China was not public, but rather arranged by each family, so that married couples continued to share a residence with his parents, increasing the pressure for sons. Finally, lacking pensions, elderly people in rural areas continued to rely on sons for support in their old age. As a result, the one-child policy was put on a collision course with the reform-era measures in the countryside, catching women in their reproductive years squarely at the center of the crash.

The government immediately confronted conflicts that erupted when rural officials enforced the one-child policy, and in rural areas the birth quota was raised to allow two children for couples whose first child was a girl. Still, resistance to the one-child family policy persisted, as evidenced by highly skewed sex ratios in rural areas. The phenomenon of "missing" girls became still more alarming in the 1990s, as access to ultrasound technologies made sex-selective abortion an option for families strategizing for at least one son (Junhong Chu 2001). These technologies were roundly criticized by the government, although its insistence that every child should be a wanted child (a foundation of the one-child policy) made its opposition to parental decision making and gender preference problematic (Junhong Chu 2001). The central government overall has generally ignored or paid little attention to the gendered consequences of the one-child policy, except to express concern about certain fallout from skewed sex ratios, particularly the problem of young men unable to find brides and the need to support an aging population (Greenhalgh 2008:264–268). In interviews with Chinese officials, anthropologist Susan Greenhalgh was astonished to find none who anticipated the consequences of the one-child policy for rural women. On the contrary, she found, government officials expected only positive results, mainly because the party's key concerns were macrodemographic: to reduce population growth. The party assumed that the new policies would liberate women from feudal bonds of the "traditional patriarchal family" and improve their health by delaying marriage and limiting births. Here, as Greenhalgh points out, the unconscious urban and class biases of Chinese Communist Party (CCP) policy planners and even members of the Women's Federation came into play and went unchallenged, not to mention "assumptions of male superiority" that were "commonsense notions" in the larger culture (2008:268). Only one population specialist interviewed by Greenhalgh in late 1999, when she was surveying feminists and Women's Federation leaders, alluded to problems that the skewed sex ratio and "excess female mortality" posed for the future. Pointing out that the "real victims of the restrictive policy are women," this specialist named kidnapping and sale of marriageable women alongside abandonment and death of infant girls as the most negative consequences of the one-child policy (Greenhalgh 2001:872). Concern about rootless single males and their unruly behavior has also surfaced in the Chinese press and sociological literature in recent years, echoing age-old concerns about the importance of marriage to social order in the discourses of the imperial government.

The early effects of the one-child family policy were drastic for girls and women, especially in areas where impoverished or hard-pressed couples were most desperate for a male heir and male labor. After the dramatic gains of the Maoist era, education for girls, especially in rural areas, suffered a serious setback in the early 1980s. But research shows that Chinese women and girls still want to do what men do and can often do it better. A study of girls' education in the city of Wuhan in the 1990s found "no gender differences" in the education of girls and boys. In fact, according to the researchers, "the high parental expectations and high family spending on girls' education may have increased girl-only children's sense of their right to a good education" (Tsui and Rich 2002:90). Data from the same surveys showed that parents of only daughters put more pressure on them to succeed than parents of only sons (termed "naughty" slackers by some parents), praised their daughters less often (their expectations were higher), and even spent more money on their daughters. As the study's authors remarked (2002:89): "While our survey does not reveal how typical this [naughty, lazy] behavior pattern is for boys, some of our findings suggest that boys are more likely than girls to waste the money their families spend on their education." Even in the countryside, research on education for girls has revealed a surprising reversal of the downward trends of the early years of the reform era. Emily Hannum's data on rural education from 1971 to 1997, for instance, revealed "steep increases [in enrollments at both primary and secondary levels] from the mid-1970s . . . , with a downturn at the time of market reforms and a subsequent resumption of the increasing trend by the mid-1980s" (Hannum 2005:288). She found that girls remained more vulnerable than boys to opportunity costs and family financial difficulty. But she also showed that, to the extent that reform programs raised family income and promoted non-farm occupations that rewarded more education for girls, the prospects for expanding girls' education were improving.

During the late 1980s, in other words, the economic and social concerns prompting female infanticide began to abate. Schools for girls rebounded and investment in female education increased (Lavely et al. 1990). A decline in village exogamy (the requirement that a daughter marry outside her home village) and growing evidence that daughters provide for their parents in old age when sons are distant or absent (Parish et al. 1996) also signaled a shift in reproductive decision making, tilting more in favor of daughters. As a new generation of couples confronts the policy, in other words, there are signs that pragmatism in rural areas has reduced pressures to have a son and has even encouraged adaptations to an only daughter. In addition to the rise in village endogamy, new research has also found increasing acceptance of uxorilocal marriage (Hong Zhang 2007). Parents everywhere, facing a future in which one child is their "only hope," are investing as never before in education and opportunities for "singletons" of either sex (Vanessa Fong 2004). Evidence is mounting that parents of only daughters are welcoming the emotional support of daughters and their apparent willingness to work harder than sons to repay parental investment in their education and training. As Hong Zhang (2007) pointed out, all of this evidence of new reproductive norms sounds good, especially in terms of its implications for gender equality. But it is accompanied by a harsh new market-generated pressure to produce "high-quality" children who can thrive in a competitive modern world. These kinds of pressures on parents and children are replacing some of the old pressures that drove up rates of infanticide. Their long-term effect has yet to be measured.

PART III

GENDER, SEXUALITY, AND THE OTHER

7   Same-sex relationships and transgendered performance

For true sensuality in the mortal world, one ought not search among womankind. Why pass through each and every brothel. . . . In selecting smiles and summoning music [seeking sensual pleasure], one must seek out the Chrysanthemum Registry [the world of actors].
Record of the Flowers of Beijing's Stage, nineteenth century
(Joshua Goldstein 2007:39)

The operas began in the afternoon of the first day. . . . Whenever a portion was performed that brought blushes to the women and the young folks in the audience and smirks to the grown men, a servant with a stentorian voice would come out on the stage and read from a festively red slip of paper: "The Honourable Mr. So-and-so presents to such-and-such an actor the sum of so-much!" And the lucky actor (invariably a female impersonator) would at once profusely thank his donor, while the beneficent gentleman beamed with pompous satisfaction. But even this did not satisfy the honourable guests. When an opera was over, the actors who had been rewarded had to drink with them at their tables, still wearing their make-up and costumes. The honourable gentlemen fondled the performers and filled them with wine; they behaved with such crass vulgarity that the younger guests were shocked and the servants whispered among themselves.
Ba Jin, *Family* (1972 [1931]:245–246)

It is only since the Republican period that China's long history of cultural tolerance of same-sex eroticism began to fade. In the process of Westernization, what Chinese intellectuals have accepted is not homophobia per se but a scientific discourse of biological determinism that marginalizes and pathologizes all nonreproductive sexuality.
Wah-shan Chou (2000:54)

137

"Global gayness," with its assumptions about the similitude of
identity, the homogeneity of values, and a sliding scale of identity
development, fails to capture the intricate complexity... of gay
life in Beijing.... While the visions of many Chinese gay men
in China about what it means to be gay are certainly connected
to the knowledge that gay people exist all over the world, these
men do not simply imagine a global community of horizontal
comradeship.

Lisa Rofel (2007:109–110)

In Chinese natural philosophy, a healthy body displayed the right balance
between *yin* and *yang*, and that balance shifted throughout the life cycle
of females and males (Furth 1999). In Qing times, as Yi-Li Wu has
shown, the human body was "infinitive" – that is, a physical body could
"conjugate" many forms: male or female, young or old, robust or delicate
(Wu 2010:232–233). Before the twentieth century, therefore, Chinese
medical specialists and intellectuals were not invited to view the human
body in binary terms as *either* male *or* female (Barlow 1994). Instead
classical Chinese medicine represented sex and gender as indeterminate
and fluid. Benign tropes pointing to ancient tales of romance or love
between, say, an emperor and a courtier ("cut sleeve," "shared peach")
were widely used as euphemisms for sexual relations between men. With
transgendered performance and opposite-gender role-playing widely in
evidence in late imperial times and right through the first half of the
twentieth century, the notion of "same-sex" relationships had limited
social or cultural meaning (Sang 2003:30–34). At the same time, as this
chapter shows, people clearly recognized the difference between male-
male sex and heterosexual sex. Why did sex between men receive so
much attention in late imperial times? What kind of attention was it?
And how have homosexual identities (gay and lesbian) developed in the
twentieth-century global context? These questions frame this chapter.

In Chinese culture as elsewhere, we know much more about men than
we do about women in same-sex relationships. Classical language and folk
sayings gave names to sexual relationships and feelings between men. In
late imperial China, sex between men was referred to in literary sources as
nan feng or *nan se* ("southern custom" or "southern lust"), punning on the
characters for "south" (南) and "male" (男), which are both pronounced
nan. By calling male homosexuality a southern custom, writers from
the northern and central parts of China distanced themselves from it and
exoticized it (Volpp 2001a). Their focus on the south was partly the result
of political gossip: the far southeastern province of Fujian was home to

a religious cult that government officials had been ordered to suppress. The cult's followers worshipped Hu Tianbao, a deity enshrined in the coastal port city of Fuzhou who granted the wishes of older men seeking sex with young boys (Szonyi 1998). The zealous northern bureaucrat Zhu Gui (1731–1807), who held office in Fujian for a time, became so incensed by the "licentious cult," as he called it, that he chopped up the plaster image of the god along with the god's wooden tablet and flung them into a river.

Arguments about the Hu Tianbao case filled many pages in the days and years following Zhu Gui's campaign, helping us to see that Zhu's opinion of the cult was by no means universal. In fact, opinions about sex between men ranged widely in the late eighteenth century. For most people, it appears, the worrisome thing about homosexual relations was the stigma attached to men or boys who were penetrated during sexual intercourse. Many wondered if a man's willingness or wish to be penetrated signaled a problem. Perhaps he was tricked, deceived, or brainwashed. Bad karma from a previous life might ruin the present one, people thought, or some young men simply had allowed their desires to get out of control. These were the kinds of explanations people produced when they encountered same-sex relations between men. They reserved speculation and gossip for the boys and youthful men who allowed themselves to be penetrated, especially actors who impersonated females on stage. Elite men who patronized boy actors, including influential literati like the poet Yuan Mei (1716–1798), also became occasional targets of gossip (Waley 1956:98–100). But an elite man was always presumed to be the superior partner (i.e., penetrator) in any homosexual relationship, and keeping company with boy actors was no more noteworthy than keeping company with singing girls. In other words, sexual relations between men were understood in terms of status differences rather than as expressions of mutual love, or, as Bret Hinsch puts it, people perceived homosexual acts "in terms of social relationships rather than erotic essence" (Hinsch 1990:21).

On the other hand, tales of powerful men who became infatuated with a young male lover show that emotional bonds surely played a role in at least some of these relationships. The trope of the cut sleeve, a euphemism for male-male sex, comes from the story of Emperor Ai of the Han dynasty (r. 6 BCE–1 CE), who cut off the sleeve of his robe rather than awaken his lover Dong Xian while Dong slept with his head on the emperor's arm. The tale of the shared peach, found in a text from the third century BCE, shows a boy favorite of the ruler of the state of Wei giving half of a delicious peach to his lord. The glimpses of tenderness in these stories of same-sex relationships are unmistakable, and the sexual preferences of certain rulers drew attention. Of Emperor Ai, the historian Ban Gu observed that "by nature [he] did not care for women" (Hinsch 1990:52–53). Bisexuality and homosexuality, as "identities" we now name, were unknown to Ban Gu and his successor historians, but their observations give us insight into sexual behavior and practice that is vital to any history of sexuality.

Because phallic penetration was such a powerful status symbol in same-sex relationships, assumptions about hierarchy and power were implicit in most historical accounts of male-male sex. Fictional references to young male lovers were often patronizing or dismissive, sometimes noting that a young man who took a passive (inferior) role in male-male sex would eventually move on to heterosexual relationships in which he would be the penetrator, sometimes treating male lovers as a convenient substitute for inaccessible cloistered females. Often the assumption was that in all-male company, whether a secret society, a schoolroom, a ship's crew, or a labor gang, same-sex relationships were to be expected – because there were no women available. We also have hints of nonconsensual sex: for example, references to abuse of male students by their teachers.

Same-sex relationships between women, by contrast, received little attention in late imperial writings, perhaps because they had so little social significance. Sex between women, after all, did not involve phallic penetration and did not threaten the purity of lineage blood lines. Female same-sex ties came under scrutiny mainly in certain localities where "local customs" marked a departure from normative family practice (Hinsch 1990:173–178, has a brief overview; see also McGough 1985:185–186). During the nineteenth century, in Shunde and Panyu counties in the Canton delta, the custom we have encountered called "delayed transfer marriage" allowed women to live in girls' houses rather than moving into the home of a husband following betrothal, sometimes postponing the move for long periods of time or at least until the birth of a child conceived during a conjugal visit. Women living together spoke of sex between women ("grinding bean curd" [*mo doufu*]), and one anthropologist studying the area in the mid-twentieth century reported the use of silk dildos filled with bean curd (Topley 1975:76–77). In the case of these Canton Delta women, same-sex relationships were seen as an alternative to, and sometimes as resistance to, arranged marriage, and they were obviously encouraged by local custom (Stockard 1989). Moreover, women from this area who did not marry could, under certain circumstances, arrange a marriage ceremony with another woman: the female partners to these rituals were called *zishu nü* (自梳女), which means "women who bind up their own hair," referring to the chignon that a married woman wore in place of her youthful braids (Topley 1975:82–83).

27. Two women in an amorous embrace. *Source:* John Byron, *Portrait of a Chinese Paradise: Erotica and Sexual Customs of the Late Qing Period.* London: Quartet Books, 1987, color pl. 171.

In another local custom, the "women's script" preserved exclusively by the women of a county in Hunan allowed them to communicate pledges of intimate emotional support and to swear sisterhood in secrecy. Their stories have been reinvented in contemporary fiction (Silber 1994; in recent fiction, See 2005). Anecdotes about romantic love between two women also appear in a famous memoir by Shen Fu (b. 1763), whose wife arranged for him a concubine whom she herself found sexually attractive (Shen 1986). A late-nineteenth-century print from the commercial market features two women in an amorous erotic pose (see Figure 27). These fragmentary references reveal same-sex relationships among women, at the same time dramatizing the general silence in the written record.

Sex between women was often connected to men's pleasure: sex manuals explained how a man might benefit from the *yin* essence of two females at once if they had sex with each other before he joined them. "Spring pictures" and novels often portray more than one woman in scenes of heterosexual intercourse: a maid may support or prop up her mistress to facilitate a coupling. Manuals, prints, and novels, of course, do not tell us much about audience or reception; what they do reveal are notions of desire, articulated through fantasy and imagination in the consumer marketplace.

Homosociality

To understand sexuality in late imperial China, we must remember that most people spent most of their time in same-sex company. Social convention and the division of labor kept women off the street and inside their homes and courtyards as much as possible. In the home, as we have seen, women kept company with children and elders of both sexes. Able-bodied males over the age of twelve, however, had limited contact with women. Their social skills, their emotional bonds, and their talents – whether physical or intellectual – were all developed in the company of men (Mann 2000). For this reason, classical Chinese writings on emotional and intellectual intimacy among men are rich. Famous novels like *Romance of the Three Kingdoms* (*Sanguo yan yi*) and *All Men Are Brothers* (*Shuihu zhuan*) celebrated comradeship and brotherhood, focusing almost exclusively on men. China's great tradition of biographical writing, a centerpiece of the historical record, depended on the keen appreciation of individual intimate relationships among men. The collected works of scholars invariably included nostalgic character sketches of beloved male friends, or copies of intense correspondence in which a circle of male friends exchanged views on moral or philosophical issues.

Social organizations also facilitated homosocial bonds among men of every social class. For the educated elite, patronage networks gathered clusters of talented men into the service of officials and wealthy scholars and merchants, where they served as "tent-friends" (*muyou*, a term derived from military history) or as "guests" (*ke*). Paul Rouzer (2006), who has studied the historical origins of these patronage networks, has pointed out that a patron brought his *ke* under his control – indeed, into a kind of service-onto-death – by extending gracious favor even when a guest threatened or insulted his host. Such "friendships" were constructed hierarchically, based on favor extended and obligation owed.

So an "intimate friend" (*zhiji*, or "one who knows me") was a patron who trusted his guests absolutely to be loyal to him. Friendship, in this view, was a way of exerting social control over possibly unruly men who could be called to the patron's standard by his own magnanimity and "understanding." The *muyou* networks of the Qing period were more professionalized than their early prototypes, to be sure, but nevertheless they served as fields of power in which talented men sought protection, sparred with their minds, and competed with their skills to win praise and "fame" in certain circles (Folsom 1968).

Scholars of literature like Martin Huang have argued that the *muyou* role became crucial in the late seventeenth and eighteenth centuries, when highly educated men were fiercely competing for prestige and power. As commercial wealth produced more and more students struggling to win civil service degrees, more and more elite men had to find employment outside the prestigious official bureaucracy. These men turned to medicine, to teaching, and – increasingly – to working as a *muyou* for a powerful patron. Such positions could even provide creative outlets for poets and calligraphers, because many official patrons prized the company of talented literati and loved to indulge and display their good taste as connoisseurs. These positions, however, were clearly positions of dependency that advertised a scholar's state of unemployment to the rest of the world, and in that sense they represented a marginal status. Huang suggests that these marginal roles affected notions of masculinity in the Qing period: that working as a *muyou* could be a "feminizing experience" – a "faceless existence, similar to the case of a concubine" (Huang 2003:94). His point is that a scholar's literary or intellectual output as a *muyou* went to the credit of his employer, not himself, just as the child born of a concubine was declared the offspring of the first wife. As an alternative, the masculine identity of a physician was superior. A physician, like a scholar, could operate as an independent person of talent, capable of healing (bringing civilization to) aboriginal people and curing (giving intimate service to) members of the imperial family.

Self-doubt and insecurity caused by competitive pressures, Martin Huang argues, also led many scholars to turn to autobiographical writing in fiction and drama, and to become fascinated by the theater and the many fictional roles played by characters on the stage (Huang 2003:97–87; see also Huang 1995:21–44). The shy and reclusive poet Huang Jingren (1749–1783), for example, loved to perform amateur opera (Huang 1995:39). So the competition for scarce official positions in the nineteenth century expanded the domain of homosociality for men, while at the same time challenging men to construct different models of manly responsibility. Poetry clubs supplied still another important space for homosocial interaction among educated men in late imperial China. Although such clubs often implicitly clustered around a master, they operated independently of official patronage networks. Publications of work by members of these clubs (with titles like "Chanting Poems Together in the XX Studio"), with eloquent prefaces and commemorative paintings, show how meaningful these bonding experiences were to the men who enjoyed them, and even how central to social and political identity membership in poetry clubs could be (Polachek 1992:39–61).

Because elite male relationships were so vividly recorded in collected prose and poetry writings, some scholars have inferred that same-sex friendships included sexual relations (Hinsch 1990:131–132); others insist that male friendship among literati did not extend to sexual relations (McDermott 1992:70). The sexual hierarchies associated with penetration, arguably, would have encouraged literati to think of homosexual relations in a different register from friendship between peers. On these points there is little evidence in the historical record, apart from allegations of rape or abuse involving male-male sex that came before the courts. A fragment of evidence for homosexual relationships among commoners comes from depositions taken from pirates captured off the coast of Guangdong and tried in local courts. Transcribed in summaries sent by the Guangdong government to the imperial court between 1796 and 1801, twenty-two of fifty-six cases mention homosexual acts involving 102 individuals. Most of these cases alleged that the penetrated person was coerced (Murray 1992:128). Yet Matthew Sommer's research on consensual sex described in legal cases suggests that commoner men sought sexual comfort and affection from both men and women (Sommer 2000:154–162). The nature and extent of sex between men remains, however, a difficult subject to study in the premodern era, although we can uncover a range of attitudes toward it, from romanticization and celebration to condescension and even disgust.

Theater and monastery

Brotherhoods, merchant guilds, theaters, and monasteries all served as venues for male homosociality. Opera performances were often hosted or sponsored by local brotherhoods, and the opera stage was a central feature of the urban guild hall. By the end of the eighteenth century, moreover, opera was performed largely by all-male casts. Aesthetics of the theater, as we have seen, celebrated the *dan* (female impersonator) actor's ability to capture perfectly the essence of female purity and sexuality, including the wavering steps of a delicate young woman with bound feet. This captured essence was the measure of a *dan*'s greatness. At the same time, connoisseurship of the *dan* and his talent became a major pastime of highly educated literati, who vied with one another to see and be seen with the most exciting current *dan* performers (Volpp 2002). During the nineteenth century, the leisure pastime of *dan* patronage combined erudition (familiarity with opera scripts and roles), critical sensibilities, and a good deal of pleasurable entertainment. The nineteenth-century novel *A Precious Mirror for Judging Flowers* (*Pinhua baojian*) details the escapades of the "flowers," the comely *dan* awaiting the appreciative judgment of male patrons. In titillating plotlines of this kind, women were entirely displaced from the erotic male imagination.

The scenes in *Precious Mirror* describe what became known as the *xianggong* (male courtesan) system. Originally *xianggong* meant "prime minister"; then the term became a general referent for "young master of a noble house," or "handsome young man." By the late eighteenth century, *xianggong* referred exclusively to beautiful young actors who were admired and coveted by elite men seeking entertainment and pleasure (Ruan 1991:114–115). One story traces the playful use of the term *xianggong* as a name for a male courtesan to the seventieth birthday party of the Qianlong Emperor in 1779. The imperial court had banned female opera performers in 1772, as a belated part of the larger ongoing effort to remove female entertainers from official venues, and as a result only female impersonators appeared on the opera stage at the capital. For the imperial birthday party in 1779, the all-male opera troupe of the famed *dan* Wei Changsheng performed at the court, and the appreciative emperor rewarded the young actors lavishly. This imperial gesture became an emblem of the refined relationship between discriminating elite men and the *xianggong* (Chao-Jung Wu 2007:55). Qing rulers frowned on the popular entertainments offered by female courtesans, but they had no objection to the flirtatious relationships that developed between scholar-officials and the *xianggong* who kept company with them. By the middle of the nineteenth century, Beijing was known for its *xianggong tangzi*, houses of male prostitution staffed by *dan* actors (Hui-ling Chou 1997:137).

By removing women from the gaze of elite men, the *dan* and the *xianggong* system created a sexualized and romanticized homosocial space at the theater for members of the scholar-official elite. But removing women from public entertainment may have had complicated psychological and emotional consequences. As one scholar of nineteenth-century fiction has observed:

Borrowing romantic clichés to describe the virtues of love and fidelity among male courtesans/actors and their patrons, [fiction such as *Precious Mirror*] nevertheless [deals] just as much with women as with men. The displacement of gender and gender-oriented rhetoric paradoxically calls attention to the absence of woman: through the mediation of masqueraded homoerotic romance, it exposes how "woman" has been treated both as an idealized object of a male-centered fantasy and as a social "position" so subordinate that it can be filled even by men. (David Der-wei Wang 1997:60)

In other words, the kinds of public spaces that opened for male-male romantic and sexual relationships also affected men's perceptions of women. One can speculate about these effects, which surely expanded the figurative moral space between cloistered women of virtue and women who were sexually available. If elite men were criticized for patronizing courtesans but admired for patronizing *xianggong*, then the *xianggong* system must have captured at least some of the market for female entertainment and sexual favors.

In the theater, where costume and gesture defined gender roles, same-sex relationships were not only tolerated; they were integrated into the consumer culture of the capital and other major cities. By contrast, same-sex relationships in Buddhist and Daoist monasteries and convents figured in jokes, slurs, and even political vendettas. As homosocial spaces where men lived with men and women with women, convents and monasteries stood outside of and challenged the values of Confucian family life. And as we have seen, Daoist and Buddhist nuns – along with fortunetellers, matchmakers, healers, and other suspect women – were listed among the "three aunties and six grannies" (*san gu liu po*) who were never to set foot inside the house of respectable women (Despeux and Kohn 2003:151). County officials warned women in their jurisdiction not to visit temples, where they would be seduced by monks, if not by opportunistic commoners (Djang 1984:608–609). Fiction writers used convents and temples as settings for erotic scenes featuring monks and nuns, with sexual orgies, both heterosexual and homosexual, described in salacious detail (Ruan 1991:90). Lascivious nuns and monks as "sex adepts" were stock characters in erotic romances of the eighteenth century (McMahon 1995:139–142). In the theater too, monasteries suggested seduction, as West and Idema observe in their analysis of the play *The Western Wing*: "As a place where, theoretically, the urges of sexuality have been cleaned away, the monks' cloister . . . is a cauldron of barely concealed lust and homosexuality" (West and Idema 1991:83–84).

In both China and Japan, male same-sex relationships in Buddhist monastic communities were well recognized, structured according to age in passive or active (penetrated or penetrator) roles (Faure 1998:215ff.). Unlike the discourse in Japan, however, the Chinese discourse on monastic male love was not articulated and valorized as a way of being. Only in the late imperial theater were playful relationships between elite men and their *dan* courtesans indulged and valorized, and even there mainly as a form of entertainment and leisured pleasure.

Critiques and anxieties in the nineteenth century

Late imperial Chinese culture, as we have seen, showed few discernible traces of what today is described as homophobia. In the late Ming, love between men and love between women both received sympathetic treatment at the hands of the best fiction writers (Pi-Ching Hsu 2006:112–118, Sang 2003:66–95, 281–287). In the Qing period distinguished literati often kept company with young men whom they took as sexual partners. On the other hand, early-eighteenth-century Qing law banning rape, whether homosexual or heterosexual, may have influenced attitudes toward same-sex relations between men, which in legal casework acquired the derogatory label *jijian* (chicken lewdness) when marginal males were involved (Faure 1998:218–219, Sommer 2000, 2005). Fear of marginal men as rapists has been clearly identified by Matthew Sommer as a factor in eighteenth-century court cases. But marginal men ("bare sticks") were only one source of sexual danger for young men and boys. Monasteries, as we have seen, were also targets of suspicion. Of still greater concern to literati families were the schools and academies where young boys studied for the civil service exams under the strict discipline of a male teacher. These classes presented opportunities for both same-sex attraction and same-sex abuse, illustrated in well-known vignettes from the great eighteenth-century novel *Dream of the Red Chamber*.

It is possible that attitudes toward same-sex relationships became more negative following the criminalization of same-sex relations after 1740. We see the impact of the new laws, for example, in numerous legal cases brought by parents of young boys who had sex with a teacher (Meijer 1985). The stigma attached to being penetrated made such cases inflammatory in families of the educated elite. Evidence points to an emerging consciousness of sexual abuse in schools as a political and moral issue in the late Qing period, as in Yeh Wen-hsin's dramatic account of the sodomizing of boy students by male teachers in a village school (located, ironically, in a Buddhist temple). In one case cited by Yeh, sexual abuse by a teacher sparked a young man's revolutionary consciousness, as Shi Cuntong confronted his disillusionment with Confucian moral instruction (Yeh 1996:108–109). Still, in the late empire, sex as consumption, sex as emotional bonding, sex as physical appetite, and sex for health – all were available to elite men, with a person of the same sex or the opposite sex. For men the significant constraint on same-sex relationships was the presumption that phallic penetration was reserved for social inferiors in status and in age. Evidence suggests that the stigma attached to penetration was so powerful among the elite that it placed sexual intercourse in a regime of human interaction distant from emotional intimacy and closer to patronage, entertainment, or indulgence (as we saw above in the brief discussion of male friendship).

Twentieth-century shifts

Views of same-sex relationships that prevailed in the Qing period confronted Western representations of sexuality in law and science at the end of the nineteenth century, as translations of missionary tracts and social Darwinist treatises introduced a new vocabulary for same-sex relationships that labeled them harmful to health and the social order. New conceptions of "normal" sex placed same-sex relationships in a marginal position where they were pathologized, criminalized, or tainted with notions of sin (see, for example, Chen Dongyuan 1937:300 passim). As Wenqing Kang has stressed, these Western critiques of homosexuality, and Western homophobia, found receptive ground in the concerns and anxieties about same-sex relationships described earlier in this chapter (Kang 2009:19–59). Even so, Western-inspired condemnation of same-sex relationships did not win a wide following in China. On the contrary, as Tze-lan Sang has shown, ideas about same-sex relationships continued to range widely and eclectically throughout the twentieth century. The introduction of evolutionary theory and social Darwinism, in fact, suggested to some Chinese that males and females were becoming more alike all the time – a trend that pointed to the increasing likelihood of same-sex attraction (Sang 1999b:288–289). Over the objections of "Dr. Sex" (Zhang Jingsheng), author of a detailed report on sexual behavior in China during the 1920s, the dominant discourse at the time translated Western terms for homosexuality as *tongxing lian'ai* – "same-sex *love*." In an era when free love and mate choice were valorized as the key to modernity and building a strong citizenry, this rhetorical move continued to anchor homosexual discourses in a benign, even positive, register. Columbia-educated sociologist Pan Guangdan voiced these benign attitudes when he commented in 1946 that whereas homosexual attraction might be rare among young people in the co-educational schools of Europe and America, "in the schools in China ten or twenty years ago, same-sex love between male students occurred quite a bit. . . . After co-education became popular in China, of course, such incidents have become fewer and fewer. Still, even in co-ed schools, we can find many instances of same-sex love between female school-mates" (Sang 1999b:296). Pan subscribed to the view that homosexual attraction was primarily a function of stage in the life cycle and other particular conditions, and that heterosexual marriage was the ultimate "natural" path of most people. In that sense he was very much in tune with the attitudes toward homosexuality in the culture as a whole, which understood sexual attraction as relational and situational, not biologically determined (Sang 1999b:297).

Western critiques of homosexuality did begin to influence Chinese performing arts by the end of the nineteenth century, however, as the celebrated *dan* were edged aside by the new fans of *laosheng* (older male) actors in Peking opera. *Laosheng* became "models of late Qing mas-culinity" who kept Peking opera popular, even as the *dan* role came under critical scrutiny (Joshua Goldstein 2007:6). By contrast with the *dan* stars of the eighteenth-century stage, *laosheng* actors fit the milita-rized popular culture of the last half of the nineteenth century, era of rebellions (Taiping, *nian*, and Muslim) and wars with European powers (Joshua Goldstein 2007:18–19). Citing the crises of masculine identity that accompanied these conflicts, Goldstein notes: "This was a time when the two pillars of Chinese masculine identity – the *wen* of culture and the *wu* of military prowess – were being directly challenged by imperialism" (2007:54; see Louie 2002 and Louise Edwards 1995). Mei Lanfang, the *dan* who drew international adulation in the twentieth century (between 1912 and 1937), helped to restore the *dan* to cultural visibility (Kang 2009). But Mei Lanfang also underscored the very complex gender shifts that accompanied the turn of the twentieth century:

The dismantling of the *xianggong* system provides one example of an assertion of biological sex over gender. The *xianggong* was now viewed as evidence of how the Qing's oppressive patriarchal polity distorted the ideal of male equality and perverted male desire, a perversion the Republic should expunge. . . . This meant shifting the *dan* from a position as a courtesan and sex worker to status as a "respectable artist and citizen" who could take his place in literary magazines with support from respectable literary patrons. (Joshua Goldstein 2007:113)

Changes in male actors' roles in the early twentieth century had impli-cations for actresses, who now returned to the stage. The first women's acting troupe in Shanghai, founded in the 1870s by a former Peking opera performer, was just the beginning. After 1911 female performers

appeared regularly in the new teahouses of Shanghai. These female performers cross-dressed to portray men on stage, and their cross-dressing
inspired new fashion among young women drawn to revolutionary ideas
about women's roles. At the same time, cross-dressed actors and actresses
became stars in new revolutionary theater featuring free-thinking young
intellectuals of both sexes (Hui-ling Chou 1997:147). Meanwhile, local
opera troupes from outside the city – particularly Yue opera, the theater
of Zhejiang province that attracted a huge following in early-twentieth-
century Shanghai – began to build an urban audience, using all-female
casts recruited in the countryside (Jiang 2009:46–59). Their audience of
female "petty urbanites," mostly from the Ningbo-Shaoxing area, where
Yue opera originated, created a new "public women's culture" in Shanghai during the first half of the twentieth century (Jiang 2009:259). This
female audience, which ranged from factory and domestic workers to
middle-class housewives and white-collar workers, was also the audience
for the discourses on new women, modern girls, and nuclear families that
became the groundwork for the coming Communist revolution (Jiang
2009:258–262).

Gay cultures in the twentieth century

During the Republican era (1911–1949), research on the history of sexuality began in earnest, partly in response to the questions posed by
Western sexology.[1] The history of lesbianism, for example, made an
appearance in Chen Dongyuan's *History of the Lives of Chinese Women*,
first published in 1937. Chen, a prominent educational reformer and
writer in the 1930s, was inspired by the "woman question" to write this
book, which he concluded with a brief catalog of sexual and gender practices from different parts of the country. A description (quoted by Chen
from a notebook on Guangdong customs published in 1827 by Zhang
Xintai [*Yue you xiao zhi*]) of one such local practice follows:

Many girls in Guangdong join what are called Golden Lotus Clubs. After a girl
has been married, she will return to her natal family and not go back to her

---

[1] In China proper, the heavy influence of Marxism constrained the development of gay
cultures and knowledge about them after the revolution of 1949. Although pioneering
work by Li Yinhe, Pan Suiming, and others has to some degree broken through these
constraints, there is a certain localism to discussions of gay cultures in twentieth-century
Chinese societies (Hinsch 2005). In Taiwan, for example, views of same-sex relationships
in the academy and beyond have been largely influenced by Western culture and especially
theory. In Hong Kong, where postcolonial taboos slowed research, Hong Kong University
Press launched its new "Queer Asia" series in 2009.

husband's family, even to the point where they do not live together as husband and wife. They will wait until every single girl in the club has been married out before they will move in with their husbands. If the pressure on them becomes too great, all the girls will make a pact to withhold themselves [from their marital obligations]. (Chen 1937:300)

Chen also described practices in Shunde county that, he claimed, had spread into neighboring Panyu and other areas, including the provincial capital. His book introduced readers to partnerships in which two women lived together as a couple, with one of them taking the part of the husband. This was known locally, Chen said, as "bowing to an intimate" or "pledging intimacy" (*bai xiangzhi*). He continued: "After taking such a vow, they [the couple] would delight in being bound together like husband and wife[2] and they would pass the time with lutes large and small[3] and in this manner go to the end of their days without ever marrying" (Chen 1937:300).

Chen's comments on these ethnographic discoveries placed them in the cultural context of Republican social Darwinism and Western-influenced sexology. He called them "unnatural" and also "very harmful to a girl's health" (Chen 1937:300). He was even more concerned that as the economy and modes of earning a living changed, homosexuality among women who remained unmarried would become increasingly common. He must have feared that women who got jobs to support themselves would have no economic need to marry a man or rely on children. Here he touched on nationalist concerns – the need to build a strong nation with strong, reproductively successful mothers – that peaked in 1937 as the Japanese occupation of China's heartland began. Much more research is needed on the relationship between "semi-colonialism" in China and negative views of homosexuality, which were developing rapidly by that time. Chen's work is just one example.

The Communist government after 1949 held rigid views on sexuality and gender performance that, in effect, removed sexuality from the arena of "modernization" and folded it into a campaign to clean up prostitution and shore up monogamous marriage (Hershatter 1996). Explicit policies regulating same-sex relationships were formulated in 1956, when homosexual acts were criminalized in the legal code, making "hooliganism" (i.e., sodomy) a crime if it involved violence, coercion, or

---

[2] The phrase is "*chou mou*" – from the *Classic of Poetry* air of the same title (Mao Ode 118; Legge 1991:179), meaning "tightly bound" firewood. The poem is about a couple delighting in their unexpected happy union.

[3] "*Qin seng*," another allusion to the *Classic of Poetry* from the first air, which celebrates the harmony of husband and wife.

a minor. The reference to hooliganism comes from Marx and Engels, who referred to homosexual men as hooligans, but the pejorative term echoes the late imperial government's marginalization of politically disruptive single men (bare sticks). Not until 1984, with the post-Mao reforms, did the government stop punishing homosexual acts as crimes, and only in 1997 was sodomy removed from the criminal code.[4] Removing hooliganism from the criminal code did not, however, remove the stigma attached to homosexual acts in the modern scientific discourses of the post-Mao reform era. Until 2001 the term *tongxinglianbing* classified homosexuality as a form of mental illness, although it no longer appears in Chinese psychiatric texts as a mental disorder. (To escape punishment for sodomy, some men actually sought a diagnosis of mental illness so they would be subject to medical treatment instead of criminal punishment.)

In the contemporary People's Republic of China, there are no laws against what is once again termed "same-sex love" (*tongxinglian*) (Yinhe Li 2006). Consensual homosexual relations between adults, if private, are unlikely to attract legal or punitive sanctions. Nonetheless they may encounter social stigma and prejudice, which – according to sexologist Li Yinhe – can lead to "administrative penalties [such as thought reform or labor, withholding wages or pay cuts, or keeping a record in the worker's file] and Party disciplinary sanctions [e.g., expulsion]" (2006:82). In other words, pressures on same-sex relations in contemporary China come not from fear of criminal conviction but from fear of losing a job or having one's sexual preferences revealed to fellow workers or, worse, family members. Li cautions that "tolerance" might be too strong a word to characterize attitudes toward male homosexuality; on the other hand, she points out, neither does one see the eruptions of hatred and homophobia found in the United States. Even if the police in China seem threatening, they are likely to let gay people off with a warning or a shrug. No one really cares that much, in other words, about consensual homosexual activity, though individuals might personally think such behavior is "mistaken" or even weird.

Beginning in the 1990s, people who called themselves "gay" began to gather in public places in China's major cities. The internet, along with other media including television and film, gave them a chance to view themselves as part of a global community. But coming out in the Chinese context produced particular forms of identity. Men who identified as gay were overwhelmingly young (under thirty), and they came of age in the

---

[4] Or, as James Farrer puts it, "the crime of 'hooliganism'" was abolished (Stewart 2007). On hooliganism (*liumangzui*) and homosexuality, see Dutton 1998:62–74.

post-Mao reform era. For them, as Lisa Rofel's research has shown, relationships to family, to the nation, and to "culture" as a whole all required careful negotiation (Rofel 1999). For example, being gay did not relieve many gay men of their deeply felt responsibility as sons to marry and produce an heir to continue the line of descent. Gay men in Hong Kong were also more conscious of the importance of having a "Chinese" (as opposed to a "foreign") way of doing things (Rofel 1999:463). And the gay community's appropriation of the term *tongzhi* (the old Communist word for "comrade") served as a bridge between Hong Kong, Taiwan, and mainland gay conversations, even as it provoked new critiques and debates about differences of class, ethnicity, culture, language, gender, and sexual practices that fractured those conversations (Wah-shan Chou 2000:286ff.). For lesbians, the complex legacies of cross-dressing and male impersonation by women shaped a different modern history. In the late 1980s, for example, a "tomboy-girl" (TB/G) culture in Hong Kong began to emerge from girls' schools, where same-sex relationships between classmates were common and virtually unremarked (Wah-shan Chou 2000:213–245). Such new sexualized identities have produced arguments and debates that pit feminist-oriented lesbians against others, and split the gay and lesbian populations in Hong Kong over issues such as sexism, phallocentrism, and political correctness (Wah-shan Chou 2000:245). These debates are part of the larger picture of emerging identities in a global context, although they are at present unique to Hong Kong. Interviewing in gay bars and other venues in the late 1990s, Lisa Rofel concluded that coming out as gay in contemporary China was an expression of modernity, but of a particular kind: a way of entering the world of global neoliberal capitalism that criticized and rejected the constraining influence of China's government (Rofel 2007).

8   Sexuality in the creative imagination

An image flashes before my mind, and I see her standing in front of me, my nearest, my dearest love – the perfect oval of her face, the high arch of her brows, the limpid gaze, the rosebud mouth, the childhood dimples... and I am driven out of my mind by the sight and left mesmerized, as if in a drunken stupor. Oh, if only we had been destined to spend one night together, a single night, my nearest, my dearest love and I.

Fu Lin, *Stones in the Sea* (*Qin hai shi*), 1906 (Hanan 1995:21)

Romantic love became one of the most important themes in popular culture as new patterns of family, gender, and sexual relationships began to emerge in twentieth-century Chinese society, which was undergoing tremendous modernization. . . . As a response to the deeply felt need to address these deeply felt changes, this culture of love in turn discursively shaped popular perceptions and understandings of changing sex and gender relationships.

Jiang Jin (2009:4)

As we have seen, romantic love was far from a new theme in twentieth-century China's popular culture. For centuries, the tension between romantic love and arranged marriage supplied endless drama for opera scripts, novels, and short stories. During the Qing period, the Manchus campaigned against eroticism and sensuality in fiction and the theater, in part to enhance their claims to legitimacy. By attacking the "decadent customs" of the former Ming dynasty, the new Qing government presented itself as a regime dedicated to restoring the proper boundaries between men and women and to promoting the Confucian family system and its rituals. To some degree, Qing rectification movements, much like the sweeping anti-rightist campaigns of the Maoist period in the People's Republic, reshaped the content of literary and visual arts. Woodblocks

154

for printing proscribed works were burned along with manuscript copies and published editions, so that many of these books are now known only from titles in bibliographies, or because they made their way into libraries outside of China (Ruan 1991:96–98). Much of the erotic painting and drawing that fills sinologist Robert van Gulik's famous book on Chinese erotica, for example, was copied in Japan, where it survived the Qing purges unscathed (Gulik 1951). Even so, and despite the Manchu court's efforts, fiction and drama from the Qing dynasty open huge windows on romantic love, sexuality, and gender performance under Manchu rule.

Fiction and drama are invaluable sources for the history of sexuality because they were written using the language spoken by ordinary people. As Patrick Hanan (1981) has emphasized, classical or literary Chinese (*wenyan*) – the language of the documents that supply most of the Qing evidence for this book – was homogeneous, conservative, and institutionalized. Classical Chinese was the language of the state, the law, medicine, and the entire corpus of literary collections left by scholars in poetry, memoir, prose, and so forth. By contrast, the vernacular of fiction and drama in late imperial times was heterogeneous, transgressive, and parochial. Fiction and drama replicated local dialects and idioms, faithfully recording patterns of speech that varied by age, sex, and class. Vernacular Chinese operated outside the institutional box, in other words, probing the lives of ordinary people and spoofing the institutions of the upper classes and the government. Finally, because of its local verisimilitude, vernacular language was constantly changing and never canonized. There is a sense, of course, in which the vernacular itself was institutionalized by genre, as seen in the conventions that governed the writing of short stories, operas, and plays. But for insight into the feelings, emotions, and gendered performance of ordinary people, historians rely almost exclusively on vernacular sources.

Much of the vernacular writing of the Qing period, like its predecessors, celebrated youthful romance, its glorious highs and its tragic lows, if largely stripped of explicit erotic content. Romantic images drew on both mythic and historical figures and their stories: the legend of the Herd Boy and the Weaving Maid, for example, or the tale of the young widow Zhuo Wenjun's seduction by the famed poet Sima Xiangru (see West and Idema 1991:77–153). Writers of fiction and drama loved to dwell on the tragic aftermath of love affairs thwarted. The sentimental image of the abandoned, inaccessible woman and her suffering (sitting alone in the chilly moonlight, frigid and remote) commanded almost as much attention as the glory days of passionate love. Thus Zhuo Wenjun, later abandoned by Sima Xiangru, was celebrated for her mournful "Ballad of White Hair." The Moon Goddess Chang'e, lonely in her

heavenly exile after drinking a forbidden elixir, longed for the return of
happier days with her consort. The Weaving Maid was forced to work
at her loom day and night except on the Double Seven, when she could
cross the starry Magpie Bridge and enjoy her yearly tryst with the Herd
Boy. The paradigmatic lovers of late imperial stage and fiction made continual appearances as versions of Yingying and her lover, Scholar Zhang.
Yingying's story became a template for exploring the tensions between
youthful romance and arranged marriage that gripped modern writers –
tensions that laced Ba Jin's novel *Family* in the early twentieth century,
and that were recalled in every marriage law passed after 1930. How
could youthful romance be reconciled with the demands of marriage and
family life? And was romance even relevant to the kind of relationships
that supported stable and lasting marriage?

In the Qing period, most young women probably encountered stories like Yingying's as readers. Women of the governing class could see
opera performed in family- or lineage-based celebrations, or as a guest
at the home of a friend. But "*reading* was the conventional image of
the governing-class woman's access to drama," as attested by women's
commentaries on the opera *The Peony Pavilion* (Carlitz 1997a:124, italics in original; Zeitlin 1994). Young women of the governing class read
nonfiction texts intended to cultivate their virtue, but those texts too –
especially those recounting the tales of faithful maidens and widows, and
martyred heroines – could be so full of passion that they read like love
stories (Carlitz 1994:125). Fascination with the strange, a leading subject
of popular fiction, enabled writers to explore bizarre or exotic or extreme
experiences that often included sexual adventures (Zeitlin 1993). Elite
readers imagined peasants who inhabited a world of sexual freedom that
was free from the constraints of the *guixiu* boudoir. So-called hill songs
collected and published by seventeenth-century writer Feng Menglong
(1574–1646) show the elite fascination with bawdy verse celebrating
sex and lust. Transcribed in local dialects from Suzhou (Jiangsu) and
Tongcheng (Anhui), many of these songs were considered faithful ren-
derings of the original Wu dialect. In the following example the singer
plays on the notion of "cleverness," the conventional term for a young
woman's artfulness with needle and thread:

> "Clever"
> Mother is clever, but her daughter is clever too.
> Mother has strewn the floor with lime.
> So I carry my boyfriend to the bed on my back.
> We leave one person's footprints on the floor.
>   (Ōki 1997:132)

Turning virtue upside down, the hill songs flaunted the sexuality of married women and spoofed ideas about fidelity:

> "Gazing"
> That young man is very bold.
> Why do you gaze back at me after passing my gate?
> My husband is not blind.
> Why not come to the back gate if you wish to see me?
>   (Ōki 1997:134)

Qing fiction and drama featured negative female images of state-topplers and shrews who also challenged the virtuous models in classical texts (West and Idema 1991:98ff.). These images too came from history and legend, such as the story of the young beauty Xi Shi, one of the state-topplers recalled by Scholar Zhang when he renounced Yingying. Xi Shi alone, legend said, brought about the downfall of one of the most powerful lords of the Spring and Autumn Period (fifth century BCE). Plucked from her rustic home in a woodcutter's village, she entered the court of the king of Yue, where she was trained in the courtesans' arts and elite womanly virtues. The Yue king then sent her as a gift to his archenemy, the king of Wu. Her charge: to seduce the Wu king and destroy his state, bringing a triumphant and final end to decades of bitter fighting. In the story's dramatic midpoint, as the Wu king is about to accept his rival's fateful gift, a prescient minister at the Wu court utters this warning:

August Sire, I entreat you not to fall into the trap that has been laid before you. . . . Please be wary, for since the dawn of history men have ever been slaves to beautiful women. By accepting these beguiling creatures from our fallen enemy, much trouble will surely befall the royal house, leading perhaps to the disintegration of our beloved State. Recall, for instance, the fall of the Xia dynasty, which was due to the tyrant Jie's beautiful concubine, Mo Xi. Again the Shang dynasty fell because of the ruler Zhou Xin's enchantress, Da Ji, while the Zhou house was overthrown through Yu Wang's favorite consort, Bao Si. These are but a few instances which may be cited to serve as a warning to us. (Shu-chiung 1981:33–34)

The bedazzled king accepted the gift anyway, immersed himself in an affair with Xi Shi, and exhausted the resources of his kingdom in mammoth projects built to please her. Meanwhile Xi Shi persuaded the king to kill his only wise advisor (the minister who counseled against admitting her into the palace in the first place), and the Wu kingdom was laid open to a devastating attack by Yue, timed in response to a secret communiqué from Xi Shi to the Yue court. Xi Shi thus stands firmly in the long historical tradition of women who ruined kingdoms, many of whom we have already met, including Bao Si. Bao Si, consort of the last ruler of the eastern Zhou in Confucius' day, was known for her dour temper. The Zhou king finally succeeded in making her smile: it amused her when the king called his feudal lords to assemble. Because this call was reserved only for dire emergencies, after repeated summons to false alarms, the Zhou lords stopped responding. The eastern Zhou court fell to invaders from the west, and the power of the Zhou house came to an end, opening the door to the Warring States (Robin Wang 2003:159–161).

Fiction and drama from the seventeenth century turned away from these grand narratives of sexual intrigue to scrutinize the dark underside of sexual relationships between ordinary people. Stories featuring shrewish wives and their henpecked husbands, although pitched as satirical entertainment, also took their plots from family pressures that exacerbated or brought out a wife's jealousy and antagonism toward her husband: pressure to bear sons; demands of a mother-in-law; isolation from her natal family and friends; a husband's attention to other women, especially a concubine; and so forth (Yenna Wu 1988). Jealousy was one of the "seven reasons for expelling a wife," according to Ming and Qing law, as we have seen, so a shrewish woman served as a cautionary tale showing how a wife could bring misfortune on her husband's family. Indeed, commentators often claimed that a shrewish wife was her husband's own fault, for indulging her too much out of fear that she would cause him to lose face, and the seventeenth-century writer Li Yu opined that a shrew was good for her husband's health because she saved him from over-indulging in sex (Yenna Wu 1988:365–368). Shrews ran the gamut from cunning to violent, and their husbands from ineffectual to despicable. What made the shrew stories work so well as fiction was the inversion of the proper relationship between *yin* and *yang*, as the female prevailed against the male. The male in these plots was hardly "effeminate" – rather, he might be brutal, he might be trying to escape his wife's sexual control, or he might be weak-willed. He was, to be sure, "feminized" in some plots when his wife forced him to do womanly work, such as cooking and serving. By the same token, she was not "masculinized" but rather made to appear gluttonous, ugly, or lustful (Yenna Wu 1988:376–377).

In still other kinds of fiction, gender inversion made fun of both gender roles by satirizing them, as in the novel *Forgotten History of the Buddhists* (*Chanzhen yishi*), in which the women of the village renamed "Town of Hens" organized an "All-Female Society" (*qun yin she*) and promulgated ten rules for "regulating the family" (*qi jia*) and "rectifying the self" (*zheng shen*). The rules were for husbands only (a spoof on Confucian family instructions that focused on women's conduct): no whoring and gambling, no mistreating your wife, no concubines without your wife's permission, no sex with the servants (male or female), no remarriage for widowers, no usurping authority from your wife, no carousing, no going out without permission, and no neglecting your wife while you seek fame or wealth. The last rule specified penalties for disobeying the first nine (Yenna Wu 1988:379–380; Yenna Wu 1995:180).

Shape-shifter fiction featuring the fox as wife and vixen enjoyed a particular vogue in the eighteenth and nineteenth centuries. The figure of the fox as a female seductress, object of lust, and – simultaneously – dutiful wife and mother was a favorite of Qing literati writers, who projected the desires and fears of their intimate relationships with women onto the figure of the fox (Huntington 2003). The scholar Ji Yun (1724–1805), whose "random jottings" ran heavily toward foxes and *femmes fatales*, loved the *zhiguai* (strange and marvelous) genre, not only for its liaisons between young aspiring male scholars and beautiful fox-maidens, but also for the detail these stories lavished on troubling ghosts and vengeful spirits and demons and monsters. Tales of the strange and supernatural circulated by word of mouth through scholarly circles and scholarly households, moving up and down the social hierarchy from maid to master, friend to friend. The texts themselves supply a lexicon of conflicting beliefs about the gods, sexuality, morality, and fate (Chan 1998, Ji 1999). Like satire, they exposed the iconoclasm and skepticism that jostled the moral strictures and institutional constraints of the Qing period. Their tone was captured in Yuan Mei's irreverent ghost story collection *Censored by Confucius* (*Zi bu yu*), which first appeared in 1788. Playing on the famous words of the sage in the seventh chapter of the *Analects* ("The Master would not speak [*zi bu yu*] of things strange, things requiring force, chaos and disorder, or the spirits"), the stories featured sex crimes, sexual pleasure, and sexual farce, among many other iconoclastic themes (Louie and Edwards 1996). All of these fictional representations show how the reading or viewing audience held up the sex and gender system to scrutiny, criticizing it, making fun of it, and identifying its tensions and challenges – even to the point of parodying Confucian language and classical forms (Yenna Wu 1995:180).

In fiction and drama about passion and romance, women took center stage. Fiction featuring male heroes, by contrast, foregrounded the hero's ability to *eschew* sexual relationships with women. The paradigmatic male hero – *yingxiong, da zhangfu, haohan* – was a great swordsman like Zhang Fei, star of the historical novel *Romance of the Three Kingdoms* (*San guo yan yi*). Zhang was big-hearted and generous to people who captured his admiration, brash and fearless in battle, and utterly uninterested in women. Heroes like this could easily be outlaws, fighting in the name of righteous loyalty to overcome a corrupt ruler, as in the novel *All Men Are*

Brothers (*Shui hu zhuan*). The "band of brothers" pledged to a common cause, like the heroes of the *Romance of the Three Kingdoms*, took the law into their own hands where corruption had distorted justice and lived on the margins of stable communities with like-minded fellows. In the stories of these heroes, *yangsheng* beliefs about the dangers of sexual depletion supported a commitment to comrades that superseded even filial duty to parents. These men broke out of the box of normative gender relations, in other words, and they occupied a space that was quite different from the space shared by other stock male figures in fiction (Ruhlmann 1960). Nor did they pose a predatory threat, unlike the bare sticks.

The very significant body of explicitly sexualized writing in late imperial fiction raises the question of pornography. Whether or not there is such a thing as pornography in Chinese art before the twentieth century is debatable.[1] Examples of erotica as political or social criticism are rare, possibly because none survive. In the late imperial period, erotic prints and drawings appeared in two kinds of publications: in fiction and in manuals detailing techniques, positions, and possibilities for sexual intercourse, whether for pleasure, health, or procreation. Gulik believed that all erotic drawings originated as a kind of medical literature, especially guides to men's health informed by Daoist alchemy, but that after the Tang such texts increasingly turned to entertainment and titillation ("Introduction" in Gulik 1951:2 passim). Song Neo-Confucian "prudery," according to Gulik, explained why Chinese artists were reluctant to depict the nude body, making erotic prints and manuals more useful for their details of intimate clothing and interior decoration that were rarely, if ever, portrayed in other media. The denatured bodies in Chinese erotic prints show a bare outline of the shape and the location of the vulva and the erect penis, but women's naked feet are never visible, and only rarely does a footbinding appear to come loose. At the same time, the verbal range of erotic texts, especially those devoted to pleasure rather than to procreation, is vast and rich, using language from the vulgar colloquial to the sublime poetic. Sex manuals were how-to guides, showing various

---

[1] For a critique of Hong Kong's pornography laws arguing that they are based on a colonial perspective and pathologize indigenous (Han Chinese) ideas about sexuality, especially same-sex relations, see M.-C. Man-Chung Chiu 2004. French historian Lynn Hunt has argued that pornography did not exist before the onset of Western modernity and its markers: the Renaissance, the scientific revolution, the Enlightenment, and the French Revolution (Hunt 1993:10–11). She defines pornography as "the explicit depiction of sexual organs and sexual practices with the aim of arousing sexual feelings" (1993:10) and observes that before 1800 it was used most often to criticize authority, whether religious or political.

positions for intercourse, including details of how feet and hands could be placed for maximum pleasure, with occasional forays into technology, illustrating the use of dildos by women having sex together, and rings for men to place at the base of the penis to sustain an erection. To add titillation, a chapter might discuss the sex life of emperors, describe sex between monks and nuns, catalog the frustrations of single men such as travelers far from home (loss of appetite, insomnia, poor health, etc.), recount stories of sex between famous men and their maids, and so forth (Gulik 1951:92–93 passim).

Sex manuals and erotica were targets of the Qing literary inquisitions, and many disappeared or were destroyed during that time, with the result that – as we have seen – Gulik had to seek his evidence from material preserved in Japan. But Keith McMahon has proposed that some of the erotic writing that survives from the Qing period, far from being pornographic, in fact represents a carefully researched and detailed description of "Confucian sexuality" (McMahon 1988; also McMahon 1995:150–175). As an example he cites the late-eighteenth-century novel *A Country Codger Puts His Words Out to Sun* (*Yesou puyan*), where the measure of the hero's moral caliber was his ability to "remain unperturbed with a woman in his arms" – especially an eager woman who was completely excited by his powerful *yang qi* (see also Martin Huang 2003:76). In novels like this, McMahon suggests, sexually arousing writing was intended "not as vicarious indulgence, but as a test of virtuous self-control" (McMahon 1988:33). The author of the novel used sex to dramatize the victory of "virtuous male energy" that also expressed itself in "vast learning" and "great martial and moral strength to correct social wrongs." The novel's hero, moreover, refused to consummate his relationship with any of the many women in his life without obtaining his mother's blessing first (McMahon 1988:39). He was opposed to homosexual intercourse because the anus was not a suitable recipient for a man's vital sexual energy (*yang qi*). In the author's statement of his "principles," introducing the guidelines he used in writing his book, topics included sexual proclivities (*chuntai*) alongside classics, morality, history, medicine, military science, and so forth. Acknowledging that some of the contents of his novel might appear to be obscene (*huixie*), the author of the novel explained that their purpose was purely to admonish and remind the reader of the moral principles governing relations between the sexes (McMahon 1988:45).

In studying shifts in the portrayal of sexuality between the late Ming, which stressed sexual pleasure and sensuality, and the mid-Qing, during which relations between men and women were increasingly sentimentalized and even intellectualized (in expressing love, for example, poetry became more important than sex), McMahon notes that Qing censorship certainly played a role (McMahon 1988:49). But he also stresses the absence of *qing* or romance in *Country Codger*, which rejected utterly the romantic tradition of fated lovers or predestined attachments that ran from *The Western Wing*, through *The Peony Pavilion*, into the scholar-beauty stories of the Qing period, and finally to *Dream of the Red Chamber*. Instead, McMahon situates the erotic novel *Country Codger* in the context of the scholarly fashion of the time: evidential research. In McMahon's reading, in other words, far from being pornographic, the novel is actually a laborious catalog of examples dramatizing an original Confucian morality based on separation of the sexes, lived and affirmed in the polygamous households of eighteenth-century literati. Sex for procreation is the goal, achieved by discipline of orgasm and denial of pleasure. The hero of the novel even has a friend who travels to Europe to spread Confucianism, so successfully that many Europeans start studying Chinese so they can read the classics, and members of a few royal families try mastering the art of "having less desire to produce more sons" (*guayu duonan*) by timing sexual intercourse according to the woman's menstrual cycle (Martin Huang 2003:91).[2]

Change in the twentieth century

During the twentieth century, the tensions foregrounded in late imperial fiction and drama – tensions between passion and arranged marriage, between eros and morality – were sprung or unleashed together with the "new woman" and the "modern girl," as writers, filmmakers, and playwrights vied to explore new romantic possibilities (Haiyan Lee 2007). Same-sex love or heterosexual love – either one posed new questions and produced new meanings, once the rules separating the sexes and upholding the old family system began to bend. Writers leaped to use the fluid gender boundaries of the late imperial era – displayed in cross-dressing, theater impersonation, and homoerotic fantasy – as media for examining love in every possible context. The knight errant, the woman warrior, the female virago, the male philanderer – all stock figures in late imperial fiction and drama – reappeared in new genres and new modes of writing, including modern poetry and drama, and new fiction by women.

---

[2] On sex-selective procreation, see Gulik 1952:126. Chances of conceiving a male were considered optimal four days after the end of the menses.

Like their parents and grandparents, twentieth-century writers were all too aware of the sexual tensions in the family system, especially problems with arranged marriage. Some of them railed against the double standard permitting men more than one sexual partner, and against patrilocal marriage (residence in the home of the husband's parents after marriage), which invited abuse of young brides by mothers-in-law. Ba Jin's classic novel *Family* (*Jia*) examined these intergenerational problems in excruciating detail. His May Fourth generation envisioned a reformed family (the conjugal family, or *xiao jiating*) in which happily married couples would also serve the nation's state-building modernization efforts. New provisions for divorce in the nationalist New Family Law of 1931, new scruples criticizing concubinage, and new platforms for mass weddings that made marriage affordable for individual couples suggested that these new families might also offer new kinds of gender roles for men and women. But evidence from the Republican period shows that ideas about wives and mothers remained pretty much untouched by reform rhetoric, beyond paying more attention to the education of women and to the importance of wives in promoting their husbands' careers (Glosser 2003). Women writers of the 1920s and 1930s wrote searching stories about the dilemmas of modern selfhood in this era of the new woman, torn by the competing and conflicting demands, hopes, and expectations of the changing political and cultural scene. Their conversations often centered on the question writer Lu Xun posed after viewing Ibsen's play *A Doll's House*: "what happened after Nora left home?" Lu Yin, one of the woman writers who responded directly to Lu Xun's rhetorical question, wrote this (in an imagined letter from correspondence between two girlfriends):

The truth is, the Chinese family system is more than enough to wear down any woman's willpower. I feel that ever since I got married, my old friends have grown fewer and fewer, while the friends I have now are either simply social friends or else relatives with whom I have no real rapport. . . . Oh, Qiongfang, it's pitiful how stupid people really are – before getting married, we dream of living full and satisfying lives after marriage, but in the reality of this flawed world, we wind up with nothing but regrets! (Dooling and Torgeson 1998:153)

Some women writers turned to the countryside and its problems instead of focusing on their own difficulties. Reform-minded intellectuals were fascinated by the rediscovery of folk culture that sometimes challenged the conventions of Confucian family life. In the early twentieth century, peasants in Ding xian, Hebei, were watching folk opera performances celebrating young couples who fell in love and took their own marriage vows, with the young girl initiating the pact. In these rural dramas, the leading characters rejected loveless arranged marriage, suffered long separation, and celebrated the competence and fortitude of wise and resourceful women (Arkush 1989). By contrast, fiction writer Lu Xun constantly portrayed the rural areas of his own homeland, Shaoxing, as a conservative and repressive cultural backwater where women were consigned to lives of sacrifice and subjugation as widows, and where the heartless rituals of Confucianism "ate people" alive. Lu Xun's harsh criticism of Confucian culture and rural backwardness became the dominant voice of the May Fourth Movement and its writers.

Meanwhile, the dangerous and powerful women of the past were recuperated during the twentieth century, as emerging women writers sought to trace their own history in literature. In Beijing (then Beiping) during the 1920s, a highly educated Chinese woman rewrote and published the lives of "four beauties" from Chinese history, including Xi Shi. She had this to say about them and about the meaning of her project:

The rigid standard of our womanhood, which has been regarded as the torchlight and guiding principle of our conduct for ages, has, with the advent of modern civilization, been somewhat relaxed. The Republic has brought marvelous emancipation to our womenfolk, but it remains to be seen whether the women of the old days, in whose very conservatism, fidelity, and virtue lie a wealth of sublime feminine qualities, can still be held as models in our time. ("Preface" in Shu-chiung 1981)

In journals, poems, and biographical sketches from the early twentieth century, women warriors of the past also reappeared in collections in which they were likened to Western heroines, especially Joan of Arc (Judge 2008:143–186).

As Chinese women writers turned increasingly to fiction in the aftermath of May Fourth, Ding Ling published her daring and explicit exploration of female sexual desire in *Miss Sophia's Diary*, which appeared in 1927 (Barlow 1989). The young heroine of her story, who was dying of tuberculosis, was smitten by an overseas Chinese youth whose physical body was his main attraction. Ding Ling dwelled at length on the details: "That tall guy is stunning. For the first time, I found myself really attracted to masculine beauty. I'd never paid much attention before. . . . But today as I watched the tall one, I saw how a man could be cast in a different, a noble, mold" (Barlow 1989:55). Miss Sophia scornfully compared the fine features and finesse of this beautiful man, whose lips she likened to delectable sweets, with the "coarse appearance and rude behavior," the insignificance and clumsiness, of her girlfriend's Chinese boyfriend. This frank physical eroticism, conflated with Westernized charms and cosmopolitan gestures (her foreign lover gave her his namecard; he offered her English lessons), marked the object of her infatuation as someone unlike the Chinese men who surrounded her – one of whom, in particular, was so in love with her that he wept every time she rejected him. While women consciously took up masculine roles – as warriors (Xie Bingying) and as new professionals (Zheng Wang's interviewees) – men in this period were reexamined as sexual beings. As John Yu Zou has pointed out, these new gendered identities or performances nonetheless remained based on romantic heterosexual love: "one of the most compelling metaphors of Chinese modernity is the irresistible love affair between consolidated heterosexual men and transgendered masculine women" (Zou 2000:9).

The political climate for literature and drama about sex grew increasingly unfriendly beyond the cosmopolitan center of Shanghai, as the Japanese invasion and civil war compelled citizens to renounce pleasure and serve the nation. In the countryside around the Communist base areas, cadres organizing support for the revolution professed themselves shocked at peasants' hill songs – the same songs that once delighted female readers of the late Ming as they reclined in their cloistered boudoirs. Hill songs were accordingly reformed and rewritten to serve the cause of the party and the revolution. In the Yan'an base area during the 1940s, the party decreed a new mission for fiction writers, spelled out in 1942 by Mao Zedong in his talks at the Yan'an Forum on Literature and Art (Mao Zedong 1965). Revolutionary writers, Mao insisted, must serve the masses, articulating the concerns of exploited laboring people, especially peasants, and forgetting the urban audience and its commercial markets. Thoroughgoing criticism and scathing ridicule of the "bourgeois" tastes of talented writers like Ding Ling quickly inspired an outpouring of socialist realist work, captured in Ding Ling's own prize-winning novel *The Sun Shines over the San'gang River*, which lionized the character of young male peasants demanding land reform, and consigned female figures to clichéd roles, not unlike the virago or the chastity martyr: the conniving, stingy landlord wife; the peasant daughter sold to feed her family; and so forth. Sex was a topic reserved for vulgarizing the figure of the landlord wife and parodying her relationship with her husband. Politically correct writing silenced or constrained literary expression on sex throughout the Maoist era.

Sexuality came sharply back into focus in Chinese fiction after the Cultural Revolution, however, when the media began circulating conversations about a phenomenon called *yinsheng yangshuai* (literally, the rise of the feminine and the decline of the masculine). This referred most immediately to the "iron girl" images featured at the peak of Cultural Revolution poster art (see Figure 28), but the general point of the conversations was a broader one: that Chinese men had become too weak,

28. Female miner (1979). The caption reads, "I contribute precious deposits to the mother country." This is one of the few images of women engaged in male pursuits still found in 1979 poster art. *Source:* Stefan Landsberger, *Chinese Propaganda Posters, from Revolution to Modernization.* Amsterdam: Pepin Press, 1995, p. 143.

while women had become too strong during the first decades of Communist rule (Zhong 2000). The claim was somewhat misplaced, given the powerful symbolism of "steel and iron" (*gangtie*) in the Mao years and the conflation of the construction of a Maoist citizen and the forging of steel, a transgendered image that featured men as well as women (Zhong 2000:44–45).

Women writers of the 1970s joined these conversations about gender and sexuality, challenging the Maoist line by publishing love stories that made female sex and sexuality explicit. Their writings touched off a storm (Louie 1991), breaking decades of silence in which women were supposed to believe either that liberation had already occurred or that liberation would have to await the emergence of a classless society, making sexual desire and female sexuality taboo subjects, marginalized in the great cause of revolution. What opened the window for the new women's writing – which criticized the Communist system and its failure to address women's issues – was the early 1970s campaign to "criticize Lin Biao, criticize Confucius." This campaign targeted persistent "feudal" practices, including the continuing oppression of women, especially rural women, giving a voice within the party line to women's own concerns. Some women writers took a hostile view of men, comparing Chinese men unfavorably with their Western counterparts. In 1980, Ding Ling's bold experiment with writing female desire reentered public discussion with the publication of an autobiographical short story by Yu Luojin, "A Winter's Fairy Tale" (Honig 1984). The author, twice-divorced, wrote passionately about her fantasies of love, which combined "emotional, intellectual, and physical intimacy," and gave her readers stark descriptions of sex without love that sounded clearly like rape (Honig 1984:259). Critics jumped to censure her, even as they looked back to defend Ding Ling. Ding Ling, critics argued, was progressive in speaking out for women's liberation in her day, when it had not yet been achieved. But, as Yu Luojin's critics put it, after thirty years of revolution, such views had become obsolete, and Ding Ling's Miss Sophia was no longer an appropriate model: "In today's society which has already undergone a radical transformation, the thinking, pursuits and spiritual life of youth have also changed" (Honig 1984:265).

That was the early 1980s. In the early 1990s, by contrast, female desire became big business in Chinese publishing, especially with the publication of novels by the Shanghai writers Wei Hui and her counterpart, Mian Mian. Their "body writing," aimed at China's own Generation X ("*xin xin renlei*," or "new new humans"), offered elaborately detailed physical accounts of sex acts and sensual desire, overlain with dark innuendos: impotence, promiscuity, seductive foreigners, and commodified bodies (Sheldon Lu 2007:53–67). Like seventeenth-century writer Li Yu's *Carnal Prayer Mat*, their books pressed sexual writing to extremes; unlike Li Yu, however, the authors had no interest in humor or satire. Their heroines were seriously obsessed by the consumer society and culture that surrounded them. They were after whatever they could get, however they could get it, in the global sex market.

In the face of these fierce new expressions of female desire, and with the repudiation of the Mao years, a new model of Chinese masculinity, the so-called real man (*nanzihan*), also entered the lexicon. This was partly a backlash against the gender-egalitarian language and imagery of the Mao years, which insisted on referring to both men and women as "comrade" (*tongzhi*), prefaced only by the gendered pronoun *nan* or *nü*. Xueping Zhong (2000) also suggests that the quest for new manhood became entangled with ideas about returning to China's cultural roots and saving the "race" (*zhong*) that were historically patriarchal, presuming male descent lines. In any case, phrases like *yinghanzi* had already been picked up by male writers by the mid-1980s, engaging questions of male sexuality "for the first time in Chinese literature" (Louie 1991:164–165). Not surprisingly, in the global context of this new literature, concerns about the emasculation of Chinese men appeared in the popular press in articles by pundits, one of whom warned of the "eunuchization" (*taijian hua*) of Chinese men (Louie 1991:166). In modeling alternative male sexualities, contemporary writers drew deeply on paradigms of *yin* and *yang* and invoked notions of containment and self-control (*keji fuli*) found in early Confucian writings on men's health, as well as Daoist prescriptions for nourishing bodily energy by avoiding ejaculation (Louie 1991:177). They also harked back to the self-enforced celibacy of heroes of the epic novel *All Men Are Brothers*, for whom (in the words of Kam Louie) "sexual abstinence became the only proof of their manhood" (Louie 1991:173; citing Hsia 1968:75–114). One result was a "homosocial masculine ideal" that was "hierarchical, decorous in terms of righteousness, and always self-controlled" (Zarrow 2003:355). Sheldon Lu has associated these new notions of masculinity with a "political and libidinal 'economics of deficits'" in which stories about the male self devolve around celibacy, masturbation, impotence, and solitude (Lu 2007:38).

Writers in China have constantly returned to questions of gender and sexuality, in language that is deeply informed by notions from classical medicine but also – in the twentieth century – by the global discourses of modern science and sexology. Historians of gender and sexuality must turn to fiction and drama for the evidence we need to do our work.

9 Sexuality and the Other

The People's Government is really something
No longer do we comb up our hair but wear it in a bun
With our headdress removed, we are free and easy
With flowers in our hair, oh so pretty.
Local customs are really no good
The headdress and long vest, no sleeves for one's arms
In this new era we must change our style
Three bamboo sticks inside the headdress
A headscarf made from an array of colors
It's unattractive and must be reformed.

Propaganda folksong, Hui'an, Fujian (Sara Friedman
2006:259–260)

His clothing was crisply ironed and neat from top to bottom, and
he'd applied lots of hair gel, too, so he looked like a brand-new,
furled umbrella. Those eyes of his seemed like the epicenter of
his body and all his energy emanated from there. A white man's
eyes.

Wei Hui, *Shanghai Baby* (2001:29–30)

Encountering an unfamiliar culture, the outsider looks for difference. Nowhere is difference more easily apprehended than in the arenas of gender and sexuality. In any cross-cultural encounter, gender roles and sexuality supply a medium for clarifying and symbolizing the essential cultural differences that separate "us" from "them." So sex – that most intimate of acts – is ironically one of the first things we think of when we imagine the remote Other. Imperial expansion aimed at economic or political conquest therefore also, and inevitably, negotiates gender relations (Stoler 1991). In the history of Western colonialism, the gender models at the civilizing center were binary and heteronormative. Encountering Chinese culture, Europeans asked: What makes women women, and what makes men men, in this place? The civilizing projects of China's own late imperial government, and of China's contemporary Communist state, posed the same questions on the borderlands and in China's heartland itself. The effect of civilizing projects, in general, has been to masculinize the dominant metropole and feminize the colonized Other, as in Wei Hui's *Shanghai Baby*, quoted above. But gender bending and confusion can also arise. Who is liberated, who is modern, who is moral, who is perverse? Cross-cultural encounters also pose these questions and demand answers.

Consider the late imperial program to incorporate southwestern borderlands in Guizhou and Yunnan into the regular bureaucratic provincial administration, a civilizing project that lasted several centuries. Collecting intelligence on the subjects of this civilizing project, the Qing court commissioned albums of illustrated ethnographic reporting on each of the eighty-two non-Han peoples in Guizhou province. Laura Hostetler's analysis of these eighteenth-century albums shows that the illustrator, and the text, paid more attention to courtship and marriage than to anything else. For court officials drafting policies to bring those territories under direct administrative control, family relationships and gender roles were a focal point of concern (Deal and Hostetler 2006: xlii–xliv). In contemporary China, gendered strategies in minority areas have varied, depending on whether the government was trying to suppress or preserve ethnic identities. In Tibet and in Xinjiang, for example, where the Chinese government sought to suppress ethnic identity, the main targets of central government state policy were religious institutions and practices dominated by men – Llamaist monasteries, Muslim family law (Dautcher 2009, Makley 2007). By contrast, in the Miao homelands of the southwest, where ethnic identities were nurtured and protected, the government has made Miao women into cultural icons who preserve and perform ethnic difference (Schein 2000).

Whatever the policy or strategy, and whatever the colonial regime, sexuality is clearly judged a crucial arena for identifying, articulating, imagining, performing, or suppressing difference in any cross-cultural encounter. We can dramatize this point by comparing illustrations from three roughly contemporaneous civilizing projects: a British caricature of Lord Macartney's mission to the Qianlong Emperor's court in 1793 (Figure 29), a Chinese album painting of local customs in a minority area of China's southwest frontier (Figure 30), and a Chinese gazetteer woodcut print showing the customs of Taiwan's indigenous people (Figure 31).

The drawing depicted in Figure 29 by late-eighteenth-century British artist James Gillray (1756–1815), titled "The Reception of the

29. James Gillray. "A caricature on Lord Macartney's Embassy to China." Hand-colored etching (s. 12 × 15 7/8 in. [31.7 × 40.2 cm.]). Published by H. Humphrey, London, September 14, 1792 (public domain). *Source:* John Merson, *Roads to Xanadu: East and West in the Making of the Modern World*. London: Weidenfeld and Nicolson, 1989, p. 145.

Diplomatique & his Suite at the Court of Pekin,"[1] is a caricature of Lord Macartney's imagined reception at the court of Qianlong. It appeared in London in 1792, a week before Macartney departed on his mission. Lord Macartney, sent by King George with a formal request that China open its ports to British trade (a request that the Qianlong Emperor was to dismiss categorically), won fame for his alleged refusal to *ketou* (kneel and then fall prostrate in a ritual sequence) before the emperor, as required by Chinese imperial court etiquette. Gillray's drawing, however, lampoons the British attempt to engage the Chinese court in any level of diplomatic exchange. He depicts Macartney kneeling absurdly before a dissolute Qing emperor, who is drawn à la Turque, in a classic Orientalist pose. The emperor (Qianlong), reclining slothfully on cushions, wearing

[1] I am indebted to Henrietta Harrison and Mark Elliott for assistance in identifying this cartoon.

30. "Hua (Flowery) Miao" (album leaf), dated sometime after 1797. *Source:* David M. Deal and Laura Hostetler, trans. *The Art of Ethnography: A Chinese "Miao Album."* Seattle: University of Washington Press, 2006, p. 26.

funny shoes, and smoking a water pipe, is palpably soft, weak, and foolish – a perfect foil for the cartoonist's Macartney. Gillray was convinced that the mission was an act of folly, and he wanted his audience to apprehend the ridiculousness of Macartney's obsequious bow. But Gillray, in his zeal to spoof Macartney's mission, unwittingly conveyed other civilizing subtexts. The Chinese emperor's pose as a decadent Oriental ruler also hints at his sex life. He must have a harem, because there are no women in sight. Women are shut up and cannot be viewed in public in a culture where they are reserved to serve the pleasure of men. And hovering behind the emperor we see a palace eunuch – a desexed man who reminds the viewer on another level that sexual indulgence (many women) is accompanied by sexual perversion (castration and paranoia about sexual access).

In the second illustration, depicted in Figure 30, we see a Han Chinese artist's depiction of courtship practices among the so-called Flowery Miao. The appended description begins with the following poem: "Dressing at dawn, she inserts a new wooden comb / And wraps colorful clothing around her body. / Blowing reeds, shaking bells – sound, movement, harmonize. / Strangers dance in moonlight. Young girls cherish spring-time." Similar themes in other album leaves feature the casual sex customary among other Miao peoples, showing women ringing bells while men play reed flutes, men and women mingling while dancing around a pole or picnicking in the woods, and even (in one case) a new year festival in which women were carried off on the backs of their suitors. Most shocking to elite Han Chinese sensibilities were accounts of betrothal rituals that *followed* sexual intercourse or even the birth of a child, carefully detailed with ethnographic precision by the text's authors (Deal and Hostetler 2006:xliii–xliv).

Echoing the British interest in costume and civilization, Chinese travelers and officials who began the process of colonizing Taiwan in the eighteenth century took time to catalog both the dress and the work habits of indigenous peoples, with a focus on gender roles. The drawing depicted in Figure 31 conveys a doubly negative message, with a bare-breasted woman and a bare-chested man working side by side pounding rice. Emma Teng, who has studied these and similar texts, points out that such illustrations were confined to the so-called savage peoples who were least influenced by Han Chinese custom (Teng 2004:152–156). Other drawings show indigenous people whose customs more closely resembled the Han conventions in dividing men's and women's labor, by way of pointing to their relatively "civilized" condition.

In colonial encounters, then, sex and gender roles become a powerful proxy for who "we" or "they" *really* are: "we" are normal, "they" are perverse or exotic. In the Jesuit encounter with Chinese culture in the seventeenth century, for example, Jesuit observers were upset by the widespread casual sex between men that they encountered in the social lives of the Chinese literati with whom they consorted, and many Jesuits composed long tracts condemning "sodomy" in China, a kind of measure of immorality that they used for other purposes to promote and justify their civilizing mission (Hinsch 1990:1–2; Vitiello 2000:251–253). Then there are counterexamples in which the colonizer imagines the sexual world of the Other to be better than his own. The mid-twentieth-century Dutch sinologist Robert van Gulik, for instance, was charmed by what he viewed as the uninhibited sex lives of the "ancient Chinese," and he used his research on Chinese sexuality to criticize Victorian sexuality, publishing his monumental study of Chinese erotica to make the point (Furth 1994). Gulik was captivated by books advising Chinese men that because women had nothing to gladden their hearts but sexual intercourse (this was Gulik's understanding, at any rate): "it is the duty of every enlightened householder to have a thorough knowledge of the Art of the Bedchamber, so that he can give complete satisfaction

31. "Pounding Rice," from the *Gazetteer of Zhuluo County* [Taiwan] (1717). *Source:* Emma Jinhua Teng, *Taiwan's Imagined Geography: Chinese Colonial Travel Writing and Pictures, 1683–1895.* Cambridge: Harvard University Press, 2004, p. 154. Teng notes that the author of this particular gazetteer was inclined to view the indigenous people's "savage customs" as benign examples of life in a primitive utopia (2004:74).

32. "Afterwards." *Source:* R. H. van Gulik, *Sexual Life in Ancient China.* Leiden: E. J. Brill, 1961, pl. XIX.

to his wives and concubines every time he copulates with them" (Gulik 1951:107).

Gulik was also struck by the frank homoeroticism he found in Chinese prints and drawings, which he collected assiduously and studied with fascination. For Gulik, the message of the colonial encounter was that "we" are uptight, "they" are liberated.

Perhaps the most potent sexualized emblems of a civilizing project, which we have encountered in previous chapters, come from the Manchu conquest that established the Qing dynasty in 1644. During the first four decades of their rule, the Manchus embarked on a civilizing mission of their own, focused on the performance of male and female roles in the Han Chinese population. On one level, this was a move to make

Han bodies signal submission to the Manchu conquest by requiring Han Chinese men to groom themselves like Manchu men and Han Chinese women like Manchu women. In a violent and exhaustive series of local campaigns, Han Chinese men were forced to abandon the topknot hairstyle that was the very essence of Han Chinese male identity, shave their foreheads, and grow a braid down the back – the Manchu style – signaling with their bodies their submission to Qing rule. (The late Frederic Wakeman, in a rhetorical coup, referred to this Manchu conquest policy as "tonsorial castration" [Wakeman 1985:I:649].) At the same time, the Manchus also banned footbinding among Chinese women because Manchu women never bound their feet. This policy they never managed to enforce, with complicated psychological consequences in the early Qing period ("men submit, women resist"). In that historical moment, bound feet became a marker of Han Chinese identity and resistance against foreign conquest, an emblem of Ming loyalism, and a sign of women's steadfast and superior moral strength (Mann 2002:437–439). A colonial encounter, in other words, can rapidly shift the meanings of customary practices and transform them into performances of cultural identity. What counts as "backward" or "conservative," after all, if the question is about civilization or barbarism?

Compounding the complexity of the Manchu conquest moment, as Mark Elliott has shown, was the Manchu concern to preserve a distinct cultural identity of their own, which led them to focus on certain gender issues within the Manchu population itself. As he puts it, the distinctive ideals for Manchu women in the Qing period tell us a lot "about the importance of women in the construction of ethnicity historically" (Elliott 1999:38). For the Qing court, for example, rewarding Manchu chaste widows alongside Han Chinese chaste widows signaled the court's willingness to let Manchu women embrace Han Chinese female virtues and to publicly recognize them for it. By contrast, the court never recognized Manchu men for the display of Han-style masculine virtue, especially in scholarship or in filiality. Instead, Manchu males were held to the old martial ideals of the Manchu Bannerman's "manly virtue" (*haha erdemu*): riding, shooting with bow and arrow, and living simply and unpretentiously (Elliott 1999:64). Similarly, Qing policy affecting Manchu women by no means aimed at their acculturation and assimilation into the Han population. On the contrary, like colonial regimes of Europe, the Manchus strictly controlled the marriage and fertility of Manchu women by requiring that they marry within the Banner system (Elliott 1999:69–71).

The gendered configuration of Manchu policies, carefully tailored to fit males and females of Manchu and Han populations, merely underscores the centrality of gender and sexuality in moments of conquest and colonial encounters. Still another example is the Qing practice of marriage exchange, in which imperial princesses were sent as consorts to live in Mongolia, especially Outer Mongolia, where their presence could serve a crucial diplomatic function (Rawski 1991:177–178, Rawski 1998:146–152). By contrast with the strict rules limiting Han Chinese and Manchu intermarriage among commoners, imperial intermarriage across ethnic lines served as a tool for extending the multiethnic empire beyond the borders of China proper. Finally, we should take note of the Qing empire's other imperial civilizing missions, documented both in fiction and in travel accounts from the Qing period. As we have seen, travelers to Taiwan in the Qing period (who, following the rules of the Chinese family system, were almost entirely male) displayed a deep fascination with sexuality, both in representations of indigenous "savage women" who were accessible and promiscuous and in critiques of indigenous men, whom they criticized as lazy and dependent (Teng 2004). As C. Patterson Giersch has observed, "In both European and Qing empires, indigenous women were represented as symbols of sexual conquest whereas indigenous men were portrayed as weak and feminine" (Giersch 2006:75). Giersch, who studied Qing expansion into Yunnan province during the early nineteenth century, noticed that Han travelers dubbed one ethnic group the "Water Baiyi," a label associated with drawings of members of this group that featured a bare-breasted woman bathing in a stream in the company of a man (Giersch 2006:75). Both the public bathing and the scanty clothing triggered titillation and shock in a Han Chinese reader; the level of civilization of the Water Baiyi did not need further elaboration.

In the late-eighteenth-century Chinese novel *A Country Codger Puts His Words Out to Sun (Yesou puyan)* – encountered in Chapter 8 – the Han Chinese protagonist travels to the southwest, where he predictably encounters sexual practices that he deems uncivilized and un-Confucian, highlighting the propriety of his own values (which some readers might have questioned in light of the pornographic content of the book). When his Miao informant (a "local wise man" [*tushenglao*]) protests that the Han Chinese "take so many precautions that the desires and longings men and women have for each other have no way to be let out" and defends "local customs" (permitting a wife to kiss and touch a male visitor to her home, sex between men and women without their parents' consent, and individual mate choice), the protagonist and others firmly disagree and dismiss the Miao informant's views as nonsense (McMahon 1988:46). The same novel elaborates the civilizing impact of Han Chinese culture on the Miao, not only as "reformed" gender relations (young couples start singing verses from the *Classic of Poetry* to one another) but also in a vignette featuring the hero's sexual encounter with a Miao girl who is "sterile" (a *shi nü*, or "stone woman"). His masculine *qi* and his *yang* energy not only awaken her sexual desire but even make her fertile by stimulating her menstrual period (see Martin Huang 2003:90). In this work of fiction, the grand civilizing mission of the "great man" (*da zhangfu*) once again casts the ethnic minorities as feminine and unlettered. In a final elegant touch, mentioned in Chapter 8, the author takes one of his Han heroes to Europe, where he embarks on a conversion program aimed at reforming sexual practices among certain members of Europe's royal families, who are taught how to time sexual intercourse according to the menstrual cycle rather than their own desires, to produce more sons (Martin Huang 2003:91).[2]

The bound foot as a marker of the Other

Western traders, missionaries, and diplomats were uniformly dismayed by what they viewed as the oppression of women in Asian cultures. Their sentiments were rooted in early-nineteenth-century values articulated by French utopian thinkers, especially Charles Fourier, who famously wrote: "As a general thesis: *Social progress ... occurs by virtue of the progress of women toward liberty, and social decline by virtue of decreases in the liberty of women*" (Leslie Goldstein 1982:100, italics original). The Chinese empire's decline, in other words, was clear to foreign observers the minute they saw women with bound feet. The bound foot was an uncontrovertible symbol of the oppression of Chinese women, which made it the emblem of the backwardness of the Chinese empire, and the ultimate sign of the uncivilized character of the Chinese people. In that guise, women's bound feet were also an inspiration and a justification for conquest (Zito 2006).

As Patricia Ebrey (1999) has pointed out, bound feet were not always regarded as an object of scorn or disgust by Western observers. Criticism sharpened in the nineteenth century, however, as observers shifted their focus from fashion and custom to pain and suffering, and to the oppression and control of females, especially female children. The rise of scientific medical views of the body, later bolstered by the new technology of the X-ray, revealed the extent of mutilation in footbinding

---

[2] In early nineteenth-century novels, fears of European imperialism replaced the heroic Confucian expansionism so robustly captured in *Country Codger*, with syphilis and opium both cast as dread "foreign diseases" (Martin Huang 2003:90–93).

and dramatized the resulting pain. This fed other concerns about child abuse fostered by the growing attention to childhood and childrearing in Euro–North American culture. All of this was ample fuel for the zeal that energized the colonial powers, as well as Christian missionaries and, ultimately, Chinese reformers at the end of the nineteenth century.

Current scholarship has been sharply revisionist in its account of the meanings of footbinding in the Chinese cultural context. Dorothy Ko (1997b), as we have seen, has stressed that bound feet stood for civility in late imperial times, part of the essential adornment reserved for the most advanced cultures, and that even the shaping of the foot itself was part of the styling of proper attire. In other words, far from representing a mutilation of the body, bound feet were considered part of the decoration of the body. In other work (2005), Ko has likened footbinding to a kind of cosmetic surgery whose appeal was enhanced by ordinary people's ordinary aspirations: the desire to be fashionable, to attract a good husband for a daughter, to be respectable, to be proper and refined, and to be correct and fit in. These are all reasons why a mother wanted to bind her daughter's feet. To be sure, young girls who were being prepared for work as courtesans or prostitutes had their feet bound with sexual or erotic appeal in mind, and in that sense, their bodies were marketed by pimps as commodities. But not so the vast majority of ordinary commoners. They were merely striving for respectability. So despite fantasies about the eroticism of bound feet, in cultural context they were viewed in much more complicated and even mundane ways. For example, the shoes embroidered to fit the feet were a display of a young woman's talent and creativity (Ko 2001). Moreover, the foot itself was always to be concealed, not only inside a shoe and bindings but also beneath a loose, long garment. In fact, concealment was the key to the erotic and aesthetic meanings of the bound foot, as shown in the very provocative drawing of a courtesan in Figure 14, above.

When foreigners insisted on X-rays to reveal the contortions that produced bound feet – when, in other words, the foot was no longer concealed, but open to view down to the bone – the "aura" and allure of concealment ended, and with it the mystique of fashion, status, and propriety that had attached itself to bound feet (see Figure 33). At the same time, loud cries condemning the weakness of Chinese women and the need to mobilize them for full participation in nation-building made footbinding appear backward as well as oppressive to patriotic reform-minded Chinese. Upper-class parents in droves refused to bind their daughters' feet, and within a few decades, bound feet had vanished from the urban elite, to be replaced by the pointy-toed heels preferred by Western female slaves to fashion. In the countryside where urban fashion and modern

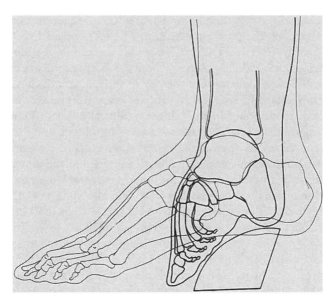

33. "A Bound Foot." *Source:* John K. Fairbank and Edwin O. Reis-
chauer, *China: Tradition and Transformation.* Boston: Houghton Mif-
flin, 1978, p. 142.

nationalist consciousness made no impact, it was left to the nationalists
or, later, the Chinese Communists to finish off footbinding, sometimes
with coercive measures.

In an age of Botox, breast implants, tattoos, and body piercing, we
can readily see that there are more ways to understand footbinding than
to condemn it as a sign of backwardness and women's oppression. That
insight alerts us again to the powerful relationships that dictate taste
and sex-gender performance in any culture. Reviewing the history of
civilizing projects, in other words, makes us ask, what counts as backward
or oppressive, and who gets to decide?

Change in the twentieth century

The relationship between gender, sexuality, and ethnicity in imperial
China closely resembles the processes and practices familiar in colonial
encounters everywhere. In the case of China's "internal colonialism,"
however, the civilizing process had its own particularly Chinese features.
One of these, rooted in mid-Qing practice, was the universalizing impe-
tus of Qing rule, which sought to hold everyone in the empire to the same

standards of civilized conduct, including proper roles for men and women (Sommer 2000).[3] Like their Qing predecessors, twentieth-century officials had similar universalizing goals, and they were well aware of the extensive local variation in gender performance and sexual practice that challenged or flouted the rules and conventions of patrilineal kinship. Certain alternative marriage forms, some of which arguably favored the emotional and personal interests of women and their loved ones, were roundly opposed by the Republican and Communist governments in their zeal to promote "modern" marriage. A survey of local customs compiled in 1922 reveals astonishment in the researcher's account of the local customs in Shunde, the area near Canton where "delayed transfer marriage" thrived:

When two women live together, although they cannot be like a man and a woman in every respect, in fact they do enjoy the pleasures of a man and a woman. Some say they use rubbing pressure, others say they use a clever mechanism [i.e., dildo]. These kinds of words are crude and difficult for highly educated men to discuss. Such couples will even select a female heir to inherit their property. Later this female heir will likewise sign a "golden lotus contract" like a daughter-in-law, just as if they had a blood relationship. Indeed but it is strange! (Hu Pu'an 1968:2:34)

Elite condescension quickly marginalized these local practices, which vanished from urban areas by the time of the 1949 Revolution. Delayed transfer marriage nonetheless survived into the 1970s in a few isolated communities, roundly scorned by residents of more economically developed areas (Siu 1990).

In urban China, where twentieth-century reformers and revolutionaries prevailed, the target of civilizing projects became the joint family system. In social Darwinist discourse, the joint family ruled by male elders represented an impediment to China's progress, which required the liberation of the energies of youth and women to build a strong nation. The civilized modern ideal, as we have seen, was the "small family" – a conjugal unit established through free mate choice in a neolocal marriage (Glosser 2003). The Republican government's promotion of the small family ideal was in part a response to long-term campaigns by reformist Christian missionaries, especially female missionaries, whose "imperial evangelism" (Hunter 1984) aimed to bring Chinese women, feet unbound, out of the home and into a public sphere where (among other things) missionaries' own Christian teachings might convert them. Many Christian missionaries noted that changing women's family roles

---

[3] Chen Hongmou's eighteenth-century campaigns to promote chaste widowhood and eradicate matrilocal marriage and the levirate among non-Han peoples show how these policies energized an especially effective Qing official (Rowe 2001:312, 424–425).

posed new problems, because Chinese culture offered no moral guidelines for respectable women to follow once they left home. Luella Miner
worried that Chinese women would need to "internalize conventions of
control" in their new sphere and suggested that Western women might
be able to teach them these new conventions. Like many other female
missionaries at the turn of the century, Miner was worried about sex and
adolescent girls (Hunter 1984:175). But this worry was conflated with
another concern: missionary schools could not risk the taint of promiscuity. The result was that missionary schools delivered a heavy dose of
moral support for marriage and compliant wives, and even unmarried
female missionaries who prided themselves on their own independence
found themselves instructing Chinese women to marry, have children,
and retreat into domesticity.

Yet the speed with which urban Chinese women embraced new roles
defied the concerns and correctives of missionary civilizing projects. Jane
Hunter suggests that this flexible adaptation to new roles had historical
and cultural roots of its own in China, where women were reared to
behave appropriately *according to* the roles they were assigned. Hunter
cites Mary Rankin's analysis of the path of the early-twentieth-century
revolutionary Qiu Jin, whose short life took her through a dizzying
sequence of disparate roles, from cloistered young lady to wife and
mother, from there to studies in Japan, and finally, to revolutionary martyrdom: "A woman who succeeded in breaking away from family bonds
and becoming a teacher, doctor, revolutionary, etc., was . . . expected
to act in accord with well-defined concepts of behavior. . . . When a
woman did enter one of these roles, she also assumed their normally
male characteristics" (Rankin 1975:64, quoted in Hunter 1984:263).

Chinese reformers and foreign missionaries may have agreed on a
model for a heteronormative nuclear family, but their interactions also
produced confusion about gender roles, particularly about notions of
masculinity and femininity. Mrinalini Sinha's work on colonial Bengal
(1995:18–19 passim) has shown how the late-nineteenth-century ideal of
the "manly Englishman" was constructed in opposition to an "effeminate
Bengali *babu*." Hunter's study of American women missionaries in turn-
of-the-century China points to a different kind of "gender confusion"
around what were seen by Chinese as the "man-like" ways of American women, and the missionaries' corresponding perception of Chinese
men as weak, effeminate, and not sexually threatening. To Chinese men,
Hunter observes, American women appeared desexed ("neither one nor
the other" [1984:214]), not only because of their free movement in public
space but also because of their unbound feet, pale hair – especially grey

hair – and long noses (1984:204–216). These observations about gender confusion resulting from colonial encounters and civilizing projects
dramatize what many scholars have now discovered: that these are the
richest areas – the most illuminating historical moments – for research on
sexuality in history, cracking open identities that are erased or concealed,
and defamiliarizing familiar evidence.

In its own civilizing project dedicated to "equality between men and
women" (*nan nü ping deng*), the Maoist Chinese Communist government brought women fully into the productive labor force alongside
men. Yet this civilizing project presumed a model of universal heterosexual marriage and reproduction that retained the household as the basic
unit of residence and livelihood. Family production remained based on
a division of labor by sex and age; patrilocal marriage and household
production secured male rights to land and women. Similar goals per-
vaded state policy in minority areas. The case of Hui'an women (in the
propaganda song that begins this chapter) shows the Chinese Communist government deciding vigorously what counts as backward. Tracing
the history of government policies toward Hui'an women also shows that
judgments about backwardness, as in the case of footbinding, are relative
and malleable, subject to other political and cultural pressures. During
the 1950s, for example, the women of Hui'an, Fujian, became the target
of intense efforts to eliminate "feudal" conditions in the peripheral parts
of China's eighteen provinces. What Hui'an women wore and how Hui'an
women worked were cited as dramatic emblems of backward practices
that hindered the building of a modern nation. A modern nation, in
the Communists' view, had to mobilize women for productive economic
activity outside the home. Women's rising economic power, so this argument went, would then also improve their status: another key goal of
the modern state. The large and cumbersome headdress that served as a
hallmark of the Hui'an woman of the southeast coast made an arresting
symbol of feudalism: it was alien and exotic to most Han Chinese, and
it was clearly an impediment to economic productivity outside the home
and an embarrassment to modern personhood as envisioned by China's
youthful women cadres.

As Sara Friedman observes, the Communist Party's attempts in the
1950s to eliminate traditional Hui'an women's headdresses, and its campaigns against female suicide in Hui'an, balanced "the state's commitment to women's liberation and its equally compelling support for rural
men and patrilineal families." Those headdresses and the suicide pacts,
along with the *dui pnua* (sisterhood) bonds they affirmed, undermined
familial control. So in preventing young women from taking their own

lives, the government was also stabilizing and reinforcing patrilineal families (Friedman 2006:84). The Communist reform agenda in Hui'an extended to other aspects of local women's culture as well. Women's collective suicide by drowning to resist marriage, for example, was a local "evil custom" celebrated in Hui'an songs and stories. This made good fodder for the Communist campaign against arranged marriage. Equally inviting as a "feudal" target was a form of Hui'an marriage in which the bride declined to move into her husband's home (the custom dubbed "extended natal residence marriage" or "delayed transfer marriage" by anthropologists). Although some scholars regard this practice as one that empowered brides, the Communists classified it as a problem for the heteronormative "modern" marriage form licensed by the government. Despite the fact that Hui'an people were officially classified as Han according to the ethnic categories drawn up in the early years of the People's Republic, such flamboyantly non-Han customs doubly stigmatized Hui'an women: Hui'an customs were both "feudal" (backward) and also "deviant" (departures from the Han patrilocal norm).

Yet all of this opposition and criticism vanished in the 1990s during the post-Mao reform era. Under the new reform policies, Hui'an women were suddenly called on to retrieve their traditional clothing from storage and revive the customs that displayed those exotic hats. The rationale for the policies was unapologetic: Han Chinese tourists loved exotic local customs, especially those involving women, and tourism was profitable. In other words, by making ethnic culture a commodity that tourists could purchase, the government also made female bodies in ethnic communities objects of new interest (Sara Friedman 2006). The Hui'an case shows how deeply questions of gender and sexuality figure in encounters with the Other, and how unstable gendered meanings can be in a volatile political environment.

Emma Teng has pointed out that Qing representations of aboriginal women emerge in new forms in modern-day tourism to Taiwan, with dance shows featuring indigenous girls, who also figure prominently as prostitutes in the Taiwan sex industry (Teng 2004:193). The rise of sex tourism in reform-era China has likewise situated minority women in frameworks of "internal Orientalism" (Schein 2000:100–131). Artists, photographers, journalists, ethnographers, officials, and tourists all flock to Guizhou province's Miao villages to see and capture images of women in ethnic (*minzu*) costume. These tourists and visitors are primarily male, and the messages they bring and take away vary from erotic fascination to paternalistic protectionism, all of it focused on Miao women, who are alternately portrayed as voluptuous and enticing or childlike and close to nature. In the ultimate commercialization of these tourist markets, local

Han Chinese women dress up as Miao to earn the money that Miao women increasingly scorn (Hyde 2007).

What makes the Hui'an women's position different from that of the Miao women described by Louisa Schein is the fact that Hui'an women identify strongly as Han and are still more reluctant to act seductively and perform publicly to meet the demands of the tourist industry (Sara Friedman 2006:227–228). Moreover, in the post-Mao era, women who "wear the headscarf" are criticized from all sides: as "feudal" (i.e., close-minded and backward, and, perhaps, excessively modest) by women who do not, and as chaotic and disruptive in their sexual behavior by men (Sara Friedman 2006:238–243). Gendered images themselves, in other words, have a multivalent quality that eludes efforts by the contemporary government to control and contain sexual performance and its meanings. The instability and fluidity of these images are powerful challenges to government "civilizing" projects aimed at securing a stable heteronormative family system.

China's recent history of cross-cultural encounters underscores the salience of sexuality and gender in defining the Other. No wonder changes in gender roles and sexuality have been central to China's twentieth-century transformations. Given the depth and range of the central government's power since 1950, the contemporary state's intense commitment to heteronormative marriage and reproduction is now displayed in projects, like the one-child policy, whose efficacy late imperial Chinese rulers would have envied.

Conclusion: Gender, sexuality, and citizenship

Of course, there are some men and women who, for the sake of idle pleasures, are unwilling to take on the responsibility of having children; such people should be educated in socialist morals, to make them understand that bringing up children is a parental responsibility, and is also every citizen's duty to the state.

Zhongguo funü (Women of China), 1955 (Evans 1995:368)

Sex is a critical site where the normalizations of cultural citizenship are being reformulated. If the passion to pursue the meaningfulness of sexual desire propels Chinese men into transnational networks, it also lies at the heart of cultural citizenship. Cultural citizenship, perhaps more so than legal subjectivity or theories of psychological personality, establishes proper and improper sex in postsocialist China.

Lisa Rofel (2007:95)

Citizens of the People's Republic of China, no longer subjects of the old imperial regime, embody notions of gender and sexuality with deep roots in the past. Even in the gay community that has grown in major urban centers, powerful affinities for family and kinship continue to dominate nascent sexual identities. The most important link that embodied citizens share with their late imperial ancestors lies in the connection between childrearing and loyalty to the government. The Qing government installed Mencian Confucianism as the prevailing orthodoxy, and it was Mencius who declared that not having a son was the most unfilial act of all. A son's foremost obligation to his parents was to have a son of his own to continue the family line. Similarly, to "seek a loyal subject in a filial son" was a maxim of late imperial governance, and the Qing court campaigned relentlessly to anchor all male subjects firmly in families in which they could be properly socialized as orderly subjects. China's

Communist government remains firmly committed to family-based citizenship, particularly in the post-Mao era.

In a family-based polity, childbearing and childrearing are the tasks of mothers, whose privileged role was vaunted and protected by late imperial policies. The Qing court bestowed honorific titles on mothers and grandmothers of successful officials. Literati memoirs never failed to pay homage to the guidance and sacrifice of mothers. And the vast medical corpus devoted to "women's medicine" elaborated the formulae and protocols for conceiving, carrying, and delivering healthy babies, especially boys (Yi-Li Wu 2010). A mother's moral character as well as her education shaped her ability to nurture a fetus, as detailed prescriptions for *taijiao* (fetal instruction) show. In that sense, a woman's fidelity to her husband's family was an integral part of her pledge of loyalty to the government. It bound her to bear and rear the offspring of the next generation, to carry on the family line and supply subjects loyal to the state – or, failing that, to supply her husband with a concubine who would bear sons for her, or see to the adoption of an heir in the event of her husband's untimely death.

During the twentieth century, the shift in gender relations signaled by the entry of women en masse into schools, jobs, politics, and intellectual life outside the home immediately called into question the relationship between motherhood and the "new woman." New conceptions of love and marriage pointed *toward* individual self-fulfillment and satisfaction, and *away* from serving parents, in-laws, and (by extension) the state. At the same time, no thought was given to replacing women's labor (reproductive and productive) in the household economy, once honored by the imperial regime. Opportunities for female employment outside the home remained limited by the slow development of industrial technologies outside a few major cities, especially Shanghai, until the post-Mao era. Schools for girls lacked female teachers, making parents extremely reluctant to release their daughters to the suspect supervision of young "modern" men. Yet from the point of view of young women, the signals in the early twentieth century all spelled excitement. From fashion to travel and from military service to the new professions, opportunities for young women in urban centers exploded. Even in the countryside, labor contractors working for urban textile factories could recruit handy numbers of young female workers by promising their parents some meager income, and young women, for their part, were not clamoring to stay at home.

The movement of women outside the home, begun in the late Qing reforms and continuing throughout the twentieth century, was clearly the most cataclysmic historical change in China's sex-gender system. But, as we have seen, fiction of the early Republic returns constantly to Nora's problem in the Ibsen play, *A Doll's House*: once a woman leaves home, then what? Women "emancipated" by natural feet and public schooling were left to invent their own lives, with luck, using resources and support from natal families or a spouse or partner. Survival for single women was difficult, if not impossible, a lesson repeated constantly in lurid tales of harassment and suicide from the contemporary press (Goodman 2005). During the Maoist period, when women's domestic roles were devalued and they were called on to be "just like men," the double burden on urban and rural women alike went virtually unremarked. In the post-Mao period, women's domestic roles have resurfaced in political discourse, as women are enjoined to withdraw from the workforce and return to wifely and motherly duties. Almost never do we hear a celebration of independent single womanhood.

So if the connections between parenting and loyalty to the government were firmly fixed in the nineteenth century, did twentieth-century changes dislodge those connections at all? This book has suggested that, far from being dislodged, links between parenting and loyalty have remained firm and even strengthened over the course of the last century. In part this is due to changes in the reach of the state. Technologies for disseminating propaganda, disciplining subjects, improving neonatal care and reproductive health, deploying labor, and counting and registering the population all expanded in scope and efficiency throughout the twentieth century. When in 1949 the new Communist government moved to organize rural and urban populations under the combined control of party and administrative personnel, the power of these technologies was brought to bear at all levels of the society. As recent research by Gail Hershatter has shown, moreover, a key to the staying power of that pervasive reach was the government's success in reaching and organizing women (Hershatter 2002, 2011). In that sense, the platform first articulated by Mao ("women hold up half the sky") was both an ideology and an organization crucial to Communism's long-term success. Because the Chinese Communist Party (CCP) left the basic structures of the family system solidly in place, the government could continue to work through kinship and household structures to deploy its new technologies. Just how effective and pervasive the family or household system is may be seen in the household registration (*hukou*) system, which – like the *baojia* and *lijia* systems of the Qing period – assigned each individual to a household unit. That conjugal couples remain the center of every household was dramatized in the 2005 sample census survey, which showed the proportion of never-married persons aged sixty-five and over to be just 2.9 percent for males and 0.2 percent for females (see Feng and Xiao

2007:8, table 4). Universal marriage for women, in other words, remains the norm, and the duty to produce a son to carry on the line continues to motivate even young men who identify as gay. Trafficking in women is still another measure of the pressures on the Chinese marriage market in an age of skewed sex ratios.

Throughout the twentieth century of cataclysmic change, with its mixed messages for women, the defining meaning of the female body – as a reproductive body – was never questioned. Further strengthening the twentieth-century nation's commitment to universal motherhood was the enduring influence of social Darwinist thinking among China's leaders, who saw themselves vying in a world of competing nation-states. They understood that the strength of the country was a function of the "quality" (*suzhi*) of the population. This kind of thinking, derived from eugenics, was first introduced into China in the 1920s by U.S.-trained scholars like Pan Guangdan (Barkey 2000), and later firmly installed in the various marriage laws of the People's Republic of China. Ideologies and practices of gender and sexuality inherited from the Qing empire supplied little ground for criticizing this social Darwinist perspective and, in many respects, encouraged and legitimized it. In this view, the values of the family are identical to those of the state: what's good for you and your children is good for the country.

If ideologies of gender and sexuality in the late Qing era laid a firm groundwork for the dramatic and sudden transition to nation-building, this groundwork was arguably strengthened by the fact that China escaped colonization. The coastal treaty ports, which expanded rapidly in scale and number after 1860, remained enclaves of "extraterritoriality" that encapsulated foreigners securely in their own space. Missionaries striving to spread European influence beyond the treaty ports into the countryside had limited contact with the Qing male elite, in formal negotiations over property or other juridical matters, and virtually no interaction with elite Chinese women. Most foreign missionary activities and programs focused on the poor, male or female. In this context, all proposals and programs for reform, especially after the end of the Taiping Rebellion, remained firmly in the hands of the Qing official elite under the (sometimes nominal) direction of the imperial court, and the most powerful reform models came to that elite from Europe or the United States via Japan.

The global effects of colonialism certainly made their mark in China through the expanding industry of translation and new media such as newspapers, which introduced foreign institutions, cultures, writings, and political agendas into the language and the thought of China's early-twentieth-century reformers and revolutionaries. The"woman question" and the new woman were part of this new language of the modern nation-state, and what to do about women became an obsession of nation-building. The obsession with women in the writings of male reformers and revolutionaries had the effect of silencing or displacing discussion about Chinese men. It may be argued, in fact, that Chinese men were spared the assault on their masculinity that so deeply affected men in colonial South Asia. In Bengal, for example, Mrinalini Sinha (1995) has argued that loss of control over property and labor, and growing dependence on employment in the British civil service, redefined the self-perception of the Bengali male elite, especially the members of the emerging new middle class. Sinha argues that in colonial Bengal, the national subject or citizen who represented modernity to the Bengalis, a model produced by the colonial government, was a construction developed in opposition and contradistinction to dominated Bengali men. The fact that China was merely "semi-colonial," in other words, may have buffered Chinese men and women, protecting them from some of the most disruptive effects of colonial domination.

The absence of colonial government in China may also shed light on the role of the woman question as a centerpiece of China's modern nation-building effort. In India the British used the woman question to further empower their legal and coercive system, arguing that the oppressive conditions inflicted on women *by indigenous men* required and helped to justify the aggressive intervention of the Crown's officials and its rule of law (Sinha 1995:44–46). Thus the urgency with which the British pressed the woman question was actually enabled by, and called prior attention to, the failures of Indian men. In China, where indigenous male elites were in charge, so to speak, of solving the woman question, addressing the question head-on and foregrounding it were power moves, not (as in India) confessions of self-criticism or failure. At the same time, the entire woman question was framed in a larger context in which becoming modern demanded renegotiating or rejecting old values. Rey Chow has offered some of the keenest insights into this process of renegotiation. Surveying the preoccupation with women in modern Chinese literature, Chow comments:

The analytical prominence of "woman" is, throughout the course of my reading [in modern Chinese literature], never an accidental one. The structure of masochism and fantasy in which woman is idealized derives its cogency from the requirement of self-sacrifice that every Chinese woman experiences as the limit of her cultural existence. If feminine self-sacrifice was the major support of traditional Chinese culture, it is not surprising that, during a period of massive social transformations, the collapse of tradition would find its most *moving* representations in the figures of those who are traditionally the most oppressed, figures that become "stand-ins" for China's traumatized *self-consciousness* in every sense of the phrase. In this way, "woman" does not simply amount to a new type of literary content but, more so, to a new agency, a dialectic of resistance-in-givenness that is constitutive of modernity in a non-Western, but Westernized, context. (1991:170)

In other words, the traditional ideal of the self-sacrificing woman became a medium through which modern male writers constructed their most impassioned and effective critiques of the past, and their anxieties about the present.

From the earliest writings about statecraft in China to the present, philosophers and political theorists have assumed that one important task of government is managing the population to make it grow and produce, by attending to everything from the food supply to marriage and reproduction. Relying heavily on normative sanctions, monetary rewards, and coercive punishments that were delivered through the family system, China's imperial government promoted universal marriage and lifelong fidelity to the marital patriline for women, stigmatized and marginalized unmarried males to reduce their chances of survival, and encouraged reproductive sex confined to married couples. The first half of the twentieth century shook loose the structures of the late imperial government gendered policies in three arenas. First, the late Qing reforms promoting women's education and the employment of women in light industry ended state programs that conjoined female respectability and purity to concealment. Although the attitudes and practices of ordinary people, especially outside the cities, perpetuated that linkage until the 1950s, without state sanction and support, values among urbanites quickly shifted. Second, the movement of women outside the home for work and education eroded parental control over marriage and residence. Third, influences from abroad, especially from Japan, poured into China through new institutions and new media. Together these sustained and supported visions of a new woman, variously imagined as a "good wife and wise mother" for the new nation's male citizenry, as a fashionable emblem of China's nascent modernity, and as a harbinger of women's emancipation from their backward state of oppression. Loudly promulgating the ideal of the new woman were male intellectuals, products of China's new universities who fancied themselves the enlightened "new youth" who would produce China's "new culture." During the May Fourth era, as women's magazines and family reform movements drew a growing urban audience, gender roles and values shifted dramatically. One of the most empowering arenas of the New Culture

Movement for men, then, was espousing liberation for Chinese women (Louise Edwards 2000). As Edwards writes, for enlightened male intellectuals, "the new woman was simultaneously the symbol of self-liberation from subordination (her original Euro-American model) and the affirmation of sociomoral values that would reestablish their right to rule (educated individuals possessing high moral principles) in the face of a cruel, commercialized, and corrupt military-dominated GMD government" (2000:128).

Identifying women as a key constituency in the new citizenry was part of the embrace of the language of Western science (Barlow 1994). During the twentieth century, sexual difference was newly understood as a biological binary, derived from the physical differences in the bodies of males and females. Yet modern scientific language had only a limited impact on the meanings of sexual difference, which remained relatively stable. As in the classical *yin* and *yang* discourses, male and female were seen as complementary partners in sexual relationships in which the male was active and vigorous and the female was responsive and weak. Men were cautioned about expending semen to preserve their health and long life, and masturbation and sexual indulgence outside of marriage were strongly condemned. Women, conversely, were taught that menstruation and childbirth made them vulnerable to weakness and infection, requiring strong protective legislation and policies to protect female fertility. And both men and women were told that sex was healthy, as long as it served the purpose of producing perfect offspring.

This coupling of gender reform with the movement to build a new nation supplied a lasting legacy for the Chinese Communist Party and its male leadership. A commitment to women's issues was and remains a centerpiece of the CCP ideology and organization. During the 1950s and 1960s, China's Communist government deployed policies and language addressed to the emerging new woman in her role as a loyal subject of a revolutionary society. Advice books and sex education in the 1950s and 1960s did not neglect the subject of sexual pleasure but viewed sexual pleasure (for men and women) as the key to harmonious marital bonds that would assure reproductive success and a robust population (Evans 1995). Until the 1980s the government dominated these discourses on sexuality. But during the reform era, the growth of a profit-making medical establishment, the explosion of media (including film, television, internet, and so forth), and new markets catering to gay and straight clients all began to deploy the language of sexuality and pleasure in ways of which the government did not necessarily approve. Still, much of the sex education that was ongoing in China during the first decades of the reform era drew heavily on information and values cultivated during the

Mao years (Evans 1995), and current research suggests that it is mainly men, and not women, who are moving outside of marriage and the family for sexual pleasure (Parish et al. 2007).

China's contemporary government since 1949, then, has taken dramatic and coercive steps to ensure that a normative heterosexual model of marriage and carefully regulated reproduction keeps the population productive and growing, at the right pace and with the right quality. Alongside this remarkable continuity of the role of the state in defining gender relations and sexuality, however, sharp ruptures have flagged the transition from nineteenth- to twentieth-century sexualities in China. Consider, for example, knowledge about sexuality and sex. During the nineteenth century, young people learned about sex from reading or listening to fiction and from reading or watching opera performances. Classical short stories, novels, and operas offered explicit accounts of romantic love and sexual pleasure and detailed information about sexual arousal and sexual awakening, especially among virginal young people, both male and female. Other fiction celebrated homoeroticism. Daoist arts of sexual self-cultivation were widely learned and practiced by both men and women. Medical texts and physicians, from at least the time of the Ming dynasty, supplied clear advice on sexual satisfaction and hygiene for both men and women (Furth 1999). Meanwhile terrifying performances of the saga "Mulian Rescues His Mother" continued to underscore the dangers of female sexuality and the threats posed by female reproductive power. Vernacular fiction and opera remained important sources of sex education for young people in the early twentieth century, as informants for a history of sex published in 1926 make clear (Zhang Jingsheng 2005; Chang Ching-sheng 1967). Beijing University professor Zhang Jingsheng's collection of personal sexual histories, with his clinical notes that anticipated Kinsey's published research by several years, shows that he himself was deeply influenced by Daoist ideas of sexual health and hygiene. These he found compatible with modern scientific notions of healthy sexuality promoted by Havelock Ellis and others that emphasized "care" and "conservation" of the sex organs and sexual energy and fluids. Zhang's informants, however – both male and female – showed enormous anxiety and ignorance about sex, and their reflections on their own sexual histories suggest that "modern" education relegated classical fiction and drama, along with texts on Daoist *yangsheng* techniques and Chinese medical arts, to the domain of the backward and unscientific, without offering anything to replace them.

Romantic fiction of the early twentieth century, meanwhile, presented sexual passion almost diffidently (Hanan 1995). The outcry that greeted Ding Ling's frank discussion of female desire in *Miss Sophia's Diary* and the despairing inchoate sexual passion repressed, denied, and censured in Ba Jin's empathic novel *Family* show how the confusions of becoming modern and scientific put a distance between twentieth-century persons and the sexual cultures of the past, even as new notions of sexual desire became politically difficult to explore. We know now, however, that the decades of the 1920s, 1930s, and 1940s were also crucial in developing an urban popular culture in which the new woman and the nuclear family became an increasingly accepted part of the changing sex and gender system (Dong 2008, Louise Edwards 2000, Glosser 2003, Jiang 2009).

The new urban popular culture of the first half of the twentieth century was essential to the rapid changes initiated after 1949, when the Communist government came to power. That government was more sympathetic to women's issues than its counterparts elsewhere, in part because of the May Fourth and modern girl values that inspired the first generation of Communist revolutionaries. Chinese Communist male leaders were strong advocates of women's suffrage, and of women's education and the development of independent personhood (*duli renge*) for women (Gilmartin 1995:33–34, Zheng Wang 1999b). To be sure, these CCP policies were not focused solely on women but rather on heterosexual marriage and reproduction.[1] From the beginning, the Chinese Communist Party was unable to make up its mind about whether women should be treated as a political constituency of their own, or whether women should be considered along with men as part of different class constituencies. Since the Mao years, differences in residency (urban vs. rural) have also divided women's interests, making it more difficult to consider such policies as the one-child family policy a women's issue, because the policy's consequences for urban women are so much more benign than they are for rural women. The underlying assumption joining all CCP policies toward women, nonetheless, has been the link between sexuality and gender. In government policy making, sexual passion is seen as a "natural" function of the biological body, and this presumption has continued to sustain gender hierarchies that subordinate women (Evans 1995). During the early 1950s, the state kept emphasizing its commitment to the "public or social importance of women's sexual and gender concerns," a commitment most clearly spelled out in the Marriage Law of 1950 and its subsequent development in the courts and in collectives and work units. In the post-Mao reform era, that same linkage between sex and gender enabled the government to "reprivatize"

---

[1] This problem was noted by Ding Ling in the early years of CCP organizing, when as editor of the literary page of *Liberation Daily*, on March 9, 1942, she published a critical essay "Thoughts on March 8" (Croll 1978:213).

women's sexual and gender concerns, relegating them to the conjugal bedroom and the domestic sphere. As a result the consumer culture of the 1990s portrayed women in public as visible victims of exploitation and abuse in the commercial marketplace, contrasting them with the "responsive, supportive, and self-sacrificing" wives whose sanctuary in the home made them dependent on a spouse for support and who committed their labor to reproduction (Evans 1995:389).

Harriet Evans, whose research has constantly called attention to the steadfast biologizing of women's bodies under both the Maoist and post-Mao regimes, also has noted, however, the intergenerational shifts that have affected women from the 1950s through the 1990s, especially the shift from silence (1950s–1960s) to speaking (1980s–1990s) about the sexed body (Evans 2008:147–159). The possibilities for change that Evans identifies – the decision not to have children, the redrawn lines between husband's and wife's responsibilities in the home, and the possibility of not marrying at all – focus on urban women, especially younger women. That these changes continue to be shaped by government policy and, increasingly, by the commercial economy that the government supports does not alter their significance for individual women's cognition and emotion. Many daughters of mothers who gave their lives over to the Cultural Revolution now ponder choices where few existed before, and in a context in which the choices encompass education, work, sports, and entertainment – not to mention commercial sex markets.

In rural China this range of options has been suppressed by the deepening feminization of agriculture since the 1980s. In the countryside, land reform and collectivization policies under Mao produced a "political culture of tough, authoritarian Chinese males" that fostered some of "the least progressive outcomes" of the Communist revolution (Friedman et al. 1991:288). The post-Mao reform-era feminization of agriculture has occurred in the context of this tough political culture, with women's interests continually marginalized. Meanwhile, the survival of the double standard and its return in the commercial sex markets of the current urban economy, the new critiques of sex hierarchies by women's organizations condemning marital rape and discrimination against single women (Evans 1995:388), and the growing risk of AIDS and HIV infection among married couples (Parish et al. 2007) all point to current tensions in China's sex-gender system generated by the conflicts between political platforms for gender equality and persistent assumptions about biologized bodies.

A number of recent studies have underscored these tensions. For example, William Parish and his collaborators found that, for urban Chinese, virginity remains the norm before marriage, with pornography and masturbation substituting for other kinds of sexual experience, and average age at first intercourse remains late. While noting the reemergence of a "strong double standard in premarital sexual behavior," Parish's research team also made the following observation and raised an important question:

Even though the gap between average age at first intercourse and first marriage for both men and women remains a year or less, the increasing willingness of women to engage in premarital sex is occurring alongside increasing use of commercial sex among men. This contrasts with the post-1960s West, where declining use of commercial sex occurred in the context of increasing mainstream acceptability of women engaging in premarital sex. A puzzle is why recently married men figure so prominently in the increased use of commercial sex. This phenomenon suggests that the nature and meaning of marriage in China are changing. But how? And how are women responding to these changes? These issues raise serious questions about the status of Chinese women in the middle of an apparent sexual revolution. In contrast to the liberating effects of the pill and the increased acceptability of premarital sex among Western women in recent decades, do these developments in China entail greater sexual freedom for women or a refashioned patriarchy? (2007:750–751)

James Farrer (2006), to cite another example, identified significant shifts in attitudes toward sexuality at the turn of the twenty-first century. Concern about the rights of homosexuals is rising in diverse constituencies that include the party itself and its officials. Since 1997 homosexual relationships of all kinds have no longer been illegal, as we have seen, even though there are no explicit legal protections for gay rights. Gay and lesbian film festivals, academic lecture courses, and international conferences on sexuality all supply forums in which people can hear and air views on the problem of sexual rights.[2] And, as Farrer has pointed out, criticisms of sexual activity do not always target sexual minority groups, or even promiscuous young people, but rather may be veiled codes for criticizing corruption in the party, because so many wealthy officials keep mistresses (Stewart 2007).

On one hand, the call for responsible parenting and citizen duty that begins this chapter, reprinted from a 1950s women's magazine, echoes the critique of sex for pleasure that was also familiar to subjects of the Qing government. On the other hand, the liberating appeal of sex for pleasure has also become a hallmark of modern citizenship in late-twentieth-century urban China. The Shanghai youth whose sexual relationships defy past patterns, and whose self-conscious displays of sexuality flout

---

[2] The Ford Foundation sponsored a conference on Chinese sexual culture in Beijing in June 2007, the proceedings of which were entirely in Chinese.

the state's messages – like the gay men in Beijing bars – see their liberated sexuality as a hallmark of becoming modern (Rofel 2007). But new sexual identities are not necessarily signs of liberation (Farrer 2006).[3] Hershatter reminds us that the sexual discourses proliferating in twentieth-century China aimed to modernize the Chinese state, not to liberate its people. National leaders, scientific sex experts, and reformist writers and intellectuals – all were preoccupied with questions of China's place in a competitive world, and not with the liberty of individual citizens (Hershatter 1996). Both Hershatter and Farrer stress, however, that within state-defined spaces and even using state-defined language, individuals can tell many kinds of different stories, some of which may be both original and empowering.

A similarly vexed relationship between modern citizenship and the state shows up in minority communities in China, particularly communities like Hui'an whose cultures have not conformed to the heteronormative binary assumptions of modern state-building. Sara Friedman (2006:245), analyzing what she calls "symbolic citizenship in a civilized nation," concludes that modernizing elites "promote an understanding of citizenship that excludes not only 'intractable' others within the nation-state but also those whose bodies and intimate practices resist the binary formulations on which such an imagined community rests." Other scholars have pointed to the problematic relationship between "notions of sexual 'innocence' and full citizenship" that are deployed in state discourses of protectionism referring to Miao and other minority communities catering to sex tourism. In these discourses, persons who "exist outside the hegemonic ideal of married heterosexuality . . . must be seen as sexually 'innocent' in order to be ushered into the charmed circle of sexual normalcy and full citizenship" (Lerum 2007:560). The publication in 1999 of *Shanghai Baby* (Wei Hui 2001), with its frank and detailed explorations of female sexual desire, and its juxtaposition of foreign male virility and Chinese male impotence, shows how inventively young female urbanites talk back to these hegemonic discourses, even as they deftly claim their own place in the commercial economy and confront their complex relationship to global discourses on sexuality.

That sexuality clearly has a place in understandings of modern citizenship – however problematic that place may be – is only one other indication of the vital importance of using sexuality as a category of analysis in studying historical change.

---

[3] He cites Foucault's concern that sexual citizens or sexual subjects are themselves "a product of modern strategies of power" subject to "modern techniques of power and regulation" (Farrer 2006:104).

Afterword: Gender and sexuality: useful categories of historical analysis?

In their close reading of the romantic drama *The Western Wing*, Stephen West and Wilt Idema paused to wonder why scholars had done so little historical research on the rich field of Chinese sexuality (1991:141–153). They blamed Confucianism and Marxism:

> In China the ascendancy of neo-Confucianism after the fifteenth century, if it did not silence the earthy voice of Chinese vernacular literature, at least drove it into a kind of silent limbo. In modern China an interest in sex is officially attributed to bourgeois decadence. While traditional critics are wont to shunt the issue aside by simply saying that a certain passage is "vulgar" (*li* 俚), the silence of modern scholars, as philologically gifted as they are, is surely due to the fact that they too are heirs to the neo-Confucian tradition. (1991:141)

Anyone can see their point: just try checking the index of standard textbooks and sourcebooks on premodern (or modern!) Chinese history for the words "sex" and "sexuality." Never mind that China's earliest philosophers were fascinated by sexual appetites, or that China's government has been constantly engaged in the process of regulating and prescribing sexual behavior. Historians seem not to be paying attention.

Sexology has not found a comfortable home in our classrooms, and attention to the historical construction of gender and sexuality is barely beginning in the China field. If the purpose of education is to create, as we often say, global citizens with broad cross-cultural proficiencies, then skipping sex as an object of inquiry invites us to remain parochial and culture-bound in the most engaging and culturally valorized arena of contemporary life. To learn how another culture treats gender and sexuality is to open one's eyes to other ways of being in the world. It goes without saying that those ways of being in the world all have a history, a history in which cross-cultural interactions and power relations – like China's early-twentieth-century encounter with Western science – are deeply and not so innocently implicated. If sex is one arena in which the results of such an encounter could be limiting or even harmful – endangering those who are homosexual, bisexual, or transsexual, for example – then studying the history of sexuality in China is a project that will benefit everyone. This is not to hold out the trap Gulik fell into – that is, Chinese sex-gender systems by no means offer some "other" utopia. Rather, it is to understand that critical historical analysis of sexuality opens the mind and frees the spirit to reflect on one's own culture with an appreciation for its dangerous limitations as well as its glorious possibilities.

Permissions

Quoted material from Rey Chow, *Woman and Chinese Modernity* (Minneapolis: University of Minnesota Press, 1991) by permission of the University of Minnesota Press.

Quoted material from Amy D. Dooling and Kristina M. Torgeson, eds., *Writing Women in Modern China* (New York: Columbia University Press, 1998) by permission of Columbia University Press.

Quoted material from Sara L. Friedman, *Intimate Politics: Marriage, the Market, and State Power in Southeastern China* (Cambridge, Mass.: Harvard University Asia Center, 2006) by permission of Harvard University Asia Center.

Quoted material from Joshua Goldstein, *Drama Kings: Players and Publics in the Re-Creation of Peking Opera, 1870–1937* (Berkeley: University of California Press, 2007) by permission of the University of California Press.

Quoted material from Patrick Hanan, *The Sea of Regret: Two Turn-of-the-Century Chinese Romantic Novels* (Honolulu: University of Hawai'i Press, 1995) by permission of the University of Hawai'i Press.

Quoted material from Maranatha Ivanova, "Commentary: Ambiguity, Absurdity, and Self-Creation in the Art of Ma Liuming." *positions: east asia cultures critique* 7, no. 1 (1999): 201–23, (Durham, N.C.: Duke University Press) by permission of Duke University Press.

Quoted material from Jin Jiang, *Women Playing Men: Yue Opera and Social Change in Twentieth-Century Shanghai* (Seattle: University of Washington Press, 2009) by permission of the University of Washington Press.

Quoted material from Sheldon H. Lu, *Chinese Modernity and Global Biopolitics: Studies in Literature and Visual Culture* (Honolulu: University of Hawai'i Press, 2007) by permission of the University of Hawai'i Press.

Quoted material from Manling Luo, "The Seduction of Authenticity: 'The Story of Yingying,'" *Nan Nü: Men, Women and Gender in China* 7, no. 1 (2005): 40–70, by permission of Koninklijke Brill NV.

Quoted material from Richard John Lynn, trans., *The Classic of Changes* (New York: Columbia University Press, 1994) by permission of Columbia University Press.

Quoted material from Susan L. Mann, trans. "Biographies of Exemplary Women," in *Hawai'i Reader in Traditional Chinese Culture*, edited by Victor

H. Mair, Nancy S. Steinhardt, and Paul R. Goldin, 607–13 (Honolulu: University of Hawai'i Press, 2005) by permission of the University of Hawai'i Press.

Quoted material from Lisa Rofel, *Desiring China: Experiments in Neoliberalism, Sexuality, and Public Culture* (Durham, N.C.: Duke University Press, 2007) by permission of Duke University Press.

Quoted material from "Shu-chiung" (pseud.), Hsi Shih, *Beauty of Beauties (A Romance of Ancient China about 495–472 B.C.)* [Singapore: Graham Brash, 1981 (1931)] by permission of Graham Brash Pte. Ltd.

Quoted material from Matthew Sommer, *Sex, Law, and Society in Late Imperial China* (Stanford, Calif.: Stanford University Press, 2000) by permission of Stanford University Press.

Quoted material from Zheng Wang, *Women in the Chinese Enlightenment: Oral and Textual Histories* (Berkeley: University of California Press, 1999) by permission of the University of California Press.

Quoted material from Burton Watson, trans., *Han Fei Tzu: Basic Writings* (New York: Columbia University Press, 1964) by permission of Columbia University Press.

Quoted material from Stephen H. West and Wilt L. Idema, ed. and trans., *The Moon and the Zither: "The Story of the Western Wing," by Wang Shifu* (Berkeley: University of California Press, 1991) by permission of the University of California Press.

Quoted material from Paola Zamperini, "Clothes That Matter: Fashioning Modernity in Late Qing Novels," *Fashion Theory* 5, no. 2 (2001a): 195–214, by permission of Berg Publishers, an imprint of A&C Black Publishers Ltd.

Quoted material from Tiantian Zheng, *Red Lights: The Lives of Sex Workers in Postsocialist China* (Minneapolis: University of Minnesota, 2009) by permission of the University of Minnesota Press.

References

Ambrica Productions. "The Mao Years, Part I." [Documentary Film]. New York: Ambrica Productions, Inc., 1994.

Ahern, Emily. "The Power and Pollution of Chinese Women." In *Women in Chinese Society*, edited by Margery Wolf and Roxane Witke, 193–214. Stanford, Calif.: Stanford University Press, 1975.

Arkush, R. David. "Love and Marriage in North Chinese Peasant Operas." In *Unofficial China: Popular Culture and Thought in the People's Republic*, edited by Perry Link, Richard Madsen, and Paul G. Pickowicz, 72–87. Boulder, Colo.: Westview Press, 1989.

Ba Jin [Pa Chin]. *Family (Jia)*. Introduction by Olga Lang. New York: Doubleday, 1972.

Bailey, Paul. "'Women Behaving Badly': Crime, Transgressive Behaviour and Gender in Early Twentieth Century China." *Nan Nü: Men, Women and Gender in China* 8, no. 1 (2006): 156–97.

Barkey, Cheryl Lynn. "Gender, Medicine, and Modernity: The Politics of Reproduction in Republican China." Ph.D. diss., University of California, Davis, 2000.

Barlow, Tani, with Gary J. Bjorge, ed. *I Myself Am a Woman: Selected Writings of Ding Ling*. Boston: Beacon Press, 1989.

Barlow, Tani E. "Theorizing Woman: *Funü, Guojia, Jiating* (Chinese Women, Chinese State, Chinese Family)." In *Body, Subject and Power in China*, edited by Angela Zito and Tani E. Barlow, 253–89. Chicago: University of Chicago Press, 1994.

Beahan, Charlotte L. "The Women's Movement and Nationalism in Late Ch'ing China." Ph.D. diss., Columbia University, 1976.

Benn, James A. *Burning for the Buddha: Self-Immolation in Chinese Buddhism*. Honolulu: University of Hawai'i Press, 2007.

Bennett, Judith M. "'Lesbian-Like' and the Social History of Lesbianisms." *Journal of the History of Sexuality* 9, no. 1/2 (2000): 1–24.

Bernhardt, Kathryn. *Women and Property in China, 960–1949*. Stanford, Calif.: Stanford University Press, 1999.

———. "Women and the Law: Divorce in the Republican Period." In *Civil Law in Qing and Republican China*, edited by Kathryn Bernhardt and Philip C. C. Huang, 187–214. Stanford, Calif.: Stanford University Press, 1994.

Birge, Bettine. *Women, Property, and Confucian Reaction in Sung and Yüan China (960–1368)*. New York: Cambridge University Press, 2002.

Black, Alison. "Gender and Cosmology in Chinese Correlative Thinking." In *Gender and Religion: On the Complexity of Symbols*, edited by Caroline W. Bynum, Stevan Harrell, and Paula Richman, 166-95. Boston: Beacon Press, 1989.

Blake, C. Fred. "Death and Abuse in Marriage Laments: The Curse of Chinese Brides." *Asian Folklore Studies* 37, no. 1 (1978): 13–33.

Boellstorff, Tom. "Queer Studies in the House of Anthropology." *Annual Review of Anthropology* 36 (2007): 17–35.

Bossler, Beverly J. *Courtesans, Concubines, and the Cult of Wifely Fidelity: Gender and Social Change in China, 1000–1400*. Cambridge, Mass.: Harvard University Asia Center, 2012.

Bray, Francesca. "The Inner Quarters: Oppression or Freedom?" In *House, Home, Family: Living and Being Chinese*, edited by Ronald G. Knapp and Kai-Yin Lo, 259–79. Honolulu: University of Hawai'i Press, 2005.

Brownell, Susan. *Training the Body for China: Sports in the Moral Order of the People's Republic*. Chicago: University of Chicago Press, 1995.

Butler, Judith. *Bodies That Matter: On the Discursive Limits of "Sex."* New York and London: Routledge, 1993.

Cahill, James. *Pictures for Use and Pleasure: Vernacular Painting in High Qing China*. Berkeley: University of California Press, 2010.

———. "The Three Changs, Yangzhou Beauties, and the Manchu Court." *Orientations* (1996): 59–68.

Carlitz, Katherine. "Desire and Writing in the Late Ming Play *Parrot Island*." In *Writing Women in Late Imperial China*, edited by Ellen Widmer and Kang-i Sun Chang, 101–30. Stanford, Calif.: Stanford University Press, 1997a.

———. "Desire, Danger, and the Body: Stories of Women's Virtue in Late Ming China." In *Engendering China: Women, Culture, and the State*, edited by Christina K. Gilmartin, Gail Hershatter, Lisa Rofel, and Tyrene White, 101–24. Cambridge, Mass.: Harvard University Press, 1994.

———. "In Praise of Martyrs: Widow-Suicide in Late-Imperial China." In *Hawai'i Reader in Traditional Chinese Culture*, edited by Victor H. Mair, Nancy S. Steinhardt, and Paul R. Goldin, 461–66. Honolulu: University of Hawai'i Press, 2005.

———. "Shrines, Governing-Class Identity, and the Cult of Widow Fidelity in Mid-Ming Jiangnan." *Journal of Asian Studies* 56, no. 3 (1997b): 612–40.

Chan, Leo Tak-hung. *The Discourse on Foxes and Ghosts: Ji Yun and Eighteenth-Century Literati Storytelling*. Honolulu: University of Hawai'i Press, 1998.

Chang Ching-sheng [Zhang Jingsheng]. *Sex Histories: China's First Modern Treatise on Sex Education*. Translated by Howard S. Levy [from the Japanese translation by Nakamura Motosuke]. Yokohama: n.p., 1967.

Chang, Kang-i Sun, and Haun Saussy, eds. *Women Writers of Traditional China: An Anthology of Poetry and Criticism*. Stanford, Calif.: Stanford University Press, 1999.

Chatterjee, Partha. *Nationalist Thought and the Colonial World: A Derivative Discourse*. Minneapolis: University of Minnesota Press, 1993.

Chen Dongyuan. *Zhongguo funü shenghuo shi* (A History of the Lives of Chinese Women). Taipei: Taiwan shangwu yinshu guan, 1997 [1937].

Chen, Tina Mai. "Dressing for the Party: Clothing, Citizenship, and Gender Formation in Mao's China." *Fashion Theory* 5, no. 2 (2001): 143–71.

Chen, Yu-shih. "The Historical Template of Pan Chao's *Nü Chieh*." *T'oung Pao*, 2nd Series 82, no. 4–5 (1996): 229–57.

Cheng, Sheung-Tak. "Epidemic Genital Retraction Syndrome: Environmental and Personal Risk Factors in Southern China." *Journal of Psychology and Human Sexuality* 9, no. 1 (1997): 57–70.

Cheng, Weikun. "Going Public through Education: Female Reformers and Girls' Schools in Late Qing Beijing." *Late Imperial China* 21, no. 1 (2000): 107–44.

Chiu, M.-C. Man-Chung. "'Censorship = Mission Impossible?': A Postcolonial Same Sex Erotic Discourse on Hong Kong Porn Law." *International Journal of the Sociology of Law* 32, no. 1 (2004): 39–63.

Chiu, Vermier Y. *Marriage Laws and Customs of China*. Hong Kong: New Asia College, Chinese University of Hong Kong, 1966.

Chiu-Duke, Josephine. "The Role of Confucian Revivalists in the Confucianization of T'ang Women." *Asia Major, 3rd Series* 8, no. 1 (1997): 51–93.

Chou, Hui-ling. "Striking Their Own Poses: The History of Cross-Dressing on the Chinese Stage." *The Drama Review* 41, no. 2 (1997): 130–52.

Chou, Wah-shan. *Tongzhi: Politics of Same-Sex Eroticism in Chinese Societies*. New York: Haworth Press, 2000.

Chow, Rey. *Woman and Chinese Modernity*. Minneapolis: University of Minnesota Press, 1991.

Chow, Tse-tsung. *The May Fourth Movement: Intellectual Revolution in Modern China*. Cambridge, Mass.: Harvard University Press, 1960.

Chu, Cordia Ming-Yeuk. "Menstrual Beliefs and Practices of Chinese Women." *Journal of the Folklore Institute* 17, no. 1 (1980): 38–55.

Chu, Junhong. "Prenatal Sex Determination and Sex-Selective Abortion in Rural Central China." *Population and Development Review* 27, no. 2 (2001): 259–81.

Ch'ü, T'ung-tsu. *Han Social Structure*. Edited by Jack L. Dull. Seattle: University of Washington Press, 1972.

Croll, Elisabeth. *Changing Identities of Chinese Women: Rhetoric, Experience, and Self-Perception in Twentieth-Century China*. London: Zed Books, 1995.

_____. *Endangered Daughters: Discrimination and Development in Asia*. London: Routledge, 2000.

_____. *Feminism and Socialism in China*. London: Routledge & Kegan Paul, 1978.

Dautcher, Jay. *Down a Narrow Road: Identity and Masculinity in a Uyghur Community in Xinjiang China*. Cambridge, Mass.: Harvard University Asia Center, 2009.

Deal, David M., and Laura Hostetler, trans. *The Art of Ethnography: A Chinese "Miao Album."* Seattle: University of Washington Press, 2006.

Despeux, Catherine, and Livia Kohn. *Women in Daoism.* Cambridge, Mass.: Three Pines Press, 2003.

Diamant, Neil J. "Between Martyrdom and Mischief: The Political and Social Predicament of CCP War Widows and Veterans, 1949–66." In *Scars of War: The Impact of Warfare on Modern China,* edited by Diana Lary and Stephen MacKinnon, 162–87. Vancouver: University of British Columbia Press, 2001.

——. *Revolutionizing the Family: Politics, Love, and Divorce in Urban and Rural China, 1949–1968.* Berkeley: University of California Press, 2000.

Dikötter, Frank. *Sex, Culture and Modernity in China: Medical Science and the Construction of Sexual Identities in the Early Republican Period.* Honolulu: University of Hawaii Press, 1995.

Djang, Chu, trans. *A Complete Book Concerning Happiness and Benevolence: A Manual for Local Magistrates in Seventeenth-Century China,* by Huang Liu-Hung. Tucson: University of Arizona Press, 1984.

Dong, Madeleine Y. "Who Is Afraid of the Chinese Modern Girl?" In *The Modern Girl around the World: Consumption, Modernity, and Globalization,* edited by Alys Eve Weinbaum, Lynn M. Thomas, Priti Ramamurthy, Uta G. Poiger, Madeleine Yue Dong, and Tani E. Barlow [The Modern Girl around the World Research Group], 194–219. Durham, N.C.: Duke University Press, 2008.

Dooling, Amy D., and Kristina M. Torgeson, ed. *Writing Women in Modern China.* New York: Columbia University Press, 1998.

Dull, Jack L. "Marriage and Divorce in Han China: A Glimpse at 'Pre-Confucian' Society." In *Chinese Family Law and Social Change in Comparative Perspective,* edited by David C. Buxbaum, 23–74. Seattle: University of Washington Press, 1978.

Dutton, Michael. *Streetlife China.* New York: Cambridge University Press, 1998.

Eberhard, Wolfram. *Guilt and Sin in Traditional China.* Berkeley: University of California Press, 1967.

Ebrey, Patricia. "Gender and Sinology: Shifting Western Interpretations of Footbinding, 1300–1890." *Late Imperial China* 20, no. 2 (1999): 1–34.

Ebrey, Patricia Buckley. *The Inner Quarters: Marriage and the Lives of Chinese Women in the Sung Period.* Berkeley: University of California Press, 1993.

Edwards, James W. "The Concern for Health in Sexual Matters in the 'Old Society' and the 'New Society' in China." *Journal of Sex Research* 12, no. 2 (1976): 88–103.

Edwards, Louise. "Policing the Modern Woman in Republican China." *Modern China* 26, no. 2 (2000): 115–47.

——. "Women Warriors and Amazons of the Mid Qing Texts *Jinghua Yuan* and *Honglou Meng.*" *Modern Asian Studies* 29, no. 2 (1995): 225–55.

Edwards, Louise P. *Men and Women in Qing China: Gender in the Red Chamber Dream.* Leiden: E. J. Brill, 1994.

Elliott, Mark C. "Manchu Widows and Ethnicity in Qing China." *Comparative Studies in Society and History* 41, no. 1 (1999): 33–71.

Engel, John W. "Marriage in the People's Republic of China: Analysis of a New Law." *Journal of Marriage and the Family* 46, no. 4 (1984): 955–61.

Epstein, Maram. *Competing Discourses: Orthodoxy, Authenticity and Engendered Meanings in Late Imperial Chinese Fiction.* Cambridge, Mass.: Harvard University Asia Center, 2001.

Evans, Harriet. "Defining Difference: The 'Scientific' Construction of Sexuality and Gender in the People's Republic of China." *Signs: Journal of Women in Culture and Society* 20, no. 2 (1995): 357–94.

————. *The Subject of Gender: Daughters and Mothers in Urban China.* Lanham, Mass.: Rowman and Littlefield, 2008.

————. *Women and Sexuality in China.* New York: Continuum, 1997.

Farrer, James. *Opening Up: Youth Sex Culture and Market Reform in Shanghai.* Chicago: University of Chicago Press, 2002.

————. "Sexual Citizenship and the Politics of Sexual Storytelling among Chinese Youth." In *Sex and Sexuality in China*, edited by Elaine Jeffreys, 102–23. London: Routledge, 2006.

Faure, Bernard. *The Red Thread: Buddhist Approaches to Sexuality.* Princeton, N.J.: Princeton University Press, 1998.

Feng, Nailin, and Ning Xiao. "Population Aging in China as Reflected by the Results of the 2005 Population Sample Survey [http://www.Ancsdaap.Org/Cencon2007/Papers/China/China_Feng.pdf]." Paper presented at the 23rd Population Census Conference: Utilization of the 2000 and 2005 rounds of Asia-Pacific Censuses, Christchurch, New Zealand, 2007.

Finnane, Antonia. *Changing Clothes in China: Fashion, History, Nation.* New York: Columbia University Press, 2008.

————. "What Should Chinese Women Wear? A National Problem." *Modern China* 22, no. 2 (1996): 99–131.

Flath, James A. *The Cult of Happiness: Nianhua, Art, and History in Rural North China.* Vancouver: University of British Columbia Press, 2004.

Folsom, Kenneth E. *Friends, Guests, and Colleagues: The Mu-Fu System in the Late Ch'ing Period.* Berkeley: University of California Press, 1968.

Fong, Grace S. "De/Constructing a Feminine Ideal in the Eighteenth Century: 'Random Records of West-Green' and the Story of Shuangqing." In *Writing Women in Late Imperial China*, edited by Ellen Widmer and Kang-i Sun Chang, 264–81. Stanford, Calif.: Stanford University Press, 1997.

————. "Signifying Bodies: The Cultural Significance of Suicide Writings by Women in Ming-Qing China." *Nan Nü: Men, Women and Gender in Early and Imperial China* 3, no. 1 (2001): 105–42.

Fong, Vanessa L. *Only Hope: Coming of Age under China's One-Child Policy.* Stanford, Calif.: Stanford University Press, 2004.

Foucault, Michel. *The History of Sexuality, Volume 1: An Introduction.* Translated by Robert Hurley. New York: Vintage Books, 1990.

———. *Security, Territory, Population: Lectures at the Collège de France, 1977–78.* Translated by Graham Burchell. Edited by Arnold I. Davidson. New York: Palgrave MacMillan, 2007.

Friedman, Edward, Paul G. Pickowicz, and Mark Selden. *Chinese Village, Socialist State.* New Haven, Conn.: Yale University Press, 1991.

Friedman, Sara L. *Intimate Politics: Marriage, the Market, and State Power in Southeastern China.* Cambridge, Mass.: Harvard University Asia Center, 2006.

Furth, Charlotte. "Androgynous Males and Deficient Females: Biology and Gender Boundaries in Sixteenth- and Seventeenth-Century China." *Late Imperial China* 9, no. 2 (1988): 1–31.

———. *A Flourishing Yin: Gender in China's Medical History, 960–1665.* Berkeley: University of California Press, 1999.

———. "The Patriarch's Legacy: Household Instructions and the Transmission of Orthodox Values." In *Orthodoxy in Late Imperial China*, edited by Kwang-Ching Liu, 187–211. Berkeley: University of California Press, 1990.

———. "Rethinking Van Gulik: Sexuality and Reproduction in Traditional Chinese Medicine." In *Engendering China: Women, Culture, and the State*, edited by Christina K. Gilmartin, Gail Hershatter, Lisa Rofel, Tyrene White, 125–46. Cambridge, Mass.: Harvard University Press, 1994.

Gamble, Sidney D. *Ting Hsien, a North China Rural Community.* New York: Institute of Pacific Relations, 1954.

Gates, Hill. "Buying Brides in China – Again." *Anthropology Today* 12, no. 4 (1996): 8–11.

Gerth, Karl. *China Made: Consumer Culture and the Creation of the Nation.* Cambridge, Mass.: Harvard University Asia Center, 2003.

Giersch, C. Patterson. *Asian Borderlands: The Transformation of Qing China's Yunnan Frontier.* Cambridge, Mass.: Harvard University Press, 2006.

Gilmartin, Christina. "Gender in the Formation of a Communist Body Politic." *Modern China* 19, no. 3 (1993): 299–329.

Gilmartin, Christina Kelley. *Engendering the Chinese Revolution: Radical Women, Communist Politics, and Mass Movements in the 1920s.* Berkeley: University of California Press, 1995.

Gimpel, Denise. "Freeing the Mind through the Body: Women's Thoughts on Physical Education in Late Qing and Early Republican China." *Nan Nü: Men, Women and Gender in China* 8, no. 2 (2006): 316–58.

Glosser, Susan L. *Chinese Visions of Family and State, 1915–1953.* Berkeley: University of California Press, 2003.

Goldstein, Joshua. *Drama Kings: Players and Publics in the Re-Creation of Peking Opera, 1870–1937.* Berkeley: University of California Press, 2007.

Goldstein, Leslie F. "Early Feminist Themes in French Utopian Socialism: The St.-Simonians and Fourier." *Journal of the History of Ideas* 43, no. 1 (1982): 91–108.

Goodman, Bryna. "The New Woman Commits Suicide: The Press, Cultural Memory and the New Republic." *Journal of Asian Studies* 64, no. 1 (2005): 67–101.

Greenhalgh, Susan. "Fresh Winds in Beijing: Chinese Feminists Speak Out on the One-Child Policy and Women's Lives." *Signs: Journal of Women in Culture and Society* 26, no. 3 (2001): 847–86.

Greenhalgh, Susan. *Just One Child: Science and Policy in Deng's China.* Berkeley: University of California Press, 2008.

Greenhalgh, Susan, and Edwin A. Winckler. *Governing China's Population: From Leninist to Neoliberal Biopolitics.* Stanford, Calif.: Stanford University Press, 2005.

Gronewold, Sue. *Beautiful Merchandise: Prostitution in China, 1860–1936.* New York: Haworth Press, 1982.

Gulik, Robert Hans van. *Erotic Colour Prints of the Ming Period, with an Essay on Chinese Sex Life from the Han to the Ch'ing Dynasty, B.C. 206–A.D. 1644.* Tokyo: Privately published in fifty copies, 1951.

———. *Sexual Life in Ancient China: A Preliminary Survey of Chinese Sex and Society from ca. 1500 B.C. till 1644 A.D.; with a New Introduction and Bibliography by Paul R. Goldin.* Leiden: Brill, 2003.

Halperin, David M. "Forgetting Foucault: Acts, Identities, and the History of Sexuality." *Representations* 63 (1998): 93–120.

Hanan, Patrick. *The Chinese Vernacular Story.* Cambridge, Mass.: Harvard University Press, 1981.

———, trans. *The Sea of Regret: Two Turn-of-the-Century Chinese Romantic Novels.* Honolulu: University of Hawai'i Press, 1995.

Handlin, Joanna F. "Lü K'un's New Audience: The Influence of Women's Literacy on Sixteenth-Century Thought." In *Women in Chinese Society*, edited by Margery Wolf and Roxane Witke, 13-18. Stanford, Calif.: Stanford University Press, 1975.

Hannum, Emily. "Market Transition, Educational Disparities, and Family Strategies in Rural China: New Evidence on Gender Stratification and Development." *Demography* 42, no. 2 (2005):275–299.

Harper, Donald. "The Sexual Arts of Ancient China as Described in a Manuscript of the Second Century B.C." *Harvard Journal of Asiatic Studies* 47, no. 2 (1987): 539–93.

Harrell, Stevan. "Introduction: Civilizing Projects and the Reaction to Them." In *Cultural Encounters on China's Ethnic Frontiers*, edited by Stevan Harrell, 3–36. Seattle: University of Washington Press, 1995.

———. "The Rich Get Children: Segmentation, Stratification, and Population in Three Chekiang Lineages, 1550–1850." In *Family and Population in East Asian History*, edited by Susan B. Hanley and Arthur P. Wolf, 81–109. Stanford, Calif.: Stanford University Press, 1985.

Hay, John. "The Body Invisible in Chinese Art?" In *Body, Subject, and Power in China*, edited by Angela Zito and Tani E. Barlow, 42–77. Chicago: University of Chicago Press, 1994.

Heinrich, Larissa N. *The Afterlife of Images: Translating the Pathological Body between China and the West.* Durham, N.C.: Duke University Press, 2008.

Henriot, Christian. *Prostitution and Sexuality in Shanghai: A Social History, 1849–1949*. Translated by Noël Castelino. Cambridge: Cambridge University Press, 2001.

Hershatter, Gail. *Dangerous Pleasures: Prostitution and Modernity in Twentieth-Century Shanghai*. Berkeley: University of California Press, 1997.

———. "The Gender of Memory: Rural Chinese Women and the 1950s." *Signs: Journal of Women in Culture and Society* 28, no. 1 (2002): 43–70.

———. *The Gender of Memory: Rural Women and China's Collective Past*. Berkeley: University of California Press, 2011.

———. "Regulating Sex in Shanghai: The Reform of Prostitution in 1920 and 1951." In *Shanghai Sojourners*, edited by Frederic Wakeman, Jr., and Wen-hsin Yeh, 145–85. Berkeley: University of California Institute of East Asian Studies, 1992.

———. "Sexing Modern China." In *Remapping China: Fissures in Historical Terrain*, edited by Gail Hershatter, Emily Honig, Jonathan N. Lipman, and Randall Stross, 77–93. Stanford, Calif.: Stanford University Press, 1996.

———. *Women in China's Long Twentieth Century*. Berkeley: Global, Area, and International Archive, University of California Press, 2007.

Hinsch, Bret. "The Origins of Separation of the Sexes in China." *Journal of the American Oriental Society* 123, no. 3 (2003): 595–616.

———. *Passions of the Cut Sleeve: The Male Homosexual Tradition in China*. Berkeley: University of California Press, 1990.

———. "Van Gulik's *Sexual Life in Ancient China* and the Matter of Homosexuality." *Nan Nü: Men, Women and Gender in China* 7, no. 1 (2005): 79–91.

Hinton, Carma, and Richard Gordon. "Small Happiness: Women of a Chinese Village." [Documentary Film]. 60 minutes. New York: Long Bow Group, 1984.

Hoang, Pierre. *Le Mariage Chinois au point de vue Légal* (Marriage in China as seen through the law). Shanghai: Imprimerie de la Mission Catholique, 1915.

Honig, Emily. "Private Issues, Public Discourse: The Life and Times of Yu Luo-Jin." *Pacific Affairs* 57, no. 2 (1984): 252–65.

———. *Sisters and Strangers: Women in the Shanghai Cotton Mills, 1919–1949*. Stanford, Calif.: Stanford University Press, 1986.

———. "Socialist Sex: The Cultural Revolution Revisited." *Modern China* 29, no. 2 (2003): 143–75.

Honig, Emily, and Gail Hershatter. *Personal Voices: Chinese Women in the 1980's*. Stanford, Calif.: Stanford University Press, 1988.

Hsia, C. T. *The Classic Chinese Novel*. New York: Columbia University Press, 1968; repr. Bloomington: Indiana University Press, 1980.

Hsiao, Kung-chuan. *Rural China: Imperial Control in the Nineteenth Century*. Seattle: University of Washington Press, 1960.

Hsiung, Ping-chen. *A Tender Voyage: Children and Childhood in China*. Stanford, Calif.: Stanford University Press, 2005.

Hsu, Pi-Ching. *Beyond Eroticism: A Historian's Reading of Humor in Feng Meng-long's "Child's Folly."* Lanham, Md.: University Press of America, 2006.

Hsu, Tao-Ching. *The Chinese Conception of the Theatre*. Seattle: University of Washington Press, 1985.

Hu Hsiao-chen. "Wenyuan, duoluo yu huaman–Wang Yunzhang zhubian shiqi (1915–1920) *Funü Zazhi* zhong 'nüxing wenxue' de guannian yu shijian" (The Writers' Garden, the Toilette Case, and the Kasumam: Theory and Practice of Women's Literature in the *Ladies' Journal* of the 1910s). *Jindai Zhongguo funü shi yanjiu* (Research on Women in Modern Chinese History) 12 (2004): 169–93.

Hu Pu'an, ed. *Zhonghua quanguo fengsu zhi* (Gazetteer of Local Customs throughout China). 2 vols. Taipei: Qixin shuju, 1968.

Hu Xiaozhen. "Ningzhi zhong de fenlie wenben: You 'Mengying Yuan' zai tan wan Qing qianqi de nüxing xushi" (Works That Break through Stagnation: A Reassessment of Women's Narrative from the Early Part of the Late Qing Period Based on 'Dream Affinities'). In *Shi bian yu wei xin: Wan Ming yu wan Qing de wenxue yishu guoji xueshu yantaohui (1999)* (Transformation and Reform: Proceedings of the International Conference on Late Ming and Late Qing Literary Arts, 1999), edited by Hu Xiaozhen. Taipei: Zhongyang yanjiuyuan wenzhesuo, 2001.

Hu, Ying. "Naming the First New Woman." *Nan Nü: Men, Women and Gender in Early and Imperial China* 3, no. 2 (2001): 196–231.

——. *Tales of Translation: Composing the New Woman in China, 1899–1918*. Stanford, Calif.: Stanford University Press, 2000.

Huang, Martin W. "From *caizi* to *yingxiong*: Imagining Masculinities in Two Qing Novels, *Yesou puyan* and *Sanfen meng quan zhuan*." *Chinese Literature: Essays, Articles, Reviews (CLEAR)* 25 (2003): 59–98.

——. *Literati and Self-Re/Presentation: Autobiographical Sensibility in the Eighteenth-Century Chinese Novel*. Stanford, Calif.: Stanford University Press, 1995.

——. *Negotiating Masculinities in Late Imperial China*. Honolulu: University of Hawai'i Press, 2006.

Huang, Philip C. C. *Code, Custom, and Legal Practice in China: The Qing and the Republic Compared*. Stanford, Calif.: Stanford University Press, 2001.

Hudson, Valerie M., and Andrea M. Den Boer. " 'Bare Branches' and Danger in Asia." *Washington Post*, Sunday, 4 July 2004, B07.

Hunt, Lynn. "Introduction: Obscenity and the Origins of Modernity, 1500–1800." In *The Invention of Pornography: Obscenity and the Origins of Modernity, 1500–1800*, edited by Lynn Hunt, 9–45. New York: Zone Books, 1993.

Hunter, Jane. *The Gospel of Gentility: American Women Missionaries in Turn-of-the-Century China*. New Haven, Conn.: Yale University Press, 1984.

Huntington, Rania. *Alien Kind: Foxes and Late Imperial Chinese Narrative*. Cambridge, Mass.: Harvard University Asia Center, 2003.

Hyde, Sandra. *Eating Spring Rice: The Cultural Politics of Aids in Southwest China*. Berkeley: University of California Press, 2007.

Idema, Wilt. *Chinese Vernacular Fiction: The Formative Period*. Leiden: E. J. Brill, 1974.

Idema, Wilt L. "'What Eyes May Light upon My Sleeping Form?': Tang Xianzu's Transformation of His Sources, with a Translation of 'Du Liniang Craves Sex and Returns to Life.'" *Asia Major, New Series* 16, no. 1 (2003): 111–43.

Ip, Hung-Yok. "Fashioning Appearances: Feminine Beauty in Chinese Communist Revolutionary Culture." *Modern China* 29, no. 3 (2003): 329–61.

Ivanova, Maranatha. "Commentary: Ambiguity, Absurdity, and Self-Creation in the Art of Ma Liuming." *positions: east asia cultures critique* 7, no. 1 (1999): 201–23.

Jacka, Tamara. *Women's Work in Rural China: Change and Continuity in an Era of Reform*. New York: Cambridge University Press, 1997.

Jankowiak, William R. *Sex, Death, and Hierarchy in a Chinese City: An Anthropological Account*. New York: Columbia University Press, 1993.

Jeffreys, Elaine. "Introduction: Talking Sex and Sexuality in China." In *Sex and Sexuality in China*, edited by Elaine Jeffreys, 1–20. London: Routledge, 2006a.

——, ed. *Sex and Sexuality in China*. London: Routledge, 2006b.

Ji Yun. *Shadows in a Chinese Landscape: The Notes of a Confucian Scholar*. Edited and translated by David L. Keenan. Armonk, N.Y.: M.E. Sharpe, 1999.

Jiang, Jin. *Women Playing Men: Yue Opera and Social Change in Twentieth-Century Shanghai*. Seattle: University of Washington Press, 2009.

Johnson, Kay, with Huang Banghan and Wang Liyao. "Infant Abandonment and Adoption, 1996–2000." In *Wanting a Daughter, Needing a Son*, edited by Kay Ann Johnson, 76–134. St. Paul, Minn.: Yeong and Yeong, 2004.

Judd, Ellen. *Gender and Power in Rural North China*. Stanford, Calif.: Stanford University Press, 1994.

Judge, Joan. *The Precious Raft of History: The Past, the West, and the Woman Question in China*. Stanford, Calif.: Stanford University Press, 2008.

——. "Talent, Virtue, and the Nation: Chinese Nationalisms and Female Subjectivities in the Early Twentieth Century." *American Historical Review* 106, no. 2 (2001): 765–803.

Kang, Wenqing. *Obsession: Male Same-Sex Relations in China, 1900–1950*. Hong Kong: Hong Kong University Press, 2009.

Karl, Rebecca. "The Violence of the Everyday in Early Twentieth-Century China." In *Everyday Modernity in China*, edited by Madeleine Yue Dong and Joshua Goldstein, 52–79. Seattle: University of Washington Press, 2006.

Kelley, David. "Temples and Tribute Fleets: The Luo Sect and Boatmen's Associations in the Eighteenth Century." *Modern China* 8, no. 3 (1982): 361–91.

Kingston, Maxine Hong. *The Woman Warrior: Memoirs of a Girlhood among Ghosts*. New York: Knopf, 1976.

Knoblock, John. *Xunzi: A Translation and Study of the Complete Works, Volume I, Books 1–6*. Stanford, Calif.: Stanford University Press, 1988.

Knoblock, John, and Jeffrey Riegel. *The Annals of Lü Buwei: A Complete Translation and Study*. Stanford, Calif.: Stanford University Press, 2000.

Ko, Dorothy. "The Body as Attire: The Shifting Meanings of Footbinding in Seventeenth-Century China." *Journal of Women's History* 8, no. 4 (1997a): 7–27.

————. *Cinderella's Sisters: A Revisionist History of Footbinding.* Berkeley: University of California Press, 2005.

————. *Every Step a Lotus: Shoes for Bound Feet.* Berkeley: University of California Press, 2001.

————. *Teachers of the Inner Chambers: Women and Culture in Seventeenth-Century China.* Stanford, Calif.: Stanford University Press, 1994.

————. "Thinking About Copulating: An Early-Qing Confucian Thinker's Problem with Emotion and Words." In *Remapping China: Fissures in Historical Terrain,* edited by Gail Hershatter, Emily Honig, Jonathan N. Lipman, and Randall Stross, 59–76. Stanford, Calif.: Stanford University Press, 1996.

————. "The Written Word and the Bound Foot: A History of the Courtesan's Aura." In *Writing Women in Late Imperial China,* edited by Ellen Widmer and Kang-i Sun Chang, 74–100. Stanford, Calif.: Stanford University Press, 1997b.

Kohrman, Matthew. *Bodies of Difference: Experiences of Disability and Institutional Advocacy in the Making of Modern China.* Berkeley: University of California Press, 2005.

Kristof, Nicholas D. "Beijing Journal; Freshest Nuance in China's Art Is (Blush) Nudes." New York Times, 9 January 1989, A4.

Kuhn, Philip A. *Soulstealers: The Chinese Sorcery Scare of 1768.* Cambridge, Mass.: Harvard University Press, 1990.

Kuriyama, Shigehisa. "The Imagination of Winds and the Development of the Chinese Conception of the Body." In *Body, Subject and Power in China,* edited by Angela Zito and Tani E. Barlow, 23–41. Chicago: University of Chicago Press, 1994.

Kutcher, Norman. "The Fifth Relationship: Dangerous Friendships in the Confucian Context." *American Historical Review* 105, no. 5 (2000): 1615–29.

————. "Practicing Kinship: Lineage and Descent in Late Imperial China." *Harvard Journal of Asiatic Studies* 64, no. 2 (2004): 492–502.

Lai, Sufen Sophia. "From Cross-Dressing Daughter to Lady Knight-Errant: The Origin and Evolution of Chinese Women Warriors." In *Presence and Presentation: Women in the Chinese Literati Tradition,* edited by Sherry J. Mou, 77–107. New York: St. Martin's Press, 1999.

Laqueur, Thomas. *Making Sex: Body and Gender from the Greeks to Freud.* Cambridge, Mass.: Harvard University Press, 1990.

Larson, Wendy. "Never This Wild: Sexing the Cultural Revolution." *Modern China* 25, no. 4 (1999): 423–50.

Lary, Diana. "A Ravaged Place: The Devastation of the Xuzhou Region, 1938." In *Scars of War: The Impact of Warfare on Modern China,* edited by Diana Lary and Stephen MacKinnon, 98–116. Vancouver: University of British Columbia Press, 2001.

Lavely, William. "Sex, Breastfeeding, and Marital Fertility in Pretransition China." *Population and Development Review* 33, no. 2 (2007): 289–320.

Lavely, William, Zhenyu Xiao, Bohua Li, and Ronald Freedman. "The Rise in Female Education in China: National and Regional Patterns." *China Quarterly* 121 (1990): 61–93.

Lavely, William R. "Age Patterns of Chinese Marital Fertility, 1950–1981." *Demography* 23, no. 3 (1986): 419–34.

Lee, Bernice J. "Female Infanticide in China." In *Women in China: Current Directions in Historical Scholarship*, edited by Richard W. Guisso and Stanley Johannesen, 163–77. Youngstown, N.Y.: Philo Press, 1981.

Lee, Haiyan. *Revolution of the Heart: A Genealogy of Love in China, 1900–1950.* Stanford, Calif.: Stanford University Press, 2007.

Lee, Sing, and Arthur Kleinman. "Suicide as Resistance in Chinese Society." In *Chinese Society: Change, Conflict, and Resistance, 2nd Edition*, edited by Elizabeth J. Perry and Mark Selden, 289–311. London: Routledge Curzon, 2003.

Legge, James, trans. *The Chinese Classics, Volume II: The Works of Mencius.* Repr. Taipei: Southern Materials Center, 1983.

―――. *The Chinese Classics, Volume IV: The She King.* Repr. Taipei: Southern Materials Center, 1991.

Lerum, Kari. "*Regulating Sex: The Politics of Intimacy and Identity*, Ed. Elizabeth Bernstein and Laurie Schaffner (Routledge, 2004)." [Review]. *Contemporary Sociology: A Journal of Reviews* 36, no. 6 (2007): 559–61.

Leung, Angela Ki Che. *Leprosy in China: A History.* New York: Columbia University Press, 2009.

―――. "Women Practicing Medicine in Premodern China." In *Chinese Women in the Imperial Past: New Perspectives*, edited by Harriet T. Zurndorfer, 101–34. Leiden: Brill, 1999.

Li, Xiaorong. "Engendering Heroism: Ming-Qing Women's Song Lyrics to the Tune *Man Jiang Hong*." *Nan Nü: Men, Women and Gender in China* 7, no. 1 (2005): 1–39.

Li, Yinhe. "Regulating Male Same-Sex Relationships in the People's Republic of China." In *Sex and Sexuality in China*, edited by Elaine Jeffreys, 82–101. London: Routledge, 2006.

Li Yu. *The Carnal Prayer Mat (Rou Putuan).* Translated by Patrick Hanan. Honolulu: University of Hawai'i Press, 1996 [1657].

Li, Yu-ning, ed. *Chinese Women through Chinese Eyes.* Armonk, N.Y.: M.E. Sharpe, 1992.

Lingat, Robert. *Les Régimes Matrimoniaux du Sud-Est de L'asie: Essai de Droit Comparé Indochinois* (Matrimonial regimes of Southeast Asia: An Essay on Comparative Law in Indochina). Hanoi: École Française d'Extrême-Orient, 1952.

Liu, Hui-chen Wang. *The Traditional Chinese Clan Rules.* Locust Valley, N.Y.: J. J. Augustin, 1959.

Lombard, Anne S. *Making Manhood: Growing Up Male in Colonial New England.* Cambridge, Mass.: Harvard University Press, 2003.

Louie, Kam. "The Macho Eunuch: The Politics of Masculinity in Jia Pingwa's 'Human Extremities.'" *Modern China* 17, no. 2 (1991): 163–87.

―――. *Theorising Chinese Masculinity: Society and Gender in China.* Cambridge: Cambridge University Press, 2002.

Louie, Kam, and Louise Edwards, ed. and trans. *Censored by Confucius: Ghost Stories by Yuan Mei*. Armonk, N.Y.: M.E. Sharpe, 1996.

Lu, Sheldon H. *Chinese Modernity and Global Biopolitics: Studies in Literature and Visual Culture*. Honolulu: University of Hawai'i Press, 2007.

Lu, Weijing. *True to Her Word: The Faithful Maiden Cult in Late Imperial China*. Stanford, Calif.: Stanford University Press, 2008.

———. "Uxorilocal Marriage among Qing Literati." *Late Imperial China* 19, no. 2 (1998): 64–110.

Lufrano, Richard John. *Honorable Merchants: Commerce and Self-Cultivation in Late Imperial China*. Honolulu: University of Hawai'i Press, 1997.

Luo, Manling. "The Seduction of Authenticity: 'The Story of Yingying.'" *Nan Nü: Men, Women and Gender in China* 7, no. 1 (2005): 40–70.

Lynn, Richard John, trans. *The Classic of Changes: A New Translation of the "I Ching" as Interpreted by Wang Bi*. New York: Columbia University Press, 1994.

Makley, Charlene E. *The Violence of Liberation: Gender and Tibetan Buddhist Revival in Post-Mao China*. Berkeley: University of California Press, 2007.

Mann, Susan. "The Cult of Domesticity in Republican Shanghai's Middle Class." *Jindai Zhongguo funü shi yanjiu* (Research on Women in Modern Chinese History) 2 (1994): 179–202.

———. "The Lady and the State: Women's Writing in Times of Trouble During the Nineteenth Century." In *The Inner Quarters and Beyond: Women Writers from Ming through Qing*, edited by Grace S. Fong and Ellen Widmer, 283–313. Leiden: Brill, 2010.

———. "The Male Bond in Chinese History and Culture." *American Historical Review* 105, no. 5 (2000): 1600–14.

———. *Precious Records: Women in China's Long Eighteenth Century*. Stanford, Calif.: Stanford University Press, 1997.

———. "Women, Families, and Gender Relations." In *The Cambridge History of China, Volume 9, Part One: The Ch'ing Dynasty to 1800*, edited by Willard J. Peterson, 428–72. New York and Cambridge: Cambridge University Press, 2002.

Mann, Susan L., trans. "Biographies of Exemplary Women." In *Hawai'i Reader in Traditional Chinese Culture*, edited by Victor H. Mair, Nancy S. Steinhardt, and Paul R. Goldin, 607–13. Honolulu: University of Hawai'i Press, 2005.

Mao Zedong. "Talks at the Yenan Forum on Literature and Art (May 1942)." In *Selected Works of Mao Tse-Tung*, 69–98. Beijing: Foreign Languages Press, 1965.

McCord, Edward A. "Burn, Kill, Rape, and Rob: Military Atrocities, Warlordism, and Anti-Warlordism in Republican China." In *Scars of War: The Impact of Warfare on Modern China*, edited by Diana Lary and Stephen MacKinnon, 18–47. Vancouver: University of British Columbia Press, 2001.

McDermott, Joseph. "Friendship and Its Friends in the Late Ming." In *Family Process and Political Process in Modern Chinese History, Part I*, edited by Institute of Modern History, Academia Sinica, 67–96. Taipei: Institute of Modern History, Academia Sinica, Taipei, Taiwan, 1992.

McGough, James. "Deviant Marriage Patterns in Chinese Society." In *Normal and Abnormal Behavior in Chinese Culture*, edited by Arthur Kleinman and Tsung-yi Lin, 171–220. Boston: R. Reidel, 1985.

McIsaac, Lee. "'Righteous Fraternities' and Honorable Men: Sworn Brotherhoods in Wartime Chongqing." *American Historical Review* 105, no. 5 (2000): 1641–55.

McMahon, Keith. "A Case for Confucian Sexuality: The Eighteenth-Century Novel *Yesou Puyan*." *Late Imperial China* 9, no. 2 (1988): 32–55.

———. *Misers, Shrews, and Polygamists: Sexuality and Male-Female Relations in Eighteenth-Century Chinese Fiction*. Durham, N.C.: Duke University Press, 1995.

———. *Polygamy and Sublime Passion: Sexuality in China on the Verge of Modernity*. Honolulu: University of Hawai'i Press, 2010.

Meijer, M. J. "Homosexual Offences in Ch'ing Law." *T'oung Pao* 71 (1985): 109–33.

———. *Marriage Law and Public Policy in the Chinese People's Republic*. Hong Kong: Hong Kong University Press, 1971.

Merson, John. *Roads to Xanadu: East and West in the Making of the Modern World*. London: Weidenfeld and Nicolson, 1989.

Mitamura, Taisuke. *Chinese Eunuchs: The Structure of Intimate Politics*. Translated by Charles A. Pomeroy. Rutland, Vt.: Tuttle, 1970.

Mou, Sherry J. *Gentlemen's Prescriptions for Women's Lives: A Thousand Years of Biographies of Chinese Women*. Armonk, N.Y.: M.E. Sharpe, 2004.

Murray, Dian. *The Origins of the Tiandihui: The Chinese Triads in Legend and History*. Stanford, Calif.: Stanford University Press, 1994.

———. *Pirates of the South China Coast, 1790–1810*. Stanford, Calif.: Stanford University Press, 1987.

———. "The Practice of Homosexuality among the Pirates of Late 18th and Early 19th Century China." *International Journal of Maritime History* 4, no. 1 (1992): 121–30.

Najmabadi, Afsaneh. "Beyond the Americas: Are Gender and Sexuality Useful Categories of Historical Analysis?" *Journal of Women's History* 18, no. 1 (2006): 11–21.

———. *Women with Mustaches and Men without Beards: Gender and Sexual Anxieties of Iranian Modernity*. Berkeley: University of California Press, 2005.

Needham, Joseph. *Science and Civilisation in China: Volume 2, History of Scientific Thought*. Cambridge: Cambridge University Press, 1956.

———. *Science and Civilisation in China, Volume 5: Chemistry and Chemical Technology, Part V: Spagyrical Discovery and Invention: Physiological Alchemy*. Cambridge: Cambridge University Press, 1983.

Ng, Vivien W. "Ideology and Sexuality: Rape Laws in Qing China." *Journal of Asian Studies* 46, no. 1 (1987): 57–70.

"Nude Modelling, Business or Art?" *Shanghai Star*, 30 January 2004, www.chinadaily.com.

Nylan, Michael. "On the Politics of Pleasure." *Asia Major, New Series* 14, no. 1 (2001): 73–124.

O'Hara, Albert Richard. *The Position of Woman in Early China According to the Lieh Nü Chuan, "The Biographies of Eminent Chinese Women."* Washington, D.C.: Catholic University of America Press, 1945.

Ōki, Yasushi. "Women in Feng Menglong's 'Mountain Songs.'" In *Writing Women in Late Imperial China*, edited by Ellen Widmer and Kang-i Sun Chang, 131–43. Stanford, Calif.: Stanford University Press, 1997.

Palmer, Michael. "The Re-Emergence of Family Law in Post-Mao China: Marriage, Divorce and Reproduction." *China Quarterly* 141 (1995): 110–34.

Pan, Suiming. "Transformations in the Primary Life Cycle: The Origins and Nature of China's Sexual Revolution." In *Sex and Sexuality in China*, edited by Elaine Jeffreys, 21–42. London: Routledge, 2006.

Pao Tao, Chia-lin. "Chaste Widows and Institutions to Support Them in Late-Ch'ing China." *Asia Major, New Series* 4, no. 1 (1991): 101–19.

Parish, William L., Chonglin Shen, and Chi-hsiang Chang. "Family Support Networks in the Chinese Countryside." USC Seminar Series No. 11. Shatin, New Territories, Hong Kong: Hong Kong Institute of Asia-Pacific Studies, Chinese University of Hong Kong ,1996.

Parish, William L., Edward O. Laumann, and Sanyu A. Mojola. "Sexual Behavior in China." *Population and Development Review* 33, no. 4 (2007): 729–56.

Peterson, Barbara Bennett, ed. *Notable Women of China: Shang Dynasty to the Early Twentieth Century.* Armonk, N.Y.: M.E. Sharpe, 2000.

Phillips, M. R., X. Y. Li, and Y. P. Zhang. "Suicide Rates in China, 1995–1999." *Lancet* 359 (2002): 835–47.

Polachek, James M. *The Inner Opium War.* Cambridge, Mass.: Council on East Asian Studies, Harvard University, 1992.

Pruitt, Ida. *A Daughter of Han: The Autobiography of a Chinese Working Woman; [by Ida Pruitt] from the Story Told Her by Ning Lao T'ai-T'ai.* New Haven, Conn.: Yale University Press, 1945; repr. Stanford, Calif.: Stanford University Press, 1967.

Qian, Nanxiu. "Borrowing Foreign Mirrors and Candles to Illuminate Chinese Civilization: Xue Shaohui's Moral Vision in the *Biographies of Foreign Women.*" In *Beyond Tradition and Modernity: Gender, Genre, and Cosmopolitanism in Late Qing China*, edited by Grace S. Fong, Nanxiu Qian, and Harriet T. Zurndorfer, 60–101. Leiden: Brill, 2004.

―――. "Revitalizing the *Xianyuan* (Worthy Ladies) Tradition: Women in the 1898 Reforms." *Modern China* 29, no. 4 (2003): 399–454.

Qinding Da Qing huidian shili (Imperially endorsed collected statutes and sub-statutes of the Qing dynasty). Edition of 1899.

Ran Xiuhong, comp. *Nü'er jing xin yi* (A New Interpretation of the Women's Classic). Beijing: Zhongguo shudian, 1997.

Rankin, Mary Backus. "The Emergence of Women at the End of the Ch'ing: The Case of Ch'iu Chin." In *Women in Chinese Society*, edited by Margery Wolf and Roxane Witke, 39–66. Stanford, Calif.: Stanford University Press, 1975.

Raphals, Lisa. *Sharing the Light: Representations of Women and Virtue in Early China.* Albany: State University of New York Press, 1998.

Rawski, Evelyn S. "Ch'ing Imperial Marriage and Problems of Rulership." In *Marriage and Inequality in Chinese Society*, edited by Rubie S. Watson and Patricia Buckley Ebrey, 170–203. Berkeley: University of California Press, 1991.

————. *The Last Emperors: A Social History of Qing Imperial Institutions*. Berkeley: University of California Press, 1998.

Riegel, Jeffrey. "Eros, Introversion, and the Beginnings of *Shijing* Commentary." *Harvard Journal of Asiatic Studies* 57, no. 1 (1997): 143–77.

Riordan, James, and Jinxia Dong. "Chinese Women and Sport: Success, Sexuality and Suspicion." *China Quarterly* 145 (1996): 130–52.

Rofel, Lisa. *Desiring China: Experiments in Neoliberalism, Sexuality, and Public Culture*. Durham, N.C.: Duke University Press, 2007.

————. "Qualities of Desire: Imagining Gay Identities in China." *GLQ* 5, no. 4 (1999): 451–74.

Ropp, Paul S., Paola Zamperini, and Harriet T. Zurndorfer, ed. *Passionate Women: Female Suicide in Late Imperial China*. Leiden: Brill, 2001.

Rosenlee, Li-Hsiang Lisa. *Confucianism and Women: A Philosophical Perspective*. Albany: State University of New York Press, 2006.

————. "*Neiwai*, Civility, and Gender Distinctions." *Asian Philosophy* 14, no. 1 (2004): 41–58.

Rouzer, Paul. "The Life of the Party: Theorizing Clients and Patrons in Early China." *Comparative Literature*, winter (2006): 59–69.

Rowe, William T. *Saving the World: Chen Hongmou and Elite Consciousness in Eighteenth-Century China*. Stanford, Calif.: Stanford University Press, 2001.

Ruan, Fang-fu. *Sex in China: Studies in Sexology in Chinese Culture*. New York: Plenum Press, 1991.

Rubin, Gayle. "The Traffic in Women: Notes on the Political Economy of Sex." In *Toward an Anthropology of Women*, edited by Rayna R. Reiter, 157–210. New York: Monthly Review Press, 1975.

Ruhlmann, Robert. "Traditional Heroes in Chinese Popular Fiction." In *The Confucian Persuasion*, edited by Arthur F. Wright, 141–76. Stanford, Calif.: Stanford University Press, 1960.

Sakamoto, Hiroko. "The Formation of National Identity in Liang Qichao and Its Relationship to Gender." In *The Role of Japan in Liang Qichao's Introduction of Modern Western Civilization to China*, edited by Joshua A. Fogel, 272–89. Berkeley: Center for Chinese Studies, Institute of East Asian Studies, University of California, Berkeley, 2004.

Sang, Tze-lan D. *The Emerging Lesbian: Female Same-Sex Desire in Modern China*. Chicago: University of Chicago Press, 2003.

Sang, Tze-lan Deborah. "Feminism's Double: Lesbian Activism in the Mediated Public Sphere of Taiwan." In *Spaces of Their Own: Women's Public Sphere in Transnational China*, edited by Mayfair Mei-hui Yang, 132–61. Minneapolis: University of Minnesota Press, 1999a.

————. "Translating Homosexuality: The Discourse of Tongxing'ai in Republican China (1912–1949)." In *Tokens of Exchange: The Problem of Translation in*

Global Circulations, edited by Lydia H. Liu, 276–304. Durham, N.C.: Duke University Press, 1999b.

Schein, Louisa. *Minority Rules: The Miao and the Feminine in China's Political Culture*. Durham, N.C.: Duke University Press, 2000.

Schmidt, J. D. *Harmony Garden: The Life, Literary Criticism, and Poetry of Yuan Mei (1716–1789)*. London: Routledge Curzon, 2003.

Scott, James C. *Seeing Like a State: How Certain Schemes to Improve the Human Condition Have Failed*. New Haven, Conn.: Yale University Press, 1998.

Scott, Joan Wallach. *Gender and the Politics of History, Revised Edition*. New York: Columbia University Press, 1999.

Seaman, Gary. "The Sexual Politics of Karmic Retribution." In *The Anthropology of Taiwanese Society*, edited by Emily Martin Ahern and Hill Gates, 381–96. Stanford, Calif.: Stanford University Press, 1981.

See, Lisa. *Peony in Love*. New York: Random House, 2007.

———. *Snow Flower and the Secret Fan*. New York: Random House, 2005.

Seton, Grace Thompson. *Chinese Lanterns*. New York: Dodd, Mead, and Company, 1924.

Shen Fu. *Six Records of a Floating Life*. Translated by Leonard Pratt and Chiang Su-hui. New York: Viking Penguin, 1986.

Shih, Shu-mei. *The Lure of the Modern: Writing Modernism in Semicolonial China, 1917–1937*. Berkeley: University of California Press, 2001.

Shu-chiung [pseud.]. *Hsi Shih, Beauty of Beauties (A Romance of Ancient China about 495–472 B.C.)*. Singapore: Graham Brash, 1981 [1931].

Sigley, Gary. "Keep It in the Family: Government, Marriage, and Sex in Contemporary China." In *Borders of Being: Citizenship, Fertility, and Sexuality in Asia and the Pacific*, edited by Margaret Jolly and Kalpana Ram, 118–53. Ann Arbor: University of Michigan Press, 2001.

Silber, Cathy. "From Daughter to Daughter-in-Law in the Women's Script of Southern Hunan." In *Engendering China: Women, Culture, and the State*, edited by Christina K. Gilmartin, Gail Hershatter, Lisa Rofel, and Tyrene White, 47–68. Cambridge, Mass.: Harvard University Press, 1994.

Sinha, Mrinalini. *Colonial Masculinity: The "Manly Englishman" and the "Effeminate Bengali" in the Late Nineteenth Century*. New York: Manchester University Press, 1995.

Sinnott, Megan. "Borders, Diaspora, and Regional Connections: Trends in Asian 'Queer' Studies." *Journal of Asian Studies* 69, no. 1 (2010): 17–31.

Siu, Helen F. "Where Were the Women? Rethinking Marriage Resistance and Regional Culture in South China." *Late Imperial China* 11, no. 2 (1990): 32–62.

Skinner, G. William. "Chinese Peasants and the Closed Community: An Open and Shut Case." *Comparative Studies in Society and History* 13, no. 3 (1971): 270–81.

———. "Family Systems and Demographic Processes." In *Anthropological Demography: Toward a New Synthesis*, edited by David I. Kertzer and Tom Fricke, 53–95. Chicago: University of Chicago Press, 1997.

Sommer, Matthew H. "Making Sex Work: Polyandry as a Survival Strategy in Qing Dynasty China." In *Gender in Motion: Divisions of Labor and Cultural Change in Late Imperial and Modern China*, edited by Bryna Goodman and Wendy Larson, 29–54. Lanham, Mass.: Rowman and Littlefield, 2005.

———. *Sex, Law, and Society in Late Imperial China*. Stanford, Calif.: Stanford University Press, 2000.

Stacey, Judith. *Patriarchy and Socialist Revolution in China*. Berkeley: University of California Press, 1983.

Stent, G. Carter. "Chinese Eunuchs." *Journal of the North China Branch of the Royal Asiatic Society* 9 (n.s.) (1877): 143–84.

Stewart, Devin. "Let's Talk About Sex in China (An Interview with James Farrer about the International Conference on Chinese Sexual Culture, Beijing, June 2007)." Asia Times Online, 12 July 2007, www.atimes.com.

Stockard, Janice E. *Daughters of the Canton Delta: Marriage Patterns and Economic Strategies in South China, 1860–1930*. Stanford, Calif.: Stanford University Press, 1989.

Stoler, Ann Laura. *Carnal Knowledge and Imperial Power: Gender, Race, and Morality in Colonial Asia*. Berkeley: University of California Press, 1991.

Strasser, Ulrike, and Heidi Tinsman. "Engendering World History." *Radical History Review* 91, winter (2005): 151–64.

Struve, Lynn A., ed. and trans. *Voices from the Ming-Qing Cataclysm: China in Tigers' Jaws*. New Haven, Conn.: Yale University Press, 1993.

Sun, Lung-kee. "The Politics of Hair and the Issue of the Bob in Modern China." *Fashion Theory* 1, no. 4 (1997): 353–65.

Szonyi, Michael. "The Cult of Hu Tianbao and the Eighteenth-Century Discourse of Homosexuality." *Late Imperial China* 19, no. 1 (1998): 1–25.

Tamba, Yasuyori, Akira Ishihara, and Howard S. Levy, trans. *The Tao of Sex: An Annotated Translation of the Twenty-Eighth Section of the Essence of Medical Prescriptions (Ishimpō)*. New York: Harper and Row, 1970.

Tang Xianzu. *The Peony Pavilion: Mudanting, Second Edition*. Translated by Cyril Birch. Bloomington: Indiana University Press, 2002.

Teng, Emma Jinhua. *Taiwan's Imagined Geography: Chinese Colonial Travel Writing and Pictures, 1683–1895*. Cambridge, Mass.: Harvard University Asia Center, 2004.

Terrill, Ross. *Madame Mao: The White-Boned Demon, Revised Edition*. Stanford, Calif.: Stanford University Press, 1999.

Terry, Jennifer. "Introduction." In *An American Obsession: Science, Medicine, and Homosexuality in Modern Society*, 1–26. Chicago: University of Chicago Press, 1999.

Theiss, Janet. "Explaining the Shrew: Narratives of Spousal Violence and the Critique of Masculinity in Eighteenth-Century Criminal Cases." In *Writing and Law in Late Imperial China: Crime, Conflict, and Judgment*, edited by Robert E. Hegel and Katherine Carlitz, 44–63. Seattle: University of Washington Press, 2007.

———. "Managing Martyrdom: Female Suicide and Statecraft in Mid-Qing China." *Nan Nü: Men, Women and Gender in Early and Imperial China* 3, no. 1 (2001): 47–76.

Theiss, Janet M. *Disgraceful Matters: The Politics of Chastity in Eighteenth-Century China*. Berkeley: University of California Press, 2004.

T'ien, Ju-k'ang. *Male Anxiety and Female Chastity: A Comparative Study of Chinese Ethical Values in Ming-Ch'ing Times*. *T'oung Pao* Monograph Number XIV. Leiden: E. J. Brill, 1988.

Topley, Marjorie. "Marriage Resistance in Rural Kwangtung." In *Women in Chinese Society*, edited by Margery Wolf and Roxane Witke, 67–88. Stanford, Calif.: Stanford University Press, 1975.

Tsai, Shih-shan Henry. *The Eunuchs in the Ming Dynasty*. Albany: State University of New York Press, 1996.

Tsui, Ming, and Lynne Rich. "The Only Child and Educational Opportunity for Girls in Urban China." *Gender and Society* 16, no. 1 (2002):74–92.

van der Sprenkel, Sybille. *Legal Institutions in Manchu China: A Sociological Analysis*. London: Athlone Press, University of London, 1962.

van der Valk, Marc. *An Outline of Modern Chinese Family Law*. Peking: Henri Vetch, 1939. Reprint, Taipei: Ch'eng-wen, 1969.

Vitiello, Giovanni. "Exemplary Sodomites: Chivalry and Love in Late Ming Culture." *Nan Nü: Men, Women and Gender in Early and Imperial China* 2, no. 2 (2000): 207–57.

Volpp, Sophie. "Classifying Lust: The Seventeenth-Century Vogue for Male Love." *Harvard Journal of Asiatic Studies* 61, no. 1 (2001a): 77–117.

———. "The Discourse on Male Marriage: Li Yu's 'A Male Mencius's Mother.'" *positions: east asia cultures critique* 2, no. 1 (1994): 113–32.

———. "*Drinking Wine and Reading 'Encountering Sorrow': A Reflection in Disguise* by Wu Zao (1799–1862)." In *Under Confucian Eyes: Writings on Gender in Chinese History*, edited by Susan Mann and Yu-Yin Cheng, 239–50. Berkeley: University of California Press, 2001b.

———. "The Literary Circulation of Actors in Seventeenth-Century China." *Journal of Asian Studies* 61, no. 3 (2002): 949–84.

Wakefield, David. *Fenjia: Household Division and Inheritance in Qing and Republican China*. Honolulu: University of Hawai'i Press, 1998.

Wakeman, Frederic, Jr. *The Great Enterprise: The Manchu Reconstruction of Imperial Order in Seventeenth-Century China*. 2 vols. Berkeley: University of California Press, 1985.

Waley, Arthur. *Yuan Mei: Eighteenth Century Chinese Poet*. New York: Grove Press, 1956.

Waltner, Ann. "On Not Becoming a Heroine: Lin Dai-Yu and Cui Ying-Ying." *Signs: Journal of Women in Culture and Society* 15, no. 1 (1989): 61–78.

Wang, David Der-wei. *Fin-De-Siècle Splendor: Repressed Modernities of Late Qing Fiction, 1849–1911*. Stanford, Calif.: Stanford University Press, 1997.

Wang, Robin R., ed. *Images of Women in Chinese Thought and Culture: Writings from the Pre-Qin Period through the Song Dynasty*. Indianapolis: Hackett, 2003.

Wang, Zheng. "Research on Women in Contemporary China." In *Guide to Women's Studies in China*, edited by Gail Hershatter, Emily Honig, Susan Mann, and Lisa Rofel, 1–43. Berkeley: Center for Chinese Studies, University of California, 1999a.

———. *Women in the Chinese Enlightenment: Oral and Textual Histories*. Berkeley: University of California Press, 1999b.

Wang Zhenya. *Jiu Zhongguo tiyu jianwen* (Observations on sports in old China). Beijing: Renmin tiyu chubanshe, 1987.

Wasserstrom, Jeffery N., and Susan Brownell, ed. *Chinese Femininities, Chinese Masculinities: A Reader*. Berkeley: University of California Press, 2002.

Watson, Burton, trans. *Han Fei Tzu: Basic Writings*. New York: Columbia University Press, 1964.

Watson, Rubie S. "Wives, Concubines, and Maids: Servitude and Kinship in the Hong Kong Region, 1900–1940." In *Marriage and Inequality in Chinese Society*, edited by Rubie S. Watson and Patricia Buckley Ebrey, 231–55. Berkeley: University of California Press, 1991.

Wei Hui [Zhou Weihui]. *Shanghai Baby (Shanghai Baobei)*. Translated by Bruce Hume. New York: Pocket Books, 2001.

Wen, Jung-kwang, and Ching-lun Wang. "Shen-K'uei Syndrome: A Culture-Specific Sexual Neurosis in Taiwan." In *Normal and Abnormal Behavior in Chinese Culture*, edited by Arthur Kleinman and Tsung-yi Lin, 357–69. Boston: D. Reidel, 1980.

West, Stephen H., and Wilt L. Idema, ed. and trans. *The Moon and the Zither: "The Story of the Western Wing," by Wang Shifu*. Berkeley: University of California Press, 1991.

Widmer, Ellen. *The Beauty and the Book: Women and Fiction in Nineteenth-Century China*. Cambridge, Mass.: Harvard University Asia Center, 2006.

Witke, Roxane. "Mao Tse-Tung, Women and Suicide in the May Fourth Era." *China Quarterly* 31, July–September (1967): 128–47.

Wolf, Margery. "Women and Suicide in China." In *Women in Chinese Society*, edited by Margery Wolf and Roxane Witke, 111–41. Stanford, Calif.: Stanford University Press, 1975.

———. *Women and the Family in Rural Taiwan*. Stanford, Calif.: Stanford University Press, 1972.

Wong, R. Bin. *China Transformed: Historical Change and the Limits of European Experience*. Ithaca, N.Y.: Cornell University Press, 1997.

Woo, Margaret Y. K. "Chinese Women Workers: The Delicate Balance between Protection and Equality." In *Engendering China: Women, Culture, and the State*, edited by Christina K. Gilmartin, Gail Hershatter, Lisa Rofel, and Tyrene White, 279–95. Cambridge, Mass.: Harvard University Press, 1994.

———. "Contesting Citizenship: Marriage and Divorce in the People's Republic of China." In *Sex and Sexuality in China*, edited by Elaine Jeffreys, 62–81. London: Routledge, 2006.

———. "Law and the Gendered Citizen." In *Changing Meanings of Citizenship Modern China*, edited by Merle Goldman and Elizabeth J. Perry, 308–29. ridge, Mass.: Harvard University Press, 2001.

———. "Shaping Citizenship: Chinese Family Law and Women." *Yale Journal of Law and Feminism* 15 (2003): 75–110.

Wu, Chao-Jung. "Performing Postmodern Taiwan: Gender, Cultural Hybridity, and the Male Cross-Dressing Show." Ph.D. diss., Wesleyan University, 2007.

Wu, Cuncun. "'Beautiful Boys Made Up as Beautiful Girls': Anti-Masculine Taste in Qing China." In *Asian Masculinities: The Meaning and Practice of Manhood in China and Japan*, edited by Kam Louie and Morris Low, 19–40. London: Routledge Curzon, 2003.

Wu, Pei-yi. "Yang Miaozhen: A Woman Warrior in Thirteenth-Century China." *Nan Nü: Men, Women and Gender in Early and Imperial China* 4, no. 2 (2002): 137–69.

Wu, Yenna. *The Chinese Virago: A Literary Theme*. Cambridge, Mass.: Council on East Asian Studies, Harvard University, 1995.

———. "The Inversion of Marital Hierarchy: Shrewish Wives and Henpecked Husbands in Seventeenth-Century Chinese Literature." *Harvard Journal of Asiatic Studies* 48, no. 2 (1988): 363–82.

Wu, Yi-Li. *Reproducing Women: Medicine, Metaphor, and Childbirth in Late Imperial China*. Berkeley: University of California Press, 2010.

Xia Xiaohong. *Wan Qing nüxing yu jindai Zhongguo* (Women at the End of the Qing and Modern China). Beijing: Beijing daxue chubanshe, 2004.

———. *Wan Qing wenren funü guan* (Literati Views of Women at the End of the Qing Dynasty). Beijing: Beijing zuojia chuban she, 1995.

Yan, Yunxiang. "Making Room for Intimacy: Domestic Space and Conjugal Privacy in Rural North China." In *House, Home, Family: Living and Being Chinese*, edited by Ronald G. Knapp and Kai-Yin Lo, 373–95. Honolulu: University of Hawai'i Press, 2005.

Yang, Daqing. "Atrocities in Nanjing: Searching for Explanations." In *Scars of War: The Impact of Warfare on Modern China*, edited by Diana Lary and Stephen MacKinnon, 76–96. Vancouver: University of British Columbia Press, 2001.

Yang, Mayfair Mei-hui. "From Gender Erasure to Gender Difference: State Feminism, Consumer Sexuality, and Women's Public Sphere in China." In *Spaces of Their Own: Women's Public Sphere in Transnational China*, edited by Mayfair Mei-hui Yang, 35–67. Minneapolis: University of Minnesota Press, 1999.

Ye, Weilin. "Five Girls and One Rope." Translated by Zhou Shizong and Diane Simmons. *Fiction* 8, no. 2–3 (1987): 96–114.

Yeh, Wen-hsin. *Provincial Passages: Culture, Space, and the Origins of Chinese Communism*. Berkeley: University of California Press, 1996.

Yeung, Alison Sau-chu. "Fornication in the Late Qing Legal Reforms: Moral Teachings and Legal Principles." *Modern China* 29, no. 3 (2003): 297–328.

Yu, Pauline. "The Story of Yingying." In *Ways with Words: Writing about Reading Texts from Early China*, edited by Pauline Yu, Peter Bol, Stephen Owen, and Willard Peterson, 182–85. Berkeley: University of California Press, 2000.

Yuan Mei. *Censored by Confucius: Ghost Stories [Zi Buyu]*. Translated by Kam Louie and Louise Edwards. Armonk, N.Y.: M.E. Sharpe, 1996.

Zamperini, Paola. "Clothes That Matter: Fashioning Modernity in Late Qing Novels." *Fashion Theory* 5, no. 2 (2001a): 195–214.

———. "Untamed Hearts: Eros and Suicide in Late Imperial Chinese Fiction." *Nan Nü: Men, Women and Gender in Early and Imperial China* 3, no. 1 (2001b): 77–104.

Zarrow, Peter. "The Real Chinese Man: Review Essay." *Jindai Zhongguo funü shi yanjiu* (Research on Women in Modern Chinese History) 11 (2003): 351–72.

Zeitlin, Judith T. *Historian of the Strange: Pu Songling and the Chinese Classical Tale.* Stanford, Calif.: Stanford University Press, 1993.

———. "Shared Dreams: The Story of the Three Wives' Commentary on *Peony Pavilion*." *Harvard Journal of Asiatic Studies* 54, no. 1 (1994): 127–79.

Zhang, Heqing. "Female Sex Sellers and Public Policy in the People's Republic of China." In *Sex and Sexuality in China*, edited by Elaine Jeffreys, 139–58. London: Routledge, 2006.

Zhang, Hong. "From Resisting to 'Embracing?' the One-Child Rule: Understanding New Fertility Trends in a Central China Village." *China Quarterly* 192 (2007): 855–75.

Zhang Jingsheng. *Xing shi 1926* (A History of Sex, 1926). Taipei: Dala, 2005.

Zhang, Lijia. *"Socialism Is Great!" A Worker's Memoir of the New China.* New York: Anchor Books, 2008.

Zheng, Tiantian. *Red Lights: The Lives of Sex Workers in Postsocialist China.* Minneapolis: University of Minnesota, 2009.

Zhong, Xueping. *Masculinity Besieged? Issues of Modernity and Male Subjectivity in Chinese Literature of the Late Twentieth Century.* Durham, N.C.: Duke University Press, 2000.

Zhong, Xueping, and Zheng Wang, ed. *Some of Us: Chinese Women Growing Up in the Mao Era.* New Brunswick, N.J.: Rutgers University Press, 2001.

Zito, Angela. "Bound to be Represented: Fetishizing/Theorizing Footbinding." In *Embodied Modernities: Corporeality, Representation, and Chinese Cultures*, edited by Larissa Heinrich and Fran Martin, 29–41. Honolulu: University of Hawaii Press, 2006.

Zito, Angela, and Tani E. Barlow, ed. *Body, Subject and Power in China.* Chicago: University of Chicago Press, 1994.

Zou, Yu. "'*After Patriarchy': Masculinity and Representation in Modern Chinese Drama 1919–45.*" Ph.D. diss., University of California, Berkeley, 2000.

Index